THE ROMANTIC CHALLENGE

Other books by Sir Francis Chichester include :

Solo to Sydney (1930)
Alone Over the Tasman Sea (1946 ; originally
    Seaplane Solo, 1932)
Ride on the Wind (1937)
Astro-Navigation (1940)
Alone Across the Atlantic (1961)
The Lonely Sea and the Sky (1964)
Along the Clipper Way (1966)
Gipsy Moth Circles the World (1967)
How to Keep Fit (1969)

The success of my 'romantic challenge' hung on this boom and its
two predecessors. A photograph I took in the Caribbean Sea

FRANCIS CHICHESTER

The Romantic Challenge

CASSELL · LONDON

CASSELL & COMPANY LTD
35 Red Lion Square, London WC1
Sydney, Toronto, Johannesburg, Auckland

First published 1971

I.S.B.N. 0 304 93869 6

Made and printed in Great Britain by
William Clowes & Sons, Limited
London, Beccles and Colchester
F.1071

AUTHOR'S NOTE

There are so many people to thank and not enough space to do it adequately:

First, and always, Sheila my wife, for her strong, unstinted support and wise counsel, as well as such practical help as stowing and cataloguing the stores for my voyages. Also for her work as vice-chairman of our map-publishing business while I am away.

Giles, my son and great friend, though kept fully stretched by our business, has always happily lent a strong hand on *Gipsy Moth* as an excellent crew and 'good companion'.

Monica Cooper, friend and co-director, who copes so ably with the sales and distribution side of our business and in her private capacity gives so much help in an enterprise like this; also Michael Lewin and Douglas Johnson, our other co-directors, for their advice and support; and Ann Champion and all the other members of our staff.

George Greenfield, for whom the words 'literary agent' seem so inadequate a cover for his fertile activities on our behalf.

Robert Clark, who designed *Gipsy Moth V*, and Denis Doyle, whose Crosshaven Yard built her so well. The quality of the work of designer and shipwrights—I remember particularly the skill and care taken by Paddy O'Driscoll—can be judged by the miraculous outcome of the events described in Chapter IX. In Cork, Denis and his wife Mary were ever hospitable hosts, as were the officers, members and staff of the Royal Cork Y.C., which did me the great honour of making me an honorary life member.

Max Gunning invented my self-steering gear and Tony Morriss made it the best possible for *Gipsy Moth*. In the Beaulieu River my thanks are to Edward and Belinda Montagu; Pat Russell, who worked on the engine, propeller, electrical and plumbing installations; Stan the rigger and Frank the joiner; Mrs Martin who provided the greater part of the stores; and Enid Shortridge who started me off with the brownest, hardest-shelled eggs ever seen.

Those who helped so generously in fitting-out: John Shaw of Shaw's Wire Ropes; Perkins Engines; Richard Gatehouse of Brookes and Gatehouse; Marconi Marine; the Avon Rubber Company; Bill Whitbread, Raymond Seymour and John Fox of Whitbread for crew's comforts, in keg and on tap; the Rolex Watch Co.; Kelvin Hughes; Norman Ellis and H. C. Hebard of Aladdin; Electric Power Storage Ltd. (Exide batteries); Lewmar Marine Ltd.; Henri-Lloyd Ltd., and many others.

At Plymouth there are so many good and helpful friends; Terence

Shaw of the Royal Western Y.C. of England; his wife Ruth, and the officers, members and staff of the Club; Vice-Admiral McKaig; Air Vice-Marshal Downey (who incidentally succeeded me as navigation officer of the Empire Central Flying School in 1945); and of course Jack and Nancy Odling-Smee, Percy and Patsy Blagdon, and the Mashfords.

From the voyage I remember with gratitude the kindness of my Portuguese friends, new and old, at Bissau and Horta; Christopher Doll was, as you will see, 'in at the beginning', and has kindly given me some of his photographs for this book; Paul Berriff took some wonderful film of *Gipsy Moth V* for the BBC film *The Romantic Challenge*; Chris Brasher was the man—and the voice—behind the film, which I found thrilling and inspiring.

In Nicaragua the British Ambassador Ivor Vincent and his wife Patricia were more than generous in their hospitality and help. And at El Bluff there was Bart, of whom more in these pages and much more in my memory.

Throughout the voyage the efficient and ever-helpful GPO operators at Portishead relayed my weak radio signals to the BBC, *The Observer*, and my family. At *The Observer*, Frank Page patiently pieced together the jigsaw of my messages to tell the story, as did the reporters of the BBC Foreign Service.

Kenneth Parker of Cassell's, my British publishers, for his help with this book. Ken channelled my thoughts and the outpourings of my logbooks into a form which, he convinced me, was exactly what I had wanted anyway. I must add however that after working under his overseer's whip seven days a week since we got together in June, I finished the book in King Edward VII's Hospital for Officers. He even pursued me there, but the staff of the Hospital were so kind that I was quite sorry I had only one chapter left to write. My thanks also go to the staff of Grayshott Hall, where I am writing this as I quickly recover my health and strength.

Margaret Helps deciphered, transcribed and typed the first drafts of the book; Gil Pearson and Erica Redfern produced the final typescript.

My thanks go also to the production staffs of Cassell's and Clowes, the printers, who co-operated magnificently to get this book out on the promised date, despite the inevitable delays caused by my illness.

Lastly, a special word of thanks to Douglas Phillips-Birt, perhaps the only man who truly sensed and understood in advance the difficulties of my speed project, and was completely right in his technical assessment of them.

F.C.

September 1971

CONTENTS

ILLUSTRATIONS

(Unless otherwise acknowledged, photographs are by the author)

The third boom   *Frontispiece*

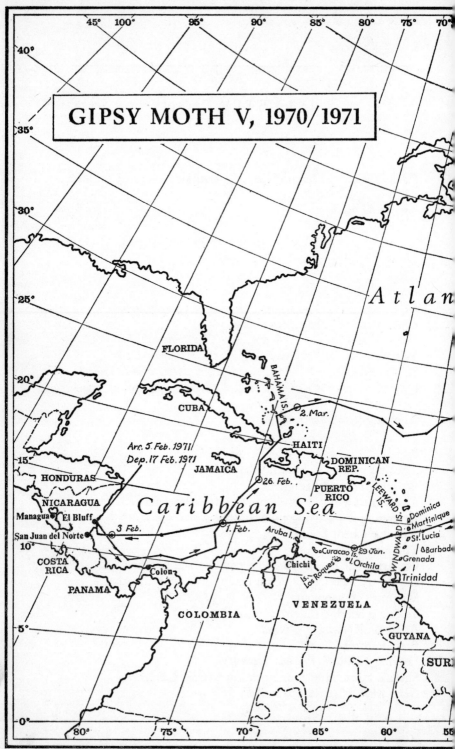

GIPSY MOTH V, 1970/1971

45° 100° 95° 90° 85° 80° 75° 70°
40°
35°
30°
25°
Atlan
20° FLORIDA
BAHAMA IS.
CUBA
2. Mar.
15° Arr. 5. Feb. 1971 HAITI
Dep. 17 Feb. 1971 DOMINICAN
JAMAICA REP.
26. Feb. PUERTO
HONDURAS RICO
Caribbean Sea LEEWARD IS.
NICARAGUA
Managua El Bluff Dominica
San Juan del Norte 3 Feb. 1. Feb. Aruba I. Martinique
Curacao Is. 29 Jan. St. Lucia
COSTA Chichi Orchila Barbado
RICA Colon Is. Grenada
PANAMA Los Roques Trinidad
VENEZUELA
COLOMBIA
5° GUYANA
SUR
0°
80° 75° 70° 65° 60° 55°

© Cassell & Co. Ltd. 1971

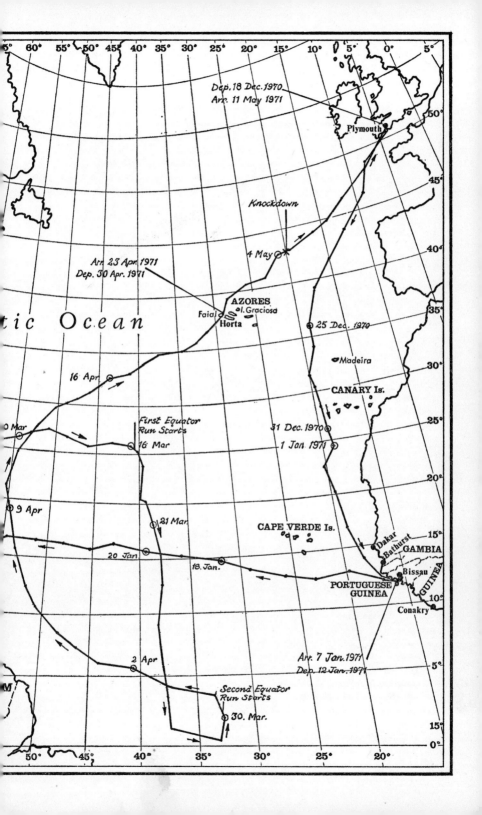

I

THE ROMANTIC CHALLENGE

I love life; this great, exciting, absorbing, intriguing, puzzling, adventurous life. But I am sixty-nine; in September 1971, before this book is published, I shall be seventy, and my lifespan is shortening. So for the past few years I have pondered time after time how I can use the remainder of this great gift of life to the full. The Buddha said that life was a gift which any man can take but none can give; I think it is wrong not to use such a gift to the utmost, wrong to bury it like an unused talent, wrong not to use it to the very end.

It was in 1959, after what seems a miraculous recovery from lung cancer, a recovery due chiefly to my wife Sheila's brave and forceful action, that my passion for life intensified and I became vividly aware of its precious quality. It was this that triggered off my taking part in the first Singlehanded Transatlantic sailing race from Plymouth to New York in 1960, and within thirty-two months of being first taken ill, I crossed the starting line for what was then the toughest yacht race ever devised, and was able to finish in 40½ days. It was a great adventure, that first solo race, and the prospect of racing alone across the Atlantic when I had never before been alone in any boat larger than a 12ft dinghy, was formidable. Five of us—five yachts—took part. Critics decried the race as too dangerous and an unnecessary risk of our lives. Before the race they said that my *Gipsy Moth III*, at 40ft, was too big for one man to handle; after the race they said that *Gipsy Moth* had won only because she was the biggest boat of the five.

Today, eleven years later, it is already difficult to understand what a daring, exciting event that first Singlehanded Transatlantic race seemed at the time. Before the race, I said to myself that nothing could better it as an adventure, that I would be content to play it as my last card. And for a few months I was content to think of it as that. But a year later I found myself craving more excitement and I set out on a solo race against time to see if *Gipsy Moth* and I could make the passage from Plymouth to New York in thirty days. We failed to reach my self-appointed target by 3 days 15 hours, but on reaching Staten Island in New York harbour I recorded that the last thousand miles along the eastern seaboard of the United States may have been the most wonderful sail I shall ever have. These two passages were joyous adventures. After each of them Sheila sailed back across the Atlantic in *Gipsy Moth* with me. And after the second our son Giles, who was then sixteen, came too.

It was after the 1962 venture that I got the urge to try sailing round the world alone. In 1931 I had failed in an attempt to fly round alone and this had been niggling away in the back of my mind; perhaps now I could achieve a solo circumnavigation sailing. The idea developed at about the time of the 1964 Single-handed Transatlantic race, and I became more ambitious. Could I at the same time pull off the first true circumnavigation by a singlehanded yacht round the three great Capes: Good Hope, Leeuwin, and the Horn? By true circumnavigation I meant one which passed through two points on the earth's surface dia-metrically opposite each other. It was a most formidable project in itself, and then I developed another ambition. I would race against time, in this case the average clipper time for the passage from England to Australia and home again, which I calculated from the records as 100 days out and then 110 days back. The voyage in *Gipsy Moth IV* turned out to be another happy ad-venture, even though I failed in my race against the clippers. In fact I passed Melbourne 99 days out from Plymouth, so I would have made the passage in 100 days if I had landed there instead of going on to Sydney. But I had set my heart on sailing into Sydney Harbour because most of my flying voyages had started or finished there, and that cost me another seven days. Romantic notions have always proved expensive in one way or another. However, in compensation I achieved a bonus in that this was the fastest true circumnavigation which has ever been made by a small craft, either with or without a crew.

My life had hardly settled down again before the same old restlessness was nagging at me. And time! time! time! was running on. How could I find one more satisfying venture? It would be difficult now to find a solo race or voyage with the thrilling romantic appeal of that first 1960 Transatlantic solo race or the 1966-7 circumnavigation. I looked back over my life to the projects or ventures which had been most satisfying; and began to ask why, and how, they stood out from the rest. I tried to see if there was a pattern running through them which would lead me to a new and perhaps last project.

The Tasman flight in 1931 was easily the greatest adventure of my life. The Tasman Sea, between New Zealand and Australia, is two-thirds the width of the Atlantic, and I set out to cross it to Australia in a Gipsy Moth seaplane which weighed 1,000lb and had a range of only 750 miles. The crossing was only possible for the little Moth if I could find and land on two islands on the way; the first, Norfolk Island, was the size of a cattle station. In order to find it without any radio aids I had to rely on sun observations with a sextant. No one then had navigated only by sextant while flying alone—and this was over the sea. I had to devise a new system of navigation for the project, a system which has now become universally accepted as the 'Find the Island' method. When the sun's altitude was at a certain height, I had to turn hard right and expect to find Norfolk Island an hour's flight away in the new direction. If my navigation was wrong and I missed the island I was lost, for I had not enough fuel to return to New Zealand, the nearest land, and no means of getting help.

The appeal of the Tasman venture was its untried newness, the demand on my brain to foresee and be prepared for the unknown snags; and then, the excitement of staking everything on the success of my system. That turn to the right over the lonely sea after flying in a different direction for hours was perhaps the most difficult action I have ever had to force myself to take.

The attraction and the satisfaction of my solo seaplane flight from Sydney to Japan in 1931 was that it had never been done before and that I would have to reckon with a succession of unforeseeable difficulties and obstacles; coupled, of course, with the romantic appeal of flying over unexplored country and alighting the seaplane at ports and islands and lagoons where the few inhabitants had never seen an aeroplane before.

The third venture which stood out in my mind was the solo flight from London to Sydney in the little Gipsy Moth in 1929. This was my first serious project and an entirely new sort of experience for me. Although the flight itself had already been made once solo by Bert Hinkler, I set out to beat his time. I failed through over-keenness and through making too big an effort which I was unable to sustain, but it was in the planning for the flight, as well as in the flight itself, that I first tasted the thrill of setting one's self in a race against time, a thrill which in my later years has become almost an obsession.

And after these flights, the highlights among the adventures of my life, came the circumnavigation, and my first two solo Transatlantic races.

It seemed clear that there were common factors in all I had set out to do in the past. At the head of the list came the attraction of doing something that had never been done before, because of the appeal of the untried, the unknown, and the excitement—as on the Tasman flight. Beyond that the adventure had to be a challenge to my mental as well as my physical capacities; the hard physical slog has no appeal to me unless I am using my brain in active support before and during the event. Secondly, the attraction of a race, and because I am by preference a solo flyer and a solo yachtsman, I preferred a race against time, an unrelenting opponent, to one against other competitors.

Speed seemed to hold a key. The distance from A to B on the earth's surface is unalterable, and once man has travelled from A to B the journey is done, finished with. Nobody else can ever know the excitement of being the first; all a man can do is travel faster.

It would have to be under sail. Flying was out of the question and I have always been intrigued by yacht speed, where travelling at 8 knots, under 10 miles an hour, produces a sensation of speed that a jet aircraft can never match. In addition, there is to me as much difference between racing a yacht and cruising it as between riding in the Grand National and going for an afternoon ride in the New Forest. Ambling around the world in a good, sturdy, seaworthy but slow craft is in its way appealing and interesting; I very much hope to do it myself with Sheila one day. But *speed*, that demands a tricky, mettlesome steed, and going faster in a yacht than anyone has done before in the same conditions has a romantic appeal all its own. In 1967, while sailing up through the Atlantic on the passage home from Sydney, *Gipsy Moth IV* made a run of 1,408 miles in eight days, 176 miles a day, which I believe was the fastest singlehanded run that had then been made.

I had hoped she would have been still faster, that she would have made good 200 miles a day in the roaring winds of the great

Southern Ocean; but her hull was cranky and I could never let her rip at her top speed down there. She would broach-to, whipping round broadside to the waves and the wind as if daring them to throw her upside down. It was rather like Russian roulette when she lay over on her beam, keel towards wind and waves, surfing on top of a 20ft breaking sea, masts horizontal and pointing to the direction in which she was travelling at a speed I judged to be 30 knots. The mastheads only had to tip into the water of the trough ahead and upside down and over she must go. Only once had I been able to let her go all out at full speed—and that was when making the passage home through the North Atlantic and I felt confident that no sea big enough and rogue enough to capsize her would build up in the 30-knot Trade Winds. So I drove her as hard as I could for eight days and nights. She was so tender that she heeled readily to 45° and sometimes to 60°, while I reckoned that the average heel during those eight days was 35°. This may not seem much, but tilt your chair 35° sideways and you will see that it means a hellish, uncomfortable existence. I would dearly have liked to carry more sail, but when I did *Gipsy Moth IV* lay over on her beam and slowed down. So although in that wild run 200 miles a day was my secret ambition, I had to be content with an average of 176, exactly a knot less.

Two hundred miles a day! If I could make such a five-day run at 200 miles a day; a thousand nautical miles in all, racing all the way. I became enchanted by the neatness, the rightness of this speed: 200 miles per day. It seemed as attractive to the solo sailor as the 10-Second Hundred Yards and the 4-Minute Mile had been to athletes before those targets were achieved. Yet the single-hander's 200 miles per day was a much more distant target than either of those had been. For some time sprinters had been within fractions of a second of the 10, while milers had been nibbling away at fifths of seconds for years. But no singlehanded run had come anywhere near 200 miles a day. I believe, though I cannot be certain, that *Gipsy Moth IV*'s 176 miles per day in 1967 was 25 miles per day faster than the previous solo fastest over 1,000 miles; but 200 miles a day was 24 miles per day, or 13·6 per cent, faster than that, which was a hell of an increase. But what a grand target to shoot at.

Records reveal that big clippers put up terrific one day runs. But fast running often meant blind running, when no astronomical fix was possible at the beginning or end of the run, and when the big ships simply ran with the weather, not caring where it took them. And I could not help wondering, as did Captain James Learmount in *Mariner's Mirror* in 1957, how often a day's run claimed as a record was followed by a meander-pace run on a dog-leg course the next day, giving an 'ordinary' average over the two days or the week. In those squarerigger days the fastest ship attracted the best cargoes and the most passengers.* What I had in mind was not distance sailed or logged in one day but a sustained run of at least 1,000 miles at 200 miles a day, measured in a straight line across the earth's surface on a Great Circle route.

Long-distance singlehanded sailing for distance alone has lost its pristine romantic appeal. At almost any one time now there must be several singlehanded yachts on passage across the Atlantic east to west or west to east—and who would have thought that twelve years ago! Even a singlehanded circumnavigation can never again have the same attraction now that several have done it. But to go after speed records in a single-handed offshore sailing yacht was an entirely new conception in sailing and a challenge that appealed to me enormously. The more I thought about it, the more I became convinced that this would be the next and a continuing phase in sailing—and nothing that has happened since my return has made me change my mind. One of the problems of offshore yacht racing as a sport in which non-participants can take an interest is that the complicated handicapping systems mean that the final result of a race may not be known for hours, even days, after the first yachts home have crossed the line and the excitement of the race has died down. The singlehanded sailor has a natural handicap that keeps him near or at the same level as his fellows. In theory, the bigger boat is always the faster boat, so the singlehander wants to go for the biggest boat he can manage. But he has to manage

---

* In spite of the great clipper claims for a record single day's run, it was the comparatively small *Cutty Sark* which put up the fastest sustained run for clippers. Twice she made six-day runs of more than 2,160 miles, which I believe have never been beaten. Her registered length was no more than 212·5 feet and she was of 2,100 tons displacement at 20ft draft. Her sail area was 32,000 sq.ft. When she made these runs she had a complement of not more than 25 hands all told.

6

her in all conditions and if he is too ambitious she will soon exhaust him to the point when he can no longer race her, and his smaller competitors will make up time against him; on the other hand, if he has a boat which is too easy to manage, she is probably too small, and a competitor with even a slightly bigger boat will probably beat him.

In search of a speed record a lot will depend on the wind and the sea, but even these will tend to even themselves out; five days hard racing in the Roaring Forties might be too tough for a singlehander, while five days in the Doldrums will not get him very far. I can foresee an intelligent search for point-to-point Great Circle stretches of ocean giving distances of 1,000, 2,000, 3,000 or 4,000 miles with the best sailing conditions, and these becoming familiar, named courses along which the single-handers will set out to better the existing record.

So this was the broad basis of the project I started scheming and planning for. It would need hard sailing and careful, constant navigation; an ideal combination from my point of view. It was a wonderful challenge, a romantic challenge with the added attraction that I would be out to break that 200 miles a day barrier for the singlehander not once, but over a sustained period of five days.

My first task was to obtain the most suitable yacht I could for the race. *Gipsy Moth IV* did not belong to me but to my cousin Tony Dulverton, who had presented her to the Greater London Council. They had put her on permanent exhibition alongside the *Cutty Sark* at Greenwich, so she was not available. Even if she had been, I knew that she was not the right craft for the job I had in mind. The winner of the third Singlehanded Transatlantic race in 1968 was Geoffrey Williams in the 57ft *Sir Thomas Lipton*. She had exactly the kind of hull design which I had originally wanted for my round-the-world speed dash in 1966, but I had been talked out of that and into *Gipsy Moth IV*. Afterwards I regretted this and when *Sir Thomas Lipton* turned up exactly what I had in mind, I decided to ask her designer, Robert Clark, to design *Gipsy Moth V* on the same lines. Robert had designed my *Gipsy Moth III*, the winner of the first Singlehanded Transatlantic race in 1960 and second boat in the 1964 race. *Gipsy Moth III* was a conventional cruiser-racer, similar to the long line of successful such yachts that Robert had already designed, and I believe that he might never have broken so radically away from it had it not been for Geoffrey Williams. Geoffrey is a clever, single-purposed, ambitious young Cornishman who had carefully read up model yacht design while teaching in New York, and he succeeded in persuading Robert to design a boat like a fast model racing yacht. I am convinced that model yacht designers are far ahead of ocean racing yacht designers. They can watch their designs sailing in every and all conditions of wind and water with great ease and can quickly make changes to the design, or can experiment with it, in a way which is impossible for the ocean-going yacht designer.

Not least of Geoffrey's accomplishments was his ability to persuade Robert to carry out the design as he wanted it. I have always found Robert difficult to deal with; he has his own views on what should be built or used and I have the impression that he does not like any suggested change in layout or equipment. For instance, Sheila specifically asked for seats in *Gipsy Moth V*'s cabin with the comfort and backward slope of a motor-car seat. What turned up? The cabin settee back actually slopes the opposite way so that one sits with one's bottom outboard under the back of the seat and one's shoulders pushed forward over the cabin table. As for the galley, the chart table, the navigation area and my bunk, for which I wanted what I considered a modern layout, they turned up without a single drawer for storage among the lot. Why, then, did I go to Robert again, and why am I now, as I write, discussing with him how to get *Gipsy Moth* going faster next year? Because I firmly believe him to be the best designer in Britain of a hull—and perhaps of the rig—for the project I had in mind. All Robert's yachts that I have had experience with or know about 'run true', which is of the greatest importance for fast singlehanded sailing. Also his designs have always had one most valuable characteristic; over the years it is possible to modernize or modify them without losing their handsome appearance or good sailing characteristics. And lastly, he has the fine record as a designer of having produced the winning yachts in two of the three Single-handed Transatlantic races and the second boat in the other.

Geoffrey invited me to come for a sail in *Sir Thomas Lipton* with him and Robert. It was a foggy, end-of-year day in the Solent with scarcely enough breeze to keep the yacht moving, but I saw enough to confirm that this was the basic design I wanted. *Sir*

Thomas Lipton was beautifully balanced. She could not enter the narrow Beaulieu River where my home mooring is, because she had no motor; so we sailed back to Cowes. Here she went aground as she was turning in to the first line of mooring piles. It was fortunate that Robert was at the helm and not me. I had invited him and Geoffrey to dinner at the Royal Yacht Squadron and as it was getting late we looked likely to miss our dinner. So I took Geoffrey with me to hearten the chef while Robert sat it out until he had floated off and moored up.

Robert had sketched me a rough sail plan for my new *Gipsy Moth* on the back of an envelope, and this 'staysail ketch rig' was completed with practically no change whatever from the sketch on his envelope; at this sort of thing he really has a touch of genius. With the stays'l ketch rig there was no mains'l but a stays'l setting between the two masts, from the top of the mizen mast to the foot of the main mast. His theory was that a normal mains'l for such a big yacht would be too big and heavy for me to handle, whereas if the same sail area was split up into mizen stays'l and tops'l I would be able to handle the rig easily. Unfortunately he carried his theory farther, and without my knowledge some of the other gear specified for the yacht was made extra light for my ease of handling. This naturally meant that its strength was that much less, which had a drastic effect on my project in, for example, the matter of the spinnaker poles. On the other hand, the sails specified for *Gipsy Moth V* were of stiff and heavy material which used up my energy and strength extravagantly when I had to handle them in stormy weather. Strength shrinks and reactions slow up with age. Undoubtedly I am much less strong than I was at nineteen when I was working in a coalmine; on the other hand, I believe that with increasing age I have developed cunning and skill in devising means of getting over difficulties without calling on brute strength; but I cannot recall Robert ever asking my opinion about heavy sea sailing, in which I have experience. If only our temperaments had allowed us to work together in 1969 and 1970 as we are at present, I think a faster and more efficient *Gipsy Moth V* would have resulted.

The design was thrashed out, contracts were drawn up, and everything was ready to start building the new yacht at the end of 1969. I thought that Rodney Warington Smyth's boatyard at Falmouth would be the yard to build it. Sheila and I like Rodney and he has a fine reputation in the boat-building world. Robert agreed but later said he feared Rodney would not be able to complete in time and produced another offer from the Crosshaven boatyard at Cork, in Ireland. The price was lower, which would compensate partly for the greater expense of flying to Cork periodically to look at the building. Also, *Gipsy Moth III* was built in Eire at Arklow, south of Dublin, and I had found that I liked working with the Irish, so I agreed.

In the end, *Gipsy Moth V* was not launched until towards the end of June 1970 instead of in March as contracted, but the delay was chiefly due to being unable to get delivery of gear from an English firm for the engine and a feathering propeller. Although *Gipsy Moth* was designed for fast deep-sea racing, she needed a motor. For one reason, Lord Montagu had given me the freedom of the Beaulieu River and a mooring there for life after my circumnavigation and the river is now so crowded with moorings that for a yacht 57ft overall and 29 tons Thames Measurement a motor is usually necessary for manœuvring up the river. Secondly, *Gipsy Moth*'s topsides have too much windage for a singlehander to haul her up to an anchor and then break it out in a near gale in a restricted anchorage without a motor or powered capstan to help. A third reason is that the Marconi Kestrel Radio/Telephone set which I have used on most of my voyages for transmitting reports to a newspaper or the BBC requires a powerful set of batteries and a motor to charge them, and I thought it best to use one motor both for propelling the yacht and for charging the batteries. The engine installation gave me more trouble than all the rest of the yacht and its gear together. To start with, the propeller used to go into forward when the gear lever was put into reverse. This caused me to go aground on the Beaulieu River bank when picking up my mooring singlehanded. It was only a matter of minutes before a Fleet Street newspaper was ringing up the Harbour Master, asking about the 'stranding'. One man's mishap may be another's joy, but in this case I was a disappointment because I got *Gipsy Moth* off the mud again unaided after a few minutes.

Another awkward episode was when I brought *Gipsy Moth* from my mooring to Buckler's Hard, where Edward Montagu wanted her to remain for a week, moored fore and aft between two piles, so that visitors to his Motor Museum at Beaulieu and

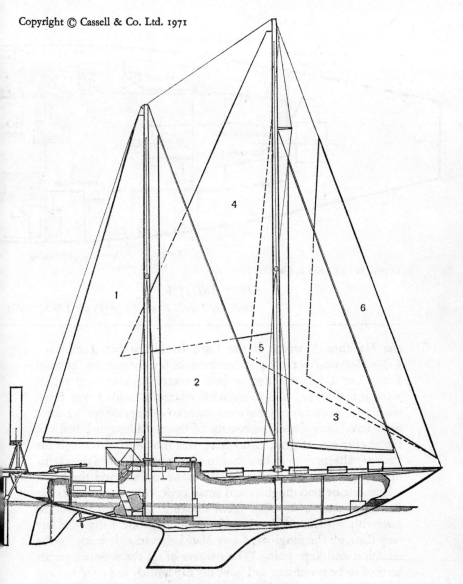

Sail plan and list of sails carried

1. Mizen (260sq.ft)   4. Main tops'l (370sq.ft)
2. Mizen stays'l (270sq.ft) 5. No. 1 jib (510sq.ft)
3. Main stays'l (220sq.ft)   6. No. 2 jib (252sq.ft)
Running heads'l 'Big Brother' (640sq.ft)

Also carried: Jib* (300sq.ft); running heads'l* (600sq.ft); storm jib (99sq.ft)

---

* *Gipsy Moth IV* sails, bought at sale.

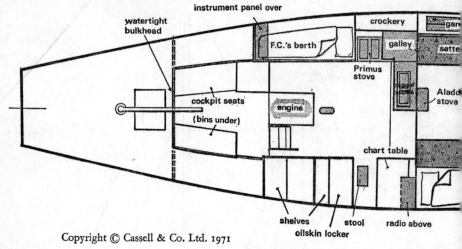

watertight bulkhead

instrument panel over

crockery

galley

F.C.'s berth

Primus stove

cockpit seats (bins under)

engine

settee

Aladd stove

gar

chart table

shelves
oilskin locker

stool

radio above

GIPSY MOTH V
Auxiliary Stays'l Ketch: LOA 57′0″; LWL 41′8″;

the Maritime Museum at the Hard could see her. I motored
Gipsy Moth up-river into position to make fast the stem to the pile;
but when I put the engine into reverse to take way off, it
went into forward and *Gipsy Moth* charged ahead. I was faced
with rows of yachts moored alongside each other; altogether there
must have been fifteen or twenty of them. Although I had put
the engine out of gear, *Gipsy Moth* was moving fast enough for
the only alternatives to be either to charge straight into the yachts
or to drive into the shallow water between them and the bank,
where one or two dinghies and small craft were moored. I chose
the latter and with *Gipsy Moth* drawing nearly 8½ft I waited
miserably for the clunk when she struck bottom. I threaded my
way through the dinghies; *Gipsy Moth* behaved as if enjoying the
situation and kept going. The owners of all the moored yachts
seemed to be watching, so I gave my cap a hitch and tried to look
as if *Gipsy Moth* was always tied up in this way. Providence or
Fate was watching benevolently and *Gipsy Moth* proceeded
gaily on her way. She went right round the outside of all the yachts
and back again into the stream without touching bottom or
another vessel; then proceeded sedately down river where
the skilful Harbour Master took the bow warp and secured her to
the pile.

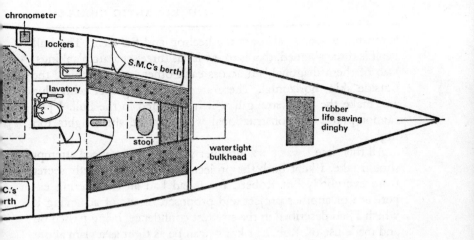

beam 12′0″; draught 8′4½″; tonnage TM 29

That was not the end of the troubles. While at Buckler's Hard the propeller shaft seized up altogether when being tested. *Gipsy Moth* had to be sailed across the Solent to Cowes, the nearest place where a hauling crane able to lift a yacht of her size out of the water was available. It was found that the propeller shaft was out of alignment and that the stern tube which ought to have had grease forced into it until it squirted out at the propeller end, was mostly filled with seawater instead of grease. As a result the white metal bearings had seized up. These troubles with the propeller, shaft, and gear continue as I write.

I want to stress that these time-delaying, irritating troubles with the motor and the design and finish of the interior accommodation were relatively trivial when compared with the excellent work of the shipwrights at Crosshaven on the hull of Robert's design, for I am convinced that a better construction job could not have been found. *Gipsy Moth* is like a big dinghy, 57ft long, waterline length 41ft 8in, beam 12ft, draught 8ft 4½in and displacement 17 tons. The Thames tonnage is, as I have said, 29 tons. She has a flattish bottom of the skimming dish type like a scow, with a fin keel and a skeg with rudder separate from the keel well aft of the cockpit. The fin is a 7½-ton lump of iron bolted to the wooden keelson. All the frames and stringers are of laminated wood, as also are the keelson and the stem. The hull itself is three-skinned, that is to say it has three separate plankings, two of them diagonal-laid across each other, and the third, the outside skin, horizontal. These are bonded together with glue and make the great strength which I wanted in the hull. I just cannot praise the constructional work by the shipwrights too highly.

All this time I was puzzling over what form my speed attempt should take. I kept both the project and my plans strictly secret from everybody but Robert, for I had had an embittering experience of another project and proposed means of achieving it which I had described in the strictest confidence, being passed on and made use of. Robert, I know, can be as tight as a clam about a client's project. Much of my spare time was spent in studying charts and weather maps, particularly the United States hydrographic pilot charts and the comparatively new British Admiralty routeing charts, which are produced one for every month of the year. Both the United States and the British charts are fine productions, most helpful to the deep-sea yachtsman. They give the average winds for a month for each rectangle of 5° of latitude and 5° longitude. It was Lieutenant Fontaine Maury of the U.S. Navy who conceived the idea of these charts in the early nineteenth century, but the Admiralty routeing charts were exceptionally valuable for my purpose. They give the average percentage of winds to be expected for the particular month for each different strength for each separate octant of the compass, the percentage expectancy of calms and variable winds, and the number of observations from which the averages have been deduced.

The 200 miles a day target was so much faster than *Gipsy Moth IV*'s 176 miles per day that I knew I must get all the help I possibly could in order to have any chance of success; I needed the most favourable site, wind conditions, weather, and current. This was going to be quite unlike previous sailing enterprises, and more like an attempt to set a high speed record in a power boat or a motor car. For these the most favourable conditions are sought after and although my problem was complicated by the timespan involved, I felt I needed exactly the same sort of support from my choice of the time of the year, site, weather, and the rest. At this stage, my interest was simply to be *somewhere* where I could sail fast for a period or periods of five days during a voyage. I thought that my best chance of finding the conditions I wanted, without going to or even considering the Pacific, which was too far away, was to make another run through the NE Trade Wind belt in the North Atlantic. It was in this that *Gipsy Moth IV* had put up her fastest run in her round-the-world voyage of 1966–7. The zone of the Trade Wind alters with the seasons of the year but lies roughly between 5°N and 25°N and stretches right across from Africa to America. Perhaps its greatest attraction was that it provides the best chance of steady, constant winds which were likely to be fresh but unlikely to be stronger than moderate gale force. January seemed the most favourable month and my first plan was to make one 1,000 mile run down to the Equator and a second run—a copy of *Gipsy Moth IV*'s speed run in 1967—from the Equator northwards.

So far all my hopes were based on *Gipsy Moth V* being swift and sure; they were little more than an optimistic vision at this stage. How often have I made plans with the greatest care, sure that every obstacle and difficulty had been foreseen, only to find when it came to putting them into practice that some vital and perhaps simple snag had been completely overlooked. I had to get *Gipsy Moth* offshore and put her through the stiffest trials. It would be vital to learn how to get the best out of her. Some yachts have their greatest success when they come brand new from the yard and straight into a race; but I suspect that this success in most cases is because their sails have at that stage perfect aerofoil shape undistorted by hard weather.

So on 14 August 1970 I set off from the Beaulieu River on a 5,000 mile trial run to Majorca in the Mediterranean and back. I invited Christopher Doll, a film producer who had made a television film about the Battle of Britain and who was now making a biographical TV film chiefly about the voyages and adventures of my *Gipsy Moths*, to sail with me to Majorca. Christopher caused me a great deal of worry; he had never been to sea in a yacht before, and never seemed able to grasp the hazards, problems, or sailing technique important for an offshore passage, or even to take a serious interest in them. He was only interested in getting good photographs and to do this he would put up with anything, clambering all over the boat and even climbing the rigging in a rough sea while being horribly seasick. Nothing requires more courage and determination than that, but

Christopher simply accepted it as part of his job, and seemed oblivious of the discomfort he created for himself for the sake of his film. Sheila flew out to Gibraltar and joined *Gipsy Moth* to sail on to Majorca. Giles flew out from England when the filming at Majorca had finished and sailed back with me, just the two of us.

I never seemed to have good luck with this voyage, which probably means that I did not plan and carry it out skilfully. For example, my chief object was to try out *Gipsy Moth* when running before the wind, not just for a few hours but during several days. What happened? On the way home with Giles, when we could confidently expect the prevailing south-westerlies, we were continually on the wind for 1,600 miles. One might go round the world several times without being close-hauled for such a stretch. Every time we turned a corner of Spain or Portugal expecting the headwind to become favourable, the wind changed direction at the same time and continued to head us. *Gipsy Moth* sailed well into wind, but this was not the object of the voyage and it was certainly not what I wanted on any speed run. In the end I never did have a sustained run to try out her speed and handling qualities in Trade Wind conditions. Once when sailing down-Channel with Christopher the wind freshened up to gale squalls and for a minute or two *Gipsy Moth* was touching 17 knots as she surfed on a wave crest with the wind from the starboard quarter. This stuffed me with optimism and I felt convinced, because I wanted to be convinced, that she could keep it up given the right conditions; that she was an exceptionally fast yacht, a veritable Arkle outstanding among all other racehorses. It was unfortunate that she had this burst of speed for a few seconds or minutes and pushed my aspirations into the clouds instead of keeping them down to earth.

It was not until 22 October that Giles and I sailed back into the Beaulieu River, and as I wanted to be in position for my speed run to the Equator by the beginning of January, I had to bustle round to get everything done in time. Sheila had her stores list for the voyage well in hand, but I had a list of 97 modifications and things to be done to *Gipsy Moth*, of which the most troublesome were still the propeller, propeller shaft, stern tube, and the engine controls.

With only six weeks to go before I should start for the Equator, the time had come to disclose my project. One of the first people I told was my friend George Greenfield, who looks after my literary business and is a connoisseur of 'strives' and adventures. When I told landsman George of what I had in mind he said, 'Wouldn't it be much more interesting if you made your speed run between two definite fixed points instead of along a 1,000 mile line across an ocean?' I said that this was quite impossible; as it stood now my project was much too difficult not to look for the most favourable conditions and site anywhere in any ocean in the world, without being tied down to going from one fixed point to another. 'For example,' I said, 'consider the Singlehanded Transatlantic Races from Plymouth to New York and Newport.' More than fifty yachts had taken part in the three races. The straight line distance from Plymouth to Newport via Cape Race was 2,840 miles. My fastest time in *Gipsy Moth III* in 1964 had been 94·6 miles per day, and the fastest passage in all three races had been that of Geoffrey Williams in *Sir Thomas Lipton* in 1968 when he crossed in 25 days 20 hours and 33 minutes, at an average speed of 109·8 miles per day. A large share of the sailing in this race was windward work because of the depressions whistling through from west to east in the North Atlantic. Two hundred miles a day was a vastly increased speed and it would be almost impossible for a singlehander to achieve it on that fixed northern route. It showed clearly why I must seek the best conditions I could find. George's comment boiled down to 'H'm'.

George's words niggled at me. Of course the whole idea was ridiculous, as any yachtsman could see at once. And yet.... A definite course between two points. A definite starting line and a definite time at which to cross it, after which you were committed to win or lose. It *was* a greater challenge, and a tougher one. I began to sit up late at night studying charts, reading Admiralty Sailing Directions and calculating distances to see if I could find some run between two fixed points which would fill the bill.

The traditional cross-Atlantic route for yachts is from the Canary Islands (29°N 13½°–17½°W) to Barbados (13°N 59½°W) in the Windward Islands of the Caribbean Sea. Hundreds of yachts have sailed over this route. I stepped off the distance on a chart and found it roughly 2,640 miles from Palma in the Canaries to Barbados. It was an intriguing possibility, a good sporting sail; but it was an old and well-worn route. Could I find something more exciting? Why not go straight through the Windward Islands and carry on into the Caribbean?

My route needed to be a straight line, that is to say a Great Circle, on the earth's surface.* I spotted a place called Chichi on the coast of Venezuela, Central America. This name sounded an auspicious tie up with mine. Supposing I started from a point near the coast between Dakar and Bathurst in West Africa, and shot through the Windward Islands, south of Grenada, to Chichi. I calculated the distance and found that it was 3,001·75 miles. Three thousand miles was certainly much more romantic than 2,640. But why stop at 3,000? I plotted route after route, getting more excited and keen to extend the distance. Could I run straight through the Caribbean, past Venezuela and the Isthmus of Panama, to Nicaragua, at the western end of it? Nicaragua seemed to have a horrid coast, strewn with cays, reefs, and islands. On top of that it had a wide belt of shallow water, which could make life very uncomfortable. On top of that again it would be a lee shore with a strong ENE wind driving right on to it; and lastly, it would also have a west-going current, trying to carry a yacht on to the beach. However, there was one place, San Juan del Norte (sometimes called Greytown), which could be approached without risk of hitting a cay. Just to the north of it the coast was indented somewhat to the west, with Corn River in the middle of this indentation. The nearest hazard north of Corn River was a rock or islet called Paxaro Bovo, fifteen miles to the north, and then there was a bunch of cays off Monkey Point, five miles farther on. Farther north was impossible. The shallow waters were sprinkled with cays and reefs and islets. There was not a single light on the coast from San Juan del Norte to El Bluff, sixty miles to the north. None of the cays or islets was lighted. Approaching Corn River from the east, it was so shallow that there were only 30 fathoms of water twenty miles offshore. San Juan was a nightmare landfall too; there was not enough depth on the bar of the estuary for *Gipsy Moth* to enter and there was a

---

* Meridians are typical Great Circles and parallels of latitude, except for the Equator, are small circles. A simple way of seeing what a Great Circle route looks like is to stretch a piece of string from one point to another on a globe. If plots are taken along the line of the string and transferred to an ordinary atlas of Mercator's projection, the results can be very instructive.

cape sticking out four and a half miles to the east of it. Approaching this coast on a dirty night with a fresh onshore breeze was enough to give a singlehanded yachtsman nightmares for the rest of his life. But, and it was a most important but, this San Juan indentation provided the longest straight stretch of water between West Africa and the west end of the Caribbean Sea. I calculated the distance from Bathurst to San Juan; it was 3,900·2 miles.

This threw me into a feverish chart hunt. I could not bear to be so close to 4,000 miles without being able to stretch the distance that far. I simply *had* to find another hundred miles of distance. On the African coast to the south of Bathurst, the capital of Gambia, the next state was Portuguese Guinea, and then the coast bore away to the south-east so that the farther south the starting point, the longer the distance would be. At Conakry, the capital of the Republic of Guinea, I should easily have the extra hundred miles of distance and more, but in January it would be in the Doldrums with no wind or fluky light airs for up to 500 miles to the west of it. That put it completely out. The only possibility was Portuguese Guinea. Here the hydrographic charts showed mostly faint airs up to 250 miles offshore, though there was a percentage of Force 3 and Force 4 breezes coming in from the north and NNE. I computed the distance from Caio at the mouth of the Canal (estuary) do Geba in Portuguese Guinea to San Juan del Norte. It was 3,956 miles. Forty-four to go. By now I was enchanted with the romantic appeal of the round figure of 4,000 miles and, carried away by it, I decided to start 47½ miles up the Geba estuary at the capital, Bissau. From there, at a point in the middle of the estuary five miles offshore from Bissau, and if I moved the 'finishing post' somewhat north of the township of San Juan del Norte to postion 11°17′N 83°47′W, about five miles off the Corn River entrance, I could get my straight line distance of just over 4,000 nautical miles.

It lay roughly along the parallel of 10°N, which put me, usefully, in the west-going North Equatorial Current. The hydrographic pilot and routeing charts showed me that January should give the strongest winds in this southern part of the North Atlantic, with a good percentage of them at Force 5 and above and comparatively few calms. The winds on the whole should be easterly, in the main between 40° and 50° abaft the beam, which would put *Gipsy Moth* on to a broad reach, a yacht's fastest point of sailing; only a small percentage was shown from astern or abeam.

This was it. What a wonderful racetrack. On the face of it, it did not look as if there was a hope of getting anything like the length anywhere else in the Atlantic, and bursting with excitement I committed myself to attempting 4,000 miles in 20 days along this track. And although I did not know it at the time, in my enthusiasm for those extra miles I had found, I had also made my first major error.

At that time, I reckoned that the whole voyage would take four months, with 9,500 miles of sailing. But after I had penetrated the Caribbean Sea I had a feeling of claustrophobia, of being encompassed and even oppressed by the land and islands surrounding it, although it is 1,650 miles from end to end. I felt 'au large' as the French put it so well, when I emerged through Crooked Island Passage into the broad Atlantic, and a primeval urge set me to sail on down to the Equator and back before being enclosed again by land on my return to the English Channel. My excuse was that I wanted to try to improve upon my five-day speed record. I did try, damned hard, but I never really believed the excuse. In the end I was to be away for five months and *Gipsy Moth* was to sail 18,581 miles.

And when in my planning I listed the difficulties and hazards of approaching the Nicaraguan shore, of beating out against strong winds and currents to escape from the Caribbean through the Windward Passage between Haiti and Cuba, and thence through the passages among the cays of the Bahamas, somehow I was not touched by the practical reality of it all. When I came to it, it turned out to be as interesting and exciting an adventure as I could wish for. Nor, while I was planning, had I any premonition of the amazing, the Providential good luck which I feel I did not deserve and which saved me and *Gipsy Moth* from disaster near the end of the voyage.

II

DOWN TO THE STARTING LINE

On 12 December 1970, Giles and his friend David Pierce helped me to sail *Gipsy Moth* from the Beaulieu River down to Plymouth. It could well have been *Gipsy Moth*'s last passage. She had such a near escape from being smashed by a steamer that my blood still runs cold when I think of it.

On a fine sunny morning in perfect visibility *Gipsy Moth* was on passage westwards from Portland Bill. Start Point was in full view ahead and bearing south-west. Abeam, three or four miles to starboard, was a steamer approaching from the N or NNE, probably out of Exmouth. *Gipsy Moth*, under sail, had right of way. I made a mental note of our closing angle, checked our course, was satisfied that all was well, and went below to cook some breakfast for the crew. It seemed only minutes later that suddenly looking up, I saw through the window on the starboard side of the doghouse the green-painted, rust-speckled iron side of a steamer a few feet away. I don't think I will ever again reach the cockpit as quickly as I did then. *Gipsy Moth*'s bows were just about to hit the broad side of the big steamer. I grabbed the helm, overriding the self-steering gear by force, and turned on to a heading parallel with the ship. The great iron mass was now eighteen inches or so from the side of *Gipsy Moth* amidships. I could not head directly away from the steamer because the stern would have swung over to starboard and been caught by the ugly steel plates and rivets sliding past. I had to keep *Gipsy Moth* sailing almost parallel to the side of the ship and between one and two feet off it. I feared that any slight roll would swing the crosstrees into the side of the steamer to knock her off course and bring the hull in contact. Giles was lying in his berth hard against the starboard side of *Gipsy Moth* amidships, and I dreaded the side being torn away by the rough iron with Giles trapped in his bunk. Yet as the steamer drew ahead I had to edge *Gipsy Moth* away, increasing the gap inches at a time, else we could have been dragged into the propellers.

One of the crew of the steamer looked down over the side at *Gipsy Moth* and I told him what I thought of *Crystal Kobus*, registered in Panama. I had reasoned that no ship would turn the Point with its busy two-way traffic without being able to cope with any problem a yacht might present. It is true that *Gipsy Moth*, like every vessel, should keep a lookout even while having right of way, but before the near miss I *had* checked the closing angle and decided that if ever there was a case where it was unnecessary for *Gipsy Moth* to keep watch on an approaching steamer, this was it. *Gipsy Moth* had not altered course nor, in the conditions, could there have been any appreciable increase or decrease in speed.

Steamers should of course be given right-of-way over smaller and normally handier yachts and sailing dinghies in land-locked waters, estuaries, or narrow sea-passages where some of the big steamers can put themselves into danger by giving way to a bull-minded racing yachtsman intent on his 'rights'. But offshore I think steamers should stick to the rules of the road when they meet sail, and should remember that a radar set is an aid to the lookout and does not replace him.

At Plymouth there was little to do. All the stores were aboard, organized by Sheila at Beaulieu; arrangements for my radio schedules and my rendezvous with Christopher Doll at Bissau were already settled. The really important item was to ask Sid Mashford, whom I regard as the most knowing judge of a yacht's likely weaknesses in storm, to look over *Gipsy Moth*. As a result of this he strengthened the stem pulpit and its fastenings; how right he was to prove to be! He also rigged a permanent radar reflector under the starboard cross-tree. While *Gipsy Moth* was at Sid's yard, BBC technicians fitted a cassette cine-camera at the forward end of the cabin top, in a gimballed container designed to stand up to rough weather. Privately I wondered how it would last, but it was certainly worth giving it a try. The camera itself had a romantic past, being ex-RAF and first used in a fighter to record air-to-air combats in the Battle of Britain.

Gipsy Moth left Plymouth on 18 December. It was a foul day with drizzle and mist, followed by heavy rain, with a nasty sea outside the breakwater. I felt gauche with the gear and in no wise like a seaman. My heart was depressed to my boots and I could not imagine anything more unpleasant than starting on a big project in the dead of winter in such weather. To make things worse Stanley Rosenfeld, one of the finest yachting photographers in the world, had been commissioned by *True* magazine in New York to take pictures during the days leading up to the start. As I left the east end of the familiar breakwater that runs across Plymouth Sound, Rosie's launch crossed my bows as I tacked and I would have rammed him had I not immediately tacked back again. I cursed him from Plymouth to hell, but he seemed quite unmoved and clicked away with his camera. I wondered if he had done it on purpose to catch me in an awkward situation.

Visibility was very bad outside the breakwater and the movement was horrible. As soon as I had got rid of Rosie I had two strong Courvoisier brandies with honey, lemon, and hot water. *Gipsy Moth* was pinched up hard on the wind, driving into a rough sea and a wind of up to 27 knots. It was dark at 1630 and the skies did not lighten again until 0845 next morning, giving sixteen hours of night sailing. In spite of a feeling that I was about to be sick—I wasn't—and all the banging, which sounded like a gale blowing up, I had a good sleep. At dawn a half moon was showing among some clear sky patches among gloomy, stormy-looking black clouds: I logged that it was thrilling to be on my way at last.

I had looked forward to using this passage from Plymouth to Bissau for trying out *Gipsy Moth*'s paces. I wanted to experiment with different sail trimmings and sail settings, and to see what speeds *Gipsy Moth* could achieve at different headings relative to the wind. Most important of all, I wanted to get my sail drill slick and fast. For three days I was chafing with impatience; there was no weather worth a damn to me and over one period of 12½ hours up till the early hours of the 20th *Gipsy Moth* averaged only 1·1 knots. Then on the morning of the 21st the wind swung round to the NE and freshened. At last I had just what I wanted. Half an hour before noon I rigged up the 25ft spinnaker pole to port and boomed out the 300sq.ft jib which I had bought back at a sale of *Gipsy Moth IV*'s sails. It took me 2¼ hours to set up the pole and boom out the sail; I had to find all the different items, the guys, outhauls, sheets, the pole rest to fit on the stem pulpit, and so on, and then to remember how to handle the complicated layout, for I had not been able to use it seriously on *Gipsy Moth V* before. All the time I had to go carefully so as not to make a mistake in a breeze now blowing at 30 knots. But the thin winter sun was shining, dolphins were surfacing within six feet of me while I worked the stemhead, and it was exciting because this rig *had* to succeed if *Gipsy Moth* was going to clock anywhere near the 200 miles per day target. One immediate benefit of poling out was that the changed air-flow put the No. 1 jib to sleep; it had been banging horribly during the night and had kept waking me from a restless night-mare in which someone was aboard *Gipsy Moth* with a whistle; but I think this noise was due to one of the stanchions, which sighed and whistled mournfully as the wind found a hole or gap in it. Two hours after noon *Gipsy Moth* was clocking 9·2 knots on the speedometer; this was a rate of 220 miles per day and I felt optimistic and excited.

At 1645 I adjusted the pole height and the guys staying it in position so that the wind pressure was even over the sail; then I hardened in on the halyard of the poled out sail to straighten its luff, and trimmed the three other sails—the No. 1 jib, the mizen stays'l and the main stays'l. This seemed to pay off and *Gipsy Moth* was doing up to 13 knots with the new windvane fitted to the self-steering gear doing splendidly; this vane was much larger than the standard size recommended for such a wind, but was necessary because of *Gipsy Moth*'s speed. Since I had poled out, *Gipsy Moth* had sailed 28·7 miles in 3 hours 12 minutes, an average of 8·95 knots, or 215 miles per day, which showed what she could do if given the wind.

From then on I was experimenting with trim, rig, and headings all the time. For instance, at midnight that night, after some try-out settings of the poled-out jib which were not right, I clapped a handy-billy on the outhaul of the boomed sail, using a rope-end stopper because the tension was too great to haul it out by hand. This took some of the curve or sag out of the jib and I thought it was then not banging so much as before when a wave slueing *Gipsy Moth*'s stern to leeward brought her up to the wind, and the leech and the foot would collapse. My handy-billies are what the old squarerig seamen called watch-tackles or tail-tackles, brought up to date. I fasten a single block with a snaphook attached to it to an eye in the deck, and a double block at the other end of the tackle has a rope tail to it which I clip on to the boomed sail out-haul by means of a couple of half-turns and a hitch.

I cooked a good supper but I felt so queasy by the time I had finished it that I turned in without eating it.

The wind was easing through the night and by the time the sky was lightening at dawn, I decided to hoist the tops'l. At noon on the 22nd *Gipsy Moth* had sailed 212·8 miles during the past twenty-four hours. I was delighted; this looked really promising. The position was now 150 miles NW of Cape Finisterre in Spain.

In the afternoon I decided to drop the boomed-out jib. For one reason it was coming aback too often as *Gipsy Moth* slued to windward; also, the poled-out sail could not be carried if the heading was brought 18° nearer the wind to set *Gipsy Moth* on the course required to pass westward of Madeira. An even more important reason for dropping it was that I wanted to test the effect of the change.

It took me about 1½ hours to drop and bag the jib and dismantle and stow all the running gear. To my surprise dropping the sail did not seem to have made any difference to the speed. The log read: 'I guess there is wind to spare and I daresay I could drop the tops'l too but I would like to keep it up for experiment.'

The sea was roughing up as the evening came on, slueing *Gipsy Moth* broadside to the wind at times. I noticed on the dial speeds of up to 14 knots. The true wind was now a few degrees N of E and 31½ knots.

By midnight the wind was gusting strongly and waves were crashing on the deck; two hours later I wrote in my log: 'So ends a mad ride. I lay in my bunk getting more and more tense and rigid but wanting to find out what would happen. A series of big breaking waves seemed to coincide with freshes of wind of up to 40 knots. *Gipsy Moth* would gripe to windward and heel over until I wondered if the sails would go into the water. Time after time the self-steering would end by bringing *Gipsy Moth* back on course. What a game beggar! It seemed miraculous that eventually it could bring back the heading through 75° with a gale forcing the boat up into the wind.'

The only snag was that the 40 knot gusts had to ease back to 25 knots before the Gunning self-steering gear could manage to do that. In the end I could not stand the strain any longer, so I hopped out and dropped the tops'l. The tops'l seemed to be the cause of the trouble: sheeted right to the stern of the boat as it was, it was pulling the stern round. For any speed run I would badly need the pull of that 370sq.ft sail, but it looked as if I could only get the extra area by poling something out. I waited to see the effect of dropping the tops'l on the speed, which had kept remarkably steady in the 14 hours since noon, the average only varying half a knot between 9·2 and 9·7 knots. For 2½ hours with the tops'l down the speed kept at 9·5 knots, but the going was so rough that I turned 30° down wind, and although the wind was still gusting up to 40 knots the speed dropped to 8·75. At 0930 I set the tops'l again, this time hoisting it only part of the way up the main mast and sheeting it to the forward end of the sheet lead track 15ft forward of the stern, hoping that it would not pull the stern round to leeward so much. However, I found that I had to alter course more to windward before I could get the speed back to 9 knots.

At noon on the 23rd the distance sailed in the previous 24 hours showed as 220·7 miles. Total for the two days, 433·5 miles. This was thrilling—but only until I calculated the fix-to-fix runs for the two days. On the first day of this run, 21/22 December, *Gipsy Moth* had sailed 212·8 miles through the water, but the fix-to-fix straight line run was only 181 miles, 15 per cent less. I was flabbergasted; thirty-one miles lost of the distance sailed was disastrous. How could it have happened? It was true that I had been only concerned with experimenting to get the maximum speed and had not been concerned to keep the track straight: true also that I had not obtained an accurate sun fix at the start of the run and that possibly the six bearings I had taken with the D/F loop of Corunna in Spain, Bordeaux, Brest, Ushant, and Round Island in the Scilly Isles had all contained an error. The two bearings of Ushant had certainly had 37 miles difference between them, but the others had met in a convincing enough 'cocked hat' triangle. The D/F (radio direction finding) fix was 30 miles ahead of my DR (dead reckoning) position and of course if that DR position had been correct, then the run 'made good' would tie in with the distance logged as sailed. Such an error was not a worry now, but if the log was going to overread the distance sailed, due to some such cause as riding up and down the surfaces of the waves, that was a serious, depressing prospect for my speed bid, for it meant that *Gipsy Moth* was a slower boat than I had thought and that many of my calculations were over-optimistic.

When I calculated the fix-to-fix run for the second day it turned out at 210 miles made good for a distance of 220·7 miles sailed. This was a drop of 4·8 per cent in the distance sailed and seemed more reasonable. Though not so good as the 220·7 miles I had been so cock-a-hoop about, it was nevertheless encouraging.

I had motor trouble. After the R/T session the evening before I had tried to start up the engine to charge the batteries. It fired for about two seconds quite normally then it turned over in a dead way as though it was sucking in water instead of fuel. The starter motor turned the engine freely enough but seemed to have no load. On the morning of the 23rd I tried the engine again but it had no kick at all. This was a setback because I had undertaken to transmit a report to the BBC every day of my speed run across the Atlantic.

My experiment of raising the tops'l only half way up the mast in order to sheet it farther forward and keep the stern from slueing round was a failure. To add to this it gave me plenty of sheeting and cordage problems in the 40 knot gusts, because when halfway up it interfered with the wind flow on to the main stays'l and the jib. I decided that it would have to be hoisted fully and sheeted to the stern, and set about doing it. At once *Gipsy Moth* was nearly out of control, coming hard up into the wind with waves crashing aboard and all the lee deck submarining under the water; I dropped the tops'l and bagged it again and was back where I started. However, this was still my experiment time.

By daybreak on the 24th the speed had dropped back to 8·7 knots and I again hoisted the tops'l. Once more it took charge, pulling the stern savagely round to leeward and heading *Gipsy Moth* into the wind. The self-steering gear could not by itself hold her or bring her back and I had to get into the cockpit with my feet against the locker seat opposite so that I could put all my strength to the tiller with both hands to get back on heading. I decided to try sheeting the tops'l to the after end of the cockpit and dropping the sail just a little lower on the mast to see what effect that had. The tops'l was the easiest of them all to set and hand, but it caused most trouble.

All that day, except when sail trimming or sailing the yacht, I worked hard and continuously at the engine. The log recorded: 'My fingers be praaper wore to the bone, like, as my Devon friends used to say, working the fuel hand-priming pump, fiddling with nuts in awkward inaccessible spots and working for hours with my head upside down looking at nuts or whatever.'

Most of the time *Gipsy Moth* was tearing through the water, lee deck under, and there was hardly a place to put a foot down in the cabin among the boxes, gear, engine casing, and tools, besides the usual boots and clothing. The fuel supply system was full of air, I expect due to running the engine while *Gipsy Moth* was bouncing about or excessively heeled so that air was under the fuel in the tank and got sucked in. I had taken a three-day course on this Perkins Diesel engine at the Peterborough works before my circumnavigation in 1966, but now I found I had forgotten everything. So I sat and looked at it between whiles for nearly two days and studied the handbooks before making any move. 'Well,' I logged, 'I shall be better able to do it another time. I must say this was rather like a sport, like fox-hunting in a small way, chasing the air bubbles from one opening to the next around the motor while trying to undo the right nut to make the right opening. However, it was wonderful to hear the motor kick again and run smoothly after it all. . . . I want to have another go at that tops'l and try sheeting it in a fresh place.'

The run to noon of the 24th was 210·9 miles sailed. Again I was to be disappointed; the calculated fix-to-fix run turned out at only 195 miles, a loss of 7·55 per cent. It was disheartening; the conditions for speed had been excellent and more than 9 knots had been averaged during three periods of the day. The lowest speed average for any one period was 8·52 knots and according to the hydrographic chart *Gipsy Moth* had been in a favourable current throughout the three days, which should have given her an extra kick along. Of course the fix-to-fix run for the two days, noon of the 22nd to noon of the 24th, at 406 miles, came to more than 200 miles per day, but conditions could hardly be better for making speed and on my 4,000-mile run I would need to be able to clock up a considerably better daily surplus than 1·5 per cent. I consoled myself with the thought that I was experimenting with different sail trims all the time, concentrating on trying to get the maximum speed and not taking much care over position fixing. I only observed the sun on two occasions to obtain two separate position lines, whereas during the actual speed run I intended to get three separate position lines to ensure accuracy in the sun fixes.

Gipsy Moth continued to sail fast; the instruments showed an average speed of over 9 knots for eight of the twelve periods in the log, and the lowest speed for the remaining four was 8·9 knots. It was rough going. At 0820 on the 25th the log read: 'I suppose it is a rough line squall passing through. A series of squally gusts up to 40 knots. *Gipsy Moth* still goes out of control of the self-steering with the tops'l up in winds over 30 knots when she has a good slap on the stern from a breaking wave. I was lying tense in my bunk at 6.30 a.m., so tense in one fierce squall that I got cramp in my neck. I had to brace myself against the side of the bunk to avoid being chucked out. *Gipsy Moth* in the worst squall heeled over 40° on her side and griped up 45° towards the wind until she was pointing 60° off the wind instead of 105°. The whole boat was shaking due to sails and gear flogging and slatting and banging, waves crashing the hull, seas racing along the lee deck. I stuck out several of these squalls but in the end there came one and I reckoned *Gipsy Moth* was not going to come out of it back to her normal heading and heel, so I got up. One has to move with great care to avoid being thrown across the cabin. I put oilskins on over my pyjamas and dropped the tops'l. It was very impressive up there in the pitch dark with the sea rushing wildly past like a cataract, dazzling white in the pool of light round the boat from the spreader lights shining down. The tops'l is pretty easy to hand and bag except for the difficulty in standing on the steep deck. After that I rigged a handy-billy tackle to the tiller so that I could haul the tiller to windward from the shelter of the companion when the self-steering was unable to control any longer. This is like I had in *Gipsy Moth IV* and needed constantly. I think it is not only the tops'l sheet pulling the stern round but also the self-steering skeg and rudder are nearly out of the water at a big angle of heel and so have greatly reduced power. Well, this is a good start to Christmas Day. I was lying thinking of boyhood Christmases, waking and emptying the pillow case "stocking" by the dim light of a small oil lamp. Also wondering how Sheila felt spending our first Christmas apart. . . .'

The run to noon of the 25th was again good at 217 miles sailed. I confidently expected as much after the consistently high speeds clocked throughout the 24 hours; but when I calculated the fix-to-fix run it was only 188 miles. This did not seem possible and I measured the distance carefully on the chart between the two fixes; the dividers made it 189 miles, a drop of 13·3 per cent in the distance sailed. So, although *Gipsy Moth* had sailed 861·4 miles in the four days, the four point-to-point runs totalled only 778 miles, which was 22 miles short of the 200 miles a day average I wanted. The position was 36°10′N 19°00′W, 205 miles WNW of Madeira.

This really was disturbing, but I decided to give my worries a rest. After all, it was my Christmas lunchtime, so I started to open one of the bottles of Champagne which Giles had given me. I had the wire off the cork when the sun peeped through the clouds. I had been trying all the morning to get a sun shot so I stood the bottle on the swinging primus cooker where it would not fall off with the heavy rolling, while I made a dash through the companion with the sextant. I was half way out of the cabin when a report like a cannon made me wonder what had crashed; of course it was the Champers bottle blowing off and firing the cork at the ceiling, and half Giles's present had foamed away before I could reach it.

Some strange things happen at sea which are difficult to explain or understand: in the middle of the night I wrote: 'Ever since noon yesterday there has been a succession of little cyclones with the wind going right round the compass, sometimes with a thunderstorm or with a rain downpour. At 3.30 a.m. I awoke because of a continuous thumping, just as if someone in the boat was trying to rouse me. I was pretty fed up by this and resisted waking for a while but it must have been "a little man" determined to wake me. When at last I gave in and came to my senses, I found that *Gipsy Moth* was tearing off for home due north at 7 or 8 knots. I don't know how long for. My previous entry was 12½ miles earlier.'

Since I was devoting the run from Plymouth to Bissau entirely to experimenting with gear, sail trimming, rig, and tactics, I ought to have been very grateful for the storm which blew up on the morning of the 27th. I learned a lot, but I realise now that I ought to have learned a lot more, deduced a lot more, from it. Twenty-four hours later, four hours after midnight on the 28th, I was to record in the log that it had been a long, hard day, and that several times I had thanked God that I had the strength and endurance to do what I did.

The gale really started for *Gipsy Moth* at 0315 when she went aback through a big and sudden windshift which made it necessary to change from a broad reach on one tack to being close-hauled on the other. Of course there was a lot of resheeting, hauling and handling of ropes, and winch work in the cockpit. It was when I went up after this to use the bilge pump under the tiller at the after end of the cockpit that I saw a dark Mother Carey's Chicken, a stormy petrel, crouching in the corner. It must have been there throughout the hour when I had been working in the cockpit. This timid, wild-looking little fellow— if fellow it was—with his soft, sooty-coloured plumage, had chosen about the only spot in the cockpit where he would not have been crushed by my unseeing foot in the dark. The bilge had to stay unpumped because the jet of water would have landed right on him.

At seven I was on deck again to drop the slatting tops'l, but I found that *Gipsy Moth* had turned right round and was heading north, so I tacked, dropped the tops'l and came hard on the wind on the port tack. The true wind was now SSE half east, $25\frac{1}{2}$ knots. This gave a relative or apparent wind of 30 knots, 45° to port of the heading. (A true wind is like a shower of rain which is falling vertically until you start walking or driving into it, when it appears *relatively* or *apparently* to be coming from ahead.)

Another squall went through at 1100 and at noon I noted that the sea began pouring over the side of the cockpit as I was trying to eat some breakfast and write up the log at the chart table. But two hours later I had the mizen down. It was a foul day, grey with heavy rain squalls and wind gusts of 35 knots.

The poor little Mother Carey's chick was still aboard but looking very sorry for himself. I wondered if I should put something there for him to clutch instead of the bare deck. Also was it any use scattering some breadcrumbs? I could try, so I gave him a length of green braided rope to perch on but he didn't seem to think much of that. Also I scattered pieces of toast and crumbs; brown, of course—only the best. But he was not taking to those while I was there, perhaps because even sea birds can get seasick, or at least feel it, when on a boat. Later I found he had nestled on the Spontex sponge under the bilge pump in the cockpit. He looked less forlorn, almost as if it had made a difference, someone trying to be nice to him.

I dropped the No. 1 jib at 1415. It took me a longish time to stow it in the special envelope-bag made to wrap round the sail on the stem so that the sail could be kept permanently hanked on the topmast stay. The object was to save bagging the sail, an exercise which can use up a lot of energy in a singlehander when it is a heavy stiff sail and seas are washing over the stem in a high wind. The foredeck sailcoat was one of Robert Clark's ideas but I had been toying with it myself for a long time and thoroughly approved of it in theory. In practice it turned out to be only troublesome, and in the end damaging. It was troublesome working the sail into the envelope so that the cover flaps could be secured round it. This had to be done thoroughly so that neither wind nor water could get in and force the cover open. The damage came later. However, I logged at that time: 'I think it may be a good thing when I get to know it.' It was very wet on deck, in the lashing rain; but the sea felt warm as it splashed in my face.

Rather than disturb the chick, I set to with the dinghy bailer to scoop into a bucket the bilge-water now running over the cabin floor with a horrid swishing noise, carrying it precariously through the boat to the cockpit. I was working my passage through the boat with my seventh bucketful when pandemonium broke out on deck! The mizen stays'l was flapping madly; something had bust. The din and the shaking of the boat under my feet and my hands was terrific. My heart sank; I thought it was the end of the sail. When I had donned my hard-weather gear and harness and sallied forth, it was not as bad as I had feared; the shackle holding the clew of the sail to the end of the boom had gone, and the sail, being loose-footed, was then free to flap as wildly as it liked. It still had one shackle in the clew thimble and was beating the boat with that. I could only see one small tear in the sail and a batten pocket starting to break away.

I could in fact have left the bilgewater to the pump because I found the chick had moved into the cabin. When I got below again after attending to the mizen he seemed quite happy. I hoped he would not occupy my bunk; but I saw him eyeing it.

By 1710 the barometer had dropped 2·5 millibars in just over two hours. With a new shackle fitted to the mizen stays'l and a handy-billy with one end anchored at the mizen mast, I was able to pull the foot of the mizen out enough to join the clew to the end of the boom and then hoist the sail. At the end of it all I was wet through again, but this time with sweat. I put the Mother

Carey's Chicken on my hand in the cockpit and held it up facing into wind in the hope that it would take off. But it only fluttered down to the cockpit sole.

There was a lull in the wind but the barometer was down another 2 millibars in $3\frac{1}{3}$ hours, and the sky looked horrible at nightfall. I thought that *Gipsy Moth* was in the centre of a small depression and that she would hit the other side of it soon.

An hour after midnight the barometer was down another 2 millibars, and on looking into the cockpit I was astonished to find the heading had swung back from 240° to 130°. The wind had suddenly backed to east and increased to 30 knots again. When I went on deck to drop the mizen I was surprised to find no chick in the cockpit. I searched thoroughly with a torch because I did not want to squash him. I hoped he would be all right and had flown away, for I had been afraid he was going to die. The large light-weather vane on the self-steering gear was taking an awful hiding so I decided I must change it for the smaller one. This proved a complicated and difficult job. It was a dark night and I could only attach the side facing away from the yacht by feel. Sometimes the stern flicked in the air and it was a strange experience to be high in the air looking down on a big sea passing under me thirty feet below.

Two hours later—at 3 a.m. according to the log—I had to take down the stays'l, the last sail I then had set. *Gipsy Moth* had been crashing through the night at 9 knots under it alone, out of control of the self-steering gear. I could hardly keep from being thrown out of my bunk. *Gipsy Moth* was fine, but there comes a limit to what anything will stand, and it looked as if more and worse was to follow. It seemed like—it was—what I would expect on the outskirts of a hurricane. The wind pressed my clothes to my body and my vision was limited because the peak of my cap was being blown hard against my nose. I saw great sheets of spray in the air, scattered like giant bucketfuls of water. The ordinary spray burst as if it were smoke from a cannon. The stays'l was like an enraged animal, and I could not work the hanks right down to the boom because the wind pressed so hard on the foot that, with the clew being secured to the other end of the pole, I could not overcome the wind which pressed the sail out into a taut curve. This was not important except that the untidy stowage meant more windage which in turn produced more movement. If only the boat could have stayed unmoving, the force of the blows from the waves would have been that much less. I was soon soaked; the wind blew the water up under my oilskin smock top, even though I had fastened it tightly round my waist. When I returned to the cockpit I spent what seemed a long time trying to coax *Gipsy Moth* to head downwind under her bare poles; but an extra fierce blast of wind with a slueing wave would start her broaching-to across wind, and the self-steering could not prevent it. Broadside on seemed to be the natural stance for her racing lines and nothing less than a man at the helm would keep her headed elsewhere. I reckon the natural stance of a boat is the safest anyway, but in this case it was much less pleasant.

By 0400 on the 28th the barometer had risen a few millibars and with it the wind increased, registering up to 60 knots. At about ten a big wave came aboard and there was a great crashing of crockery and gear as *Gipsy Moth* was flung viciously on to her side. I felt lucky that I had been forced back into my bunk and not flung out of it. As *Gipsy Moth* righted herself I clambered out, but I could not see any serious damage except for the spinnaker pole housed on the port side of the deck, which had been well and truly kyboshed by the waves. It had a big kink in it which from below I reckoned to be about 150°.

There was a lot of water in the cabin, most of which I thought had come in under the companion hatch cover. I only hoped that the fastenings of the after-peak hatches had held and that the hasps of the bins under the cockpit seats in which I kept so much of my emergency deck gear had kept the lids closed down. The upper life-line was sagging, apparently pulled down in one place, and I thought it must be where the end of the kinked pole had tangled with the foredeck net. 'The wind has eased,' I logged. 'I have not noticed it much over 50 knots lately. More important, it has not got the same savage shriek. I have often noticed the difference between two winds of the same speed. One may have a powerful, urgent, impatient note. The other, of the same speed, will not. It is some extra quality which I have never heard or read about. Anyone might wonder at my lying in my bunk instead of being on deck soaked to the skin as I was after dropping the main stays'l, but I must work up my log to deduce where *Gipsy Moth* has gotten to; and this is the only place in the yacht where I can do it at present.'

At 1900 I logged that I had headed *Gipsy Moth* dead down-wind a number of times by using tackles to the tiller, hoping that self-steering would be able to control her from there; but each time it was a failure; and watching in the cockpit, it was easy to see why. A big wave would creep up on *Gipsy Moth* and break right under her counter, picking up the stern and carrying it round as easily as a dog carrying a bone, leaving it there so that *Gipsy Moth* was broadside to the wind and the self-steering was unable to get her back on course unaided. I thought of hoisting a reefed main stays'l but in the end voted against it because the wind was still up to 60 knots. So I hauled out my brand new storm jib from the forepeak, trying hard not to let any water into the open hatch. After reeving the tops'l sheets through snatchblocks which I rigged to the big deck eyes amidships, the storm jib sheeted and set beautifully and peace reigned. *Gipsy Moth* ambled quietly down the moaning wind at 6 knots, rolling pretty drastically and with a big comber striking ever few minutes. 'Those waves—I was on the foredeck when one broke there, and I marvelled at it. It was as if a giant snowplough were forcing up a great seething, boiling curve of surf on each side to the height of my eye-level, about 12ft up.'

My 25ft spinnaker boom was a sorry sight. It had been on the deck in its usual stowage position with the gooseneck snap-hooked to a big deck eye in the angle between the side deck and the side of the doghouse. The other end of the boom lay in a curved chock on the deck forward of the mast. Now it was broken like a cardboard cylinder, with two big kinks in a 10ft length of it. If a wave could do that to a strong pole, I could not help wondering what would have happened to me if I had been stand-ing there. Would my safety harness have survived, or would the hook have pulled out? Even small waves cross the deck with a rush; when I had been sitting on the deck completing the furling of the tops'l, a wave caught me and swished me right over to the side of the boat, where my legs were in the water under the bottom life-line. No harm was done, but it reminded me forcibly of the importance of always being well attached by one's life-harness.

I presumed that the wave which bent the spinnaker pole had

also damaged the stem pulpit. All its stanchions had been pushed over to starboard and the upper rail on the port side was now pressing against the forestay. This had done some good because that stay had been slack, waiting for me to tauten it; now the pulpit rail had done the job for me. I think the damage came from the big jib being still hanked on and enveloped in the sailcoat. I ought to have realized that the pressure of a rogue wave on its bulk would be great enough to cause some damage. This was one important lesson which I learned: never to leave a sail hanked on if there was a chance of stormy weather. But I must have had a surprised and pained look on my face while handling the sail at the stem when my foot suddenly shot down over the side of the boat. The sail was not lying on the deck at all, but was suspended outboard because of the shift of the pulpit. There was a lesson in that as well.

But there was another much more important lesson staring me in the face and I failed, badly failed, to benefit from it; the spinnaker boom I wanted for my purposes *ought* to have stood up to that wave. It was not strong enough and I should have taken steps at Bissau before the 4,000 mile speed run to have it strengthened, not just repaired. Even a bamboo pole fitted inside the alloy tube could have made a world of difference to my ambitions.

Alas, there was one more tragedy to face in my tour of inspection. I saw a little black head sticking up through the duckboards covering the cockpit floor, its beak lifted to heaven as if appealing for help. My little Mother Carey's Chicken had not left during the night as I had hoped but must have sought safety under the heavy mahogany framework of slats. I had searched the cockpit carefully for him but never thought that the little bird could have squeezed into the tiny space under the boards. What it could not know is that when the cockpit is flooded by a wave breaking aboard, the duckboards float, and all the fathoms of ropes, sheet ends and gear lying there get swilled under the boards in a tangle. As the water drains away through the drainholes, the boards settle down, sometimes out of place and overlapping at the joints. This must have happened and the little chick was crushed when the boards settled down. Or had it already happened, and was the little fellow already dead when I was looking for him? I felt responsible for his death and it made me sad.

Gipsy I Moth alighting on Sydney Harbour, 1931,
during the first long-distance solo flight made
by a seaplane. She weighed only 1,100lb—and we
got as far as Japan before she crashed

Gipsy Moth II. Of 24ft
LWL she missed a prize
in the 1955 Fastnet race
by only 6 minutes.
(Some of the crew
claimed it was because
one of them stowed gun
and shooting boots right
in the stern under the
counter)

Gipsy Moth III, 28ft LWL, a Robert Clark design for cruising built by Jack Tyrrell in Arklow, Eire. The self-steering windvane was of my own design. She won the first singlehanded race from Plymouth to New York in 1960, taking 40½ days for the 3,000 miles of the Great Circle route

Gipsy Moth IV. Built for me by my cousin Tony Dulverton. Illingworth design, Camper & Nicholson build. First singlehanded small vessel to make a true circum-navigation of the three great Capes along the old Clipper Way—Plymouth–Sydney 107 days, Sydney–London 113 days; fastest run point-to-point, 1,408 miles in 8 days

Gypsy Moth V at 9½ knots

Gipsy Moth V ready for launching at Crosshaven
Boatyard, Co. Cork, in the spring of 1970

My safety harness. This photograph was taken
while we were fixing the Gunning self-steering gear
on the stern of *Gipsy Moth V*. It was an excellent
design radically different from the previous ones
I had used, and well engineered

With Sheila on the jetty at Buckler's Hard at the
end of 1970. *Gipsy Moth* can be seen between us,
moored on the trots

Gipsy Moth's three basic sails, easy and quick to hoist. Reading from the bows: main stays'l, mizen stays'l, mizen. All three sails are permanently attached to booms

All plain sail set: No. 1 jib, main stays'l, mizen stays'l with tops'l above it, mizen. The starboard sheet of the tops'l is the wrong side of the mizen shroud and I am busy changing it over. Forward and above me are the main crosstrees where I worked for an hour and a quarter in the Sargasso Sea, repairing the broken jumper stay

The clew of the No. 1 jib shows clearly, making with the attached sheet a good straight line to the lead to the cockpit winch. The tops'l sheet runs to a lead out of sight on the stern

The mizen is awkward to furl because of the wide cockpit under it, so I usually drop it first when entering port. The self-steering vane shows up well in this photograph

Ghosting under the big 640 runner—'Big
Brother'—boomed out to starboard

'31 December,' I wrote in my log. 'Is there any way that I can gybe more quickly and efficiently? I designed my running gear so that it would be safe for a singlehander to handle if a gale blew up or if the heading got out of control and the running sail came aback, and also so that one person could hoist the sail without accidents to gear in any conditions.' The spinnaker used in ocean racing I consider an unseamanlike sail, even with a full crew aboard. It is quite usual, or at least seems to be, for it or some of its gear to break up within two or three hours of the sail being set. It makes me shudder to think of what a singlehander would have to deal with if he had a big spinnaker set and his yacht broached-to in a gale squall while he was asleep.

My own scheme of booming out to windward a running sail hanked on to the topmast stay is an operation I divide into two parts. First I rig the pole and manoeuvre it into position by means of three ropes—a fore and an aft guy and a topping-lift. Having rigged the pole I then hank on the sail, attach a sheet which I lead in the usual way to the cockpit winch, then attach a line to the clew of the sail and lead this line to the outboard end of the pole, thence to the mast end of the pole and thence again down to the deck. This line is used to haul out the clew to the end of the pole. Then the sail is hoisted in the ordinary way. If a suitable jib is being used on the lee side when reaching or on the wind, only the one sail, the runner, need be hoisted in order to have a running rig. To rig the pole and hoist the running sail is no longer or more difficult an operation than the standard setting of a spinnaker on an ocean racing yacht. 'However,' I went on in my log, 'when a shift of wind demands a gybe, it takes me at present on my own between $1\frac{1}{2}$ and 2 hours of pretty intensive activity, brain as well as body. The pole has to be unshipped, unrigged and housed on the deck. Another pole has to be rigged on the other side of the yacht. The running sail has to be dropped on the starboard side, but the jib has to be dropped on the port side and shifted over to the starboard side. The big runner has to be hanked on afresh on the port side, re-sheeted and outhauled again. At present I cannot see how to improve on this except possibly by having a jib exactly the same size and shape as the big running sail; then it would not be necessary to transfer the jib from one side to the other, or the running sail. The drawback of this arrangement would be that a jib as big as the running sail would be too big for sailing to windward in a breeze and it would have to be changed down to a smaller jib if that happened.'

I was now badly handicapped by having only one pole left, which necessitated moving it from one side of the deck to the other during a gybe. Even the smaller, 22ft pole was undoubtedly an awkward customer for one person to handle on his own in a seaway.

On 1 January I wrote: 'Here is wishing folk happiness in 1971! I get the impression from the news, the newspapers, and the radio that last year folk were letting life go by without enjoying it; were wrapped up in discontent with their lot. I wish this year they may be always looking for happiness and the joy of living.' Sailing singlehanded gives one a very *detached* view of the human condition!

I watched two more gybes step by step to see if I could improve the performance; but all I could see was that having only one pole caused a big hold-up. With two poles both could be kept rigged and at the ready.

At 2000, at 23°30'N 19°30'W, I thought that *Gipsy Moth* had sailed into the real Trade Wind zone. 'The wind has a more pressing sound about it, though only two or three knots faster,' I noted. 'I don't suppose I have a hope, a faintest chance, of knocking off 4,000 miles in 20 days. *Gipsy Moth* is in the Trade Wind belt tonight, I reckon; she has 2,360sq.ft of sail set and is only making 6 to 7 knots. However, succeed or fail, I think it is a great lark, the idea, and I am looking forward to a grand sail.'

On 4 January I made a gybe in the early hours of the morning which went without a hitch and I was back in my bunk after only forty minutes for raising or dropping 1,860sq.ft of sail and trimming the sheets and vangs. 'If I can get my other pole repaired—and I believe I could if necessary get it done locally by straightening it out, cutting it at the kinks, and stuffing it closely fitted with a length of bamboo pole—I reckon I can speed up the rigging of running gear to cut the time of the operation from hours to minutes. The pole I unshipped last night for gybing is lying on the deck ready rigged and could be in place, footed to the mast and swung outboard, in 10 minutes. In one way I would like to take a month to reach Bissau so as to get my spinnaker drill really snappy. Perhaps I shall if this wind continues!'

Once when *Gipsy Moth* woke me with her old trick of coming

up in the wind out of control in a squall, I dropped the mizen. *Gipsy Moth*'s pull sideways on the hull was aft of the rudder even though the tops'l was sheeted forward of the rudder. I was sorry at having to drop the sail and turn so as to put the wind 25° aft of the beam, because *Gipsy Moth* had been tearing along with the speed I wanted. Could I think of any solution to her tricks not requiring less sail? At 0530 I altered course a little so as to be nearly wind abeam when the breeze freshened. I wanted to see if the self-steering gear had control without the mizen and whether coming up closer to the wind bettered the speed, but it looked as though the mizen was necessary to get the speed I wanted; or else I must pay off downwind and pole out. That night I led the running ends of the tiller tackles right through the companion to my bunk with the idea of controlling runaway slues from my bunk. It worked well and saved me from having to get out of the bunk, but I had to wake up several times to use the bunk controls. I thought a boomed sail would have helped. When awake I could hear a 'striker' slueing breaker coming from some way off and some time in advance. Big ones came with a roar, apparently bringing their own individual gusts with them.

By 5 January I was only a few hundred miles from the starting point of my cross-Atlantic race against the clock and keeping a good lookout for the heavy steamer traffic which closes Cape Vert on its way to and from Western Europe and the Mediterranean and the West African and Cape trade routes, traffic which has increased considerably since the closure of the Suez Canal. There were other dangers. 'I was hit by a flying fish when I stepped into the cockpit', I wrote indignantly in my log at midnight, 'and it certainly startled me in the dark. Then when I looked along the side deck with a torch, a squid glared at me with huge circular eyes. No bouillabaisse though, because when I looked later he had gone.' But my cheerfulness left me when I worked out the next noon position. A day's run of 205·5 miles seemed just tolerable enough, though I would need a greater excess over 200 miles on good days to make up for the bad ones, calms, storms, and all. But the distance made good in a straight line between sun fixes was only 187·5 miles, a drop of 18 miles below the distance sailed.

This was bad, but there was little I could do about it now and I had all my work cut out to get to the Geba Estuary. The coast of

Portuguese Guinea, low lying and heavily shoaled, has always had a bad reputation among seamen, and many ships were lost in the old days of sail as they tried to take this turning point too close or were driven on to it by contrary winds. Its lack of prominent landmarks makes pilotage difficult, and this was not helped while I was there by thick haze which clung to the sea all day. At night the warm, moisture-laden air condensed to leave a clear, starlit sky, but *Gipsy Moth*'s sails ran with streams of water, soaking me through on one occasion. There was so little wind about that my heart began to sink at the thought of starting from way up the estuary and attempting to make that magic 200 miles from the very first day. I drifted in at a wretched 2 knots, picking my way through the maze of unmarked shoals, and not even the welcoming cheerfulness of Christopher Doll and TV cameraman Paul Berriff when they came out to meet me in a Portuguese Naval patrol vessel could shift the black dog from my back.

Gipsy Moth anchored off Caio at the mouth of the Geba Estuary three hours after midnight on 7 January.

In the morning Christopher and Paul persuaded me to visit Caio so that I could pose for their cameras with the black residents and their shy, crinkly-haired young. There could hardly be a stronger contrast than between my port of departure, Plymouth, and my port of arrival with its ninety inhabitants, the heated atmosphere, the sun-baked reddish soil of the dirt roadway, and the dark green tropical trees. Just before midday *Gipsy Moth* weighed anchor and we set off for Bissau: it was a long, long passage which ended at daylight next day, and *Gipsy Moth* was not at anchor off Bissau with the sails stowed until 1030. After a brandy and a sleep for a few minutes I was visited by Commodore Bastos of the Portuguese Navy (he was also the Vice-Governor of the State), Commander Rodrigues the Chief Naval Engineer, the electronics specialist, the Police, Customs and Health Officers (the latter's title was translated to me as 'Sanitary man'). We had long discussions. The Commodore could not have been more friendly and helpful; he offered to do all the necessary repairs to *Gipsy Moth* and by mid-afternoon the two booms, the pulpit, and the BBC's cine-camera, which had had a bashing from the waves, had all been dismantled and taken to the Naval workshops. At midnight I was taken to see four craftsmen working on the boom, which was already half finished and looked to be an excellent job of work. After lunch with Tenente Luis Nogueira, a handsome man with a magnificent black beard, who had been detailed by the Naval commander to look after me and who was excellent company and surely a social lion in Cascais, his home town in Portugal, I returned to *Gipsy Moth*, which in the afternoon was swarming with craftsmen dismantling and taking away the damaged deck gear. Below deck there was hardly turning-room in the cabin because of the cameras and associated gear which Christopher and Paul were handling while they were discussing their problems in a low, quiet tone, brooding like two hens conniving to lay a joint egg.

At seven that evening I had an R/T date and was apprehensive of getting through at all from fifty miles inland, because the Naval Radio Chief said that their patrol boats had difficulty in getting through from the Geba River to the Cachew River, only a few miles farther north, outside which I had floundered among the shoals the day before I entered the Geba. But to my surprise I got through at once and after waiting my turn and switching to various frequencies before getting one free from interference, I spoke to Frank Page of *The Observer* at some length —*The Observer* was to carry an exclusive report from me each Sunday of my speed run. Then I was able to speak to Sheila and lastly to Dennis Morden of the BBC Foreign News Service, which was handling my broadcast reports.

After this Luis rushed me ashore in the Naval launch to meet the Press. Then dinner, and so to bed. I was glad and relaxed to have the promise of no visitors or commitments of any kind at all until 7 p.m. the following evening. That night I had ten hours of wonderful sleep. I had forgotten when I last had more than two or three consecutive hours during the night.

III

THE 4,000-MILE RACE

On 12 January I was ready to start on my 4,000-mile 'burn across the Atlantic' as Giles called it. The project weighed me down like lead. I knew I had blundered badly in starting from Bissau. With at least twenty days and twenty nights of continuous hard racing ahead, I had had the stupidity to lumber myself at the start with navigating a long, tricky estuary, with at best the light airs typical of the Tropics and at worst, calms. Since I arrived in Bissau I had been noting the speed of any breezes and they were mostly between 3 and 7 knots. How can one sail at 200 miles per day with ghosting breezes like that? Sheila had said forthrightly that I would be crazy not to start from Caio at the estuary mouth, and I knew she was right. But I had said that I was going to start from Bissau to make up the distance across the Atlantic to 4,000 miles and start from Bissau I would. Meanwhile, at anchor, the hot, humid, tropical air was oppressive; the muddy estuary water made fast sailing seem futile. My only hope was that by starting when the tide began to ebb I might, if only there was a breeze of, say, 10 knots from the north, reach nearly to the sea before the tide turned against me. The distance to the estuary mouth was 47·5 miles, the same as the length of the Thames from Tower Bridge to Whitstable.

It was a slow start but a very pleasant one; Commodore Bastos came aboard to farewell me and presented me with a little silk pennant flying from a miniature standard which had the device of the Commando unit on it. With him came Commander Rodrigues and Tenente Alves, who gave me a perfect little model cut out of solid brass, of a tank landing-craft, which Tenente Alves had made himself. It would be difficult to find more kind, helpful and efficient friends than these Portuguese officers.

I found the start a strain; for one thing a patrol craft of the Naval Commando was escorting me to the starting point. The Commando crew, Portuguese and experts in sea life, were watching my every move. It must have seemed interminable to them.

I was much slower and more deliberate than usual after several days of shore contacts, many meetings and many discussions. I always seem to make a clumsy switch from the talking kind of life ashore to action at sea, or vice versa. First of all I had to weigh anchor and get it aboard over the life-line. Then there was the setting of the self-steering and hoisting of sails. As usual after shore repairs, ropes were in the wrong place and sheets unrove. All this required a lot of fiddling. However, a nice light breeze got up and I was full of optimism that I would have a getaway run down to the mouth of the estuary.

The starting point I had chosen was 11°47′N 15°33′W, which was out in the estuary 5 miles S by E of Bissau. The patrol vessel went ahead and marked the spot for me, using radar bearings; this was a great help because it enabled me to concentrate on sail raising instead of having to take a series of compass bearings to establish the point.

Gipsy Moth went through the starting point at 11.30 a.m. It was hazy and the land in the offing was indistinct, the water a milky, muddy pale green. *Gipsy Moth* set off, ghosting towards the sea at 5 knots, with the big running sail poled out to starboard and five other sails set.

The patrol vessel escorted me for several miles after leaving the starting point; I daresay that they wanted to be sure that I did not charge the string of sandbanks a mile to the south. They approached and gave me a cheer, then left. A couple of hours after the start a helicopter turned up overhead and I could see Christopher Doll, Paul Berriff and Luis Nogueira aboard. It was a lovely day with a light breeze, though hazy. An hour later the breeze died down and headed *Gipsy Moth*. I had to drop the pole and running sail and *Gipsy Moth* was committed to tacking slowly into the eye of light wafts of breeze.

The Geba estuary is a wide stretch of water. At 1430 I was off Ponta Prainha, fifteen miles from the starting point, with no land in sight to the south, though there was a big three-mile long drying sandbank only five miles off. A large school of black fish, pilot whales sixteen to twenty feet long, cavorted around *Gipsy Moth*, surfacing and diving in all directions in graceful curves. I find that whales always quicken my blood-stream, even small ones like these; I remember the yachts which have been sunk by a flick of a whale's tail, particularly the yacht racing across the Tasman Sea two years ago, which sank so quickly that all seven crew were struggling in the water before they got their rubber dinghy inflated. With no food on board except a few carrots, they were indeed lucky to be picked up by a steamer days later. The captain of the steamer is reported to have asked: 'Are you carrying out a survival test?'

The temperature in the cabin was 90°F and I longed to cool off with buckets of sea water, but the Geba river water is so dirty that no one will use it even for washing, and all the drinking water I took aboard came from Portugal.

From dusk onwards I was hard at it until dawn. The current had turned, and with the turn the breeze became flukey from the west, so that *Gipsy Moth* had to tack every few minutes. All the time I was trying to fix my position in order to avoid the shoal patches down the estuary. There were seven lights along the north shore in the 45-mile stretch, placed so that one would be always in range; but they were so faint that it was difficult to locate them.* I picked up the Biombo light at 2200 and I could see land behind it when I tacked; there was moonlight above the thick haze. The Biombo light was 24 miles from Caio, so *Gipsy Moth* had not yet completed half the estuary passage. I set off again to the west but at midnight tacked to the north. The Jaime Afreixo shoal, which dries out in one place, lay ahead and I had to establish a position off Ponta Arlete before continuing westwards. I had to do a lot of thinking about how to avoid the unmarked shoals in the dark. My echo-sounder was the only navigational aid I could use and changing depths often helped fix the position; but some of the shoals were steep-to sandbanks and depth-sounding could not give enough warning in the dark.

At one point I had one of those strange, unaccountable happenings that so often occur at sea. I heard an extraordinary noise as if a million simmering peas were passing along the hull. This continued for eighteen minutes and was quite uncanny. The only cause of it that I could think of was a dense shoal of millions of shrimps or fry.

I kept on staring in to the land but could not see the Ponta

---

* That same stretch of the Thames that I have mentioned, Tower Bridge to Whitstable, has some seventy-six, excluding jetty lights, barge-mooring lights, etc.

Arlete light and began to worry. I decided that I must tack away again when I reached a depth of 5 fathoms because of the rocks lying off Arlete. At last, at two in the morning, I saw the light faintly through my night binoculars, though I could not see it without them. I carried on shorewards until the light was bearing due east, which gave me the security of getting out of the estuary without ramming a sandbank.

At 0400 *Gipsy Moth* was due south of the Caio light. My log had forty entries of changes of heading, with distances, depths and different winds. *Gipsy Moth* had only sailed 53 miles and I had been on the go non-stop for twenty-two hours—except for once, that is, when I fell asleep at the chart table and woke to find my head on the chart. That was dangerous stuff in such waters, but I believe I was only asleep for one or two minutes.

Immediately the open sea was ahead I flopped down on my bunk and slept.

By half-past eight the tops'l was up with the No. 1 jib, main stays'l, mizen stays'l and mizen. An hour later I poled Big Brother out to starboard. But I just could not keep awake and had to drop off to sleep for a few minutes. While I slept the breeze slowly died away and I woke with a start to find *Gipsy Moth* becalmed, bobbing on the sea with much banging of gear. For a few seconds I could not imagine where I was.

> First day's run to noon fix Wednesday 13 January 1971.
> Position: 12°06′N 16°55′W.
> Distance fix-to-fix: 84 miles.
> Calculated distance to finish: 3,918·5 miles.
> Days remaining: 19.

So after the first day's run *Gipsy Moth* had sailed 100·4 miles, but had made good only 84 miles fix-to-fix. Also the 84 miles was not directly towards the target because of the estuary and also because I was keeping north of the direct route in search of more speed. She was 118 miles short of the 200-mile fix-to-fix target. For the remaining nineteen days she would have to average 206·3mpd. It was no use getting depressed; it was my own fault for letting myself be trapped by a romantic notion. I must get on with the job. *Gipsy Moth* was becalmed until two hours after noon, when a gentle north-wester headed her off to the south-west. I had to drop the running sail, unship the pole, and harden up to the wind. I sluiced some bucketfuls of the Atlantic Ocean over myself in the cockpit and felt refreshed and revived, a new man. My head was still aching though, which I think was due to eyestrain from looking for the lights the night before.

In the evening I had a good R/T connection with the BBC. *Gipsy Moth* was crossing the main steamer route and while I was below on the R/T I had a bit of a fright when a steamer crossed *Gipsy Moth*'s bows. The north-west breeze had also been a disagreeable surprise to me in a zone where there ought to be a north-east Trade Wind; but I suddenly realized that it was in fact the start of the north-east Trade. The true wind was N by W and only appeared to be from the north-west due to my sailing into it. By evening it had become a gentle 12–15 knot breeze and *Gipsy Moth* was settling into her stride. As the breeze swung round from north-west to north I freed the sheets and thoroughly trimmed the sails; I had neglected this until now because I was so fagged out; then, by sailing 10–15° downwind of the course, *Gipsy Moth*'s speed-up began a proper start to her voyage. The whole scene had crept upon me unawares.

Next morning I was a reluctant starter. But the breeze had freshened at 20 knots, the heel was excessive and the tops'l sheet was pulling the stern round to leeward, causing too much weather helm for the self-steering gear to cope with, so I hauled myself out of my bunk and dropped the tops'l. By six the sky was lightening in the east and *Gipsy Moth* was well and truly in her stride; she had averaged 9·2 knots for a short period.

Soon I was again at one with the ocean life. 'Here I am,' I logged at 0800, 'reclining on my bunk like a Grand Pasha. I expect to be back on form today after a quiet night with a lot of sleep, broken only by one sail handling and one other visit above deck to trim the helm. At the moment I am lolling and lazing, drinking my morning tea with honey, which I make without even sitting up, having an Aladdin vacuum flask secured to the mizen mast within arm's length and the rest of the "doings" beside me. How excellent it is too! I am glad of a chance to re-charge my energy cells. Now I must up and trim *Gipsy Moth* to sail her proper course though I am loth to do it because I fear it will mean loss of speed.'

**Second day's run to noon fix Thursday 14 January 1971.
Position: 12°48½'N 19°38½'W.**

46

Distance fix-to-fix: 166 miles.
Calculated distance to finish: 3,755 miles.
Days remaining: 18.

The second day's run was disappointing, because *Gipsy Moth* had averaged more than her 200 miles a day in the twelve hours since midnight. Now she was 155 miles short of the two-day target, and needing to average 208·6mpd for the remaining eighteen days. Maybe I had made a fool of myself; on the other hand, a lot could happen in eighteen days.

In the afternoon I sowed the rest of my salad garden, or, put a little less grandly, the four trays which I plant with mustard and cress and keep on the shelf at the back of the settee in the main cabin. Two of these plastic trays are about 1½ft long by 4in wide and the other two about a foot long. I have developed a simple drill for the crop raising and crop rotation which seems to work well. Sheets of paper kitchen towel roll are folded up to make a pad about four inches square and these are fitted on the bottom of the tray. The correct procedure is to sow the cress first, then the mustard four days later on top of it. They should then crop together. Unfortunately I do not seem able to get cress to germinate in the Tropics, so on this voyage I had to rely on mustard only. When it is ready to cut I just lift one square paper pad and snip mustard off on to the Barmene and sliced raw onion sandwich which I make for lunch. Then I fold another sheet of paper and make a fresh sowing. I had sowed one full tray before I left Bissau but had forgotten to water it again in the flurry of beating out of the estuary and it had died by the time I got to it. Too late I remembered that I must water the seedbeds twice a day in the Tropics.

At 1800 I set Big Brother, bringing the total sail area up to 2,270sq.ft. *Gipsy Moth* was now on a broad reach, 100° off the relative wind. The excellent little self-steering gear was having trouble in controlling the heading with this amount of sail set. The big runner poled out to windward was pressing the stem away from the wind (the opposite effect from that of the tops'l) and the wind was not strong enough at 12 knots to press the windvane over, in turn to force the self-steering skeg to one side and pull the tiller to leeward, steering the yacht back to windward to its original heading. To ease the load on the self-steering gear, it was necessary to balance the wind thrust on the sails on both the windward and the leeward sides of the yacht. The delicacy of the task was to do this without losing the wind's driving force.

While I was at Bissau, Luis had brought me a huge 'hand' of about two or three hundred green bananas. We had had a long discussion about where we should put it in *Gipsy Moth*, and finally decided to hang it from the rail in Sheila's hanging cupboard, outboard of the alleyway going past the heads. This was all right while *Gipsy Moth* was at anchor, but as soon as she started bouncing about in rough seas, the bananas swung to and fro, smashing into the sides of the cupboard and the edges of the door frame, going rotten where they had been crushed and making a horrible mess of the woodwork. In pursuit of a banana after two days at sea, I discovered a slushy, rotting mess in a dark corner of the cupboard, teeming with wriggling white maggots; presently a minor plague of nasty black flies began to crawl over everything in the boat. They were a new species to me, with bodies and wings a little longer and more slender than ordinary houseflies. I did my best with an Aerosol and hung the bananas that were left in a way that would keep them safe.

By midnight it was a halcyon night, with a bright moon shining into the boat from above the stern. The shimmering silvery path on the sea and the benign looking stars in the summery sky reminded me of those wondrous nights in 1931 when I was waiting to attempt the last stage of my flight across the Tasman Sea in the Gipsy Moth seaplane which I had rebuilt at Lord Howe Island after it had been sunk in a gale in the lagoon. Nothing equals apprehension of the future for making one enjoy the unparalleled beauty and charm of the present.

Flying fish were striking the deck. Most of them thrashed their way back to the sea, but I had seen four left behind. One I picked up by the wing and I was going to throw him back, but he had already passed out, so I kept him. It is a wonder that any survive hitting the deck of a yacht. I don't know their flying speed but would think 25mph the lowest for keeping airborne with their small wings. These are narrow and long, looking as if made of shiny, transparent plastic with thin spines from body to wing-tip to keep the wings extended. They have so much body for such small wings, although they are mostly not much bigger than a pilchard.

All this romantic delight did not go with the speed I wanted. Even so, the run from noon to midnight of 90·7 miles sailed was good considering that *Gipsy Moth* had not once been up to the 8·3 knots which she had to average to make good her daily rate. I logged: 'It is difficult to sleep because it is so exciting and gripping trying to get the most speed possible. I believe that with this rig and 5 knots more wind *Gipsy Moth* could whizz along.'

From now on the log was filled with entries about changing sails or trim or course: 'Decided to drop the big runner and try hardening up to windward for more speed. It improved the speed considerably by the looks of it.' 'I set forth accoutred cap-à-pied to boom out the biggest runner, but after working out the true wind, I changed my mind; by sailing 20° to windward of the required course, *Gipsy Moth* is doing well, whereas setting up the running gear may reduce the speed, because it will entail sailing up to 20° below or downwind of the required course. Incidentally it will mean much banging of gear and a lot of work; so I have decided to leave it alone meanwhile.' 'I find I make rash and hasty decisions after being pinned down to an R/T session for 40 minutes or an hour and usually getting fussed up about that.'

Third day's run to noon fix Friday 15 January 1971.
Position: 12°29′N 22°53′W.
Distance fix-to-fix: 192 miles.
Calculated distance to finish: 3,568 miles.
Days remaining: 17.

This was better. With 192 miles made good I was only eight miles below the 200mpd target. The fact was, however, that I had failed for the third day to reach the target and was now 168 miles behind it; *Gipsy Moth* needed an average of 209·9 miles a day for the remaining seventeen days.

Working at a faster than normal pace in calculating sun fixes bred blunders. I wanted a fix to give an accurate position to the BBC; I knew there were mistakes in my calculations but I could not trace them in time. So I reverted to the old squarerigger captain's practice of using a noon latitude which does not rely on accurate times. The operation is simple enough and so is the theory: At noon the sun is on the meridian and therefore due south of the yacht. The point vertically overhead in the heavens is a point vertically above the latitude of the yacht. If the sextant is used to measure the angle between that point and the sun, and that angle is added to the latitude (which, to be academic, is called declination) of the sun, the result is the latitude of the yacht. On a fine day with a smooth sea the operation couldn't be easier.

To show how much time is needed for really accurate navigation: I had taken four separate sun observations spread over a period of six hours. Apart from the measuring of the sun's height angle above the horizon for which I would take the average of three to six shots as a rule, there was the calculating to do for each observation, and finally the plotting of a position line for each observation. Each position line would be a small section of a vast circle on the surface of the earth centred at a point vertically below the sun and with radius governed by the angle between the sun and the point vertically above the yacht. These position lines would be moved forward to the time of the last observation according to the distance and direction sailed by the yacht in the interval. Then theoretically all four position lines should meet in a point.

In this case I knew my rule of thumb latitude to be accurate and with its help I was able to decide which of the other observations was accurate and thereby get a fix to transmit to the BBC in London. I cannot bear to have a mistake put away with my calculations however, so I worked away until I found out what the blunders were. It would be difficult to find anything more silly and elementary: the first measurement of the sun's altitude demanded that the appropriate position line should be moved 22 miles towards the sun; I had moved it 22 miles away. My fourth hurried check shot observation of the sun had a simple addition error in the calculation. I have described this incident at length in order to show the immense value of taking three or four observations instead of just two, either of the sun or of stars or of planets. Incidentally, my DR position was 9 miles short of the sun fix adjusted to noon, so for the first time *Gipsy Moth* had been in a favourable instead of an adverse current since leaving Africa. 'Hurrah!' I logged.

At midnight *Gipsy Moth* had sailed exactly 100 miles in the previous twelve hours. 'It's a start! It's a start!' I wrote triumphantly. But an hour after midnight the speed had dropped to 7·3 knots and I was getting fussed; it was not fast enough. Also the heading was 24° to the north and to windward of what it should be. I went on deck and hoisted Big Brother. It is a big, awkward sail to hoist even in a pleasant light breeze of 12 knots. If it is first hauled out to the boom end, the bunt of the sail can form a great belly which beats up and down at risk of hitting the sea in front of the stem and being ridden under the keel; if it is first hoisted before being hauled out it is liable to belly out ahead of the bows and to beat to and fro on each side of the topmast stay. So I laid it out along the deck, furled it by folding it into itself and tied the long 'sausage' at intervals with lengths of soft 'rotten' caulking cotton. This enabled me to outhaul it without any trouble at all; then when I hoisted it, the stopping ties burst apart one after the other, letting the sail break out and fill.

I still had the problem however of how to coax the self-steering gear to control the yacht when running with so much sail set. I began to wonder if I could counter the effect of Big Brother's turning moment on the stem by leading the sheet of the tops'l to the end of the squared-off mizen boom.

For the moment I tried paying off the boom sail forward in hopes of keeping the wind more abeam, but as soon as the wind died down the heading always fell off downwind and the self-steering gear did not then seem to have enough power to bring the boat back on course. I tried paying the boom sail farther forward until it was forward of abeam to see if that would cure the trouble. Come the daylight I would try rigging the biggest wind vane, but I did not want to do it in the dark.

An hour later this latest trim of the sails seemed to be working all right. At least there had been no trouble and the speed was good. 'And so to bed,' I logged, 'and I hope to get some sleep after I have finished this can of pea soup which tastes delicious.' Two hours later, although I felt fagged out, I still could not sleep; I was too tired, I suppose, or else the can of soup had been a mistake.

I went on deck and thought that the mizen which I had paid well off was doing no work, so I hardened it in. The heading promptly fell off from 285° to 270° or thereabouts which threatened to put the wind dead astern. This would at once slow down the speed so I hurriedly reset the mizen as it had been before. 'If only the wind would increase from 7 to 16 knots!'

At 0700 *Gipsy Moth* gybed herself and the self-steering could not get her back on heading, so I had to wake up and rescue her. The wind had now backed a lot and *Gipsy Moth* was heading west with the wind abeam. With Big Brother poled out well forward she was doing nicely with little wind and would have done very nicely if the breeze had freshened. But the wind had been easing all night and was now down to only 10 knots; the mileage dropped short of the 200mpd rate by 8 miles and I had no hope of making it up by noon unless the speed went up to 9·7 knots.

I was hard at it day and night, continually trimming sheets and adjusting the self-steering to get more speed out of *Gipsy Moth*. On this morning I fitted a sheave at the end of the mizen boom and passed a rope through it with a narrow sheave at the end of that for outhauling the tops'l sheet to the end of the mizen boom. Also I attached a handy-billy to the outhaul of the boomed sail with a stopper on it so as to outhaul the sail as far as it would go towards the end of the boom.

> Fourth day's run to noon fix Saturday 16 January 1971.
> Position: 13°00′N 23°58′W.
> Distance fix-to-fix: 183·5 miles.
> Calculated distance to finish: 3,385·5 miles.
> Days remaining: 16.

Gipsy Moth had sailed 191·8 miles but had only made good 183·5 fix-to-fix. That was a cold slap. She was now 185·5 miles short of my four-day target and would have to average 211·6 miles a day to catch up. I certainly had fits of depression but it was no good feeling desperate; the winds should be increasing as *Gipsy Moth* sailed westwards and there should be a favourable current lift.

At 2010 my spirits got a lift. 'That's what I like to see,' I logged, 'the needle indicator of the speedometer vertical, i.e. at 10 knots. This is the first time since Bissau that it has been there. This is exciting. I was beginning to wonder if I was ever going to make the speed I wanted. I was half apologizing to the BBC spokesman tonight for my failure to reach 200 miles in a day after four days sailing.' And there were other diversions. Sheila's hanging cupboard adjoined a chest of about six drawers where I kept the ship's papers, instruments and equipment, manuals, electrical batteries, bulbs, spares and so on. Near the foot of this chest of drawers on the cabin sole, I was startled to see a big, darkish-green creature stand up square and defiant, facing me like a crab at bay with two big claws like semi-circular pincers raised ready to nip the attacking enemy. I judged he was more than an inch across. Was this fearsome looking creature a poisonous tarantula? Certainly its foreclaws were not hairy as I imagined those of a tarantula would be, but it looked dangerous and vicious. Fixing it with a beady eye, I reached for my death-ray Aerosol and directed a lethal jet at it. It turned and scurried under the chest of drawers, disappearing between a cabin floorboard and the skin of the hull. I expected to see it curl up dead where it stood but it made off at full speed. No doubt it was killed by that stream of death, and I felt a twinge of remorse; but how could I live under the threat of such a horrible creature? As it turned out, I could have spared my sorrow.

At midnight the wind was behaving very oddly. It was as if it had just been mixed in the stratosphere and was being poured on to the earth from a vast jug. Near calms gave place in a few seconds to spurts of 20 knots coming from any direction between north and east. One moment all the sails, the booms and the gear seemed to be in a banging turmoil, the next moment they were all asleep and *Gipsy Moth* was sailing fast, slipping through the balmy night. ' "On such a night"—it made me think of Jessica and Lorenzo's night together in "The Merchant of Venice".'

At 0335 I brought *Gipsy Moth*'s heading up 15° closer to the wind which increased the speed a knot, but half of that increase was lost as the breeze eased during the night. I thought that, come daylight, I must try the half-sized running sail and pole it well forward of abeam so that *Gipsy Moth* could sail with the relative wind slightly forward of abeam. That was where the speed seemed to lurk in a light 10–12 knot breeze.

I had unpleasant, nightmarish dreams mixed with one that I was wanted on deck. In my dream I was worried and sad about Dorothy Parker, 'the wittiest woman in the world', the title of her biography I had been reading in one of my sackful of newspapers. She divorced her drink-prone husband while he was away at the war, and he, unknowing, came back full of love on the day of the wedding breakfast of his beloved wife to her new husband. How I suffered for that man in my dreams! I woke at 0400 to find the speed was $\frac{1}{4}$ knot better, so I decided to leave the pole rig alone till dawn.

Two hours later I awoke and wondered again what could be

done with the foresails to improve the speed. I first thought of poling out the 300 jib instead of Big Brother, but when I arrived on deck I decided it would be best to drop the latter altogether and harden up to windward so as to put the wind forward of the beam. But while I was at work on deck the wind veered and I could not get the wind forward of the beam without steering north; so I reckoned I had made a blunder and re-set Big Brother. I trimmed it better than before though and thoroughly checked all sail settings.

Padding around the deck barefooted during the night, I had collected two flying fish. At dawn I found three more; and when I went to prepare my breakfast I was startled to find one lying in the galley sink. It could only have arrived there by shooting through the skylight in the roof of the cabin, and that when I was on deck because there must have been an infernal row. This seemed such an extraordinary thing that when I was talking that evening to the BBC I said nothing about it, for fear they should think I was trying to pull their legs.

Fifth day's run to noon fix Sunday 17 January 1971.
Position: 13°41′N 28°55′W.
Distance fix-to-fix: 180 miles.
Calculated distance to finish: 3,210·5 miles.
Days remaining: 15.

Although *Gipsy Moth* has sailed 196·9 miles, the 180 miles fix-to-fix was still 10 per cent below the 200mpd target.

Immediately after noon I rigged the big windvane. The medium-sized one seemed unable to activate the self-steering rudder when *Gipsy Moth* was carrying a lot of sail in light airs, and she had lost several miles in the morning by coming up to the wind or, more frequently, falling off until the wind was dead astern, or even a-lee. I could have continued with the medium-sized vane if I had balanced the sail area, but the balanced result deprived the mizen of its pulling power, which meant a considerable loss in speed. This big vane was 5ft high and broad at the top. It looked wobbly and it was. I rigged a small cord shroud from each side at the top of the leading edge to stay the vane to the bracket in which it was fitted. This looked like being successful and I noted that it would probably be a good thing to rig another pair of stays to the top of the trailing edge.

The big vane seemed to keep *Gipsy Moth* on course to within a few degrees. Its drawback was its obvious fragility if the wind piped up. It needed to be built much stronger because of its big area, but then it would have been too heavy for the lead counter-weights I had.

All morning I had been working stripped of clothes, but now it was time to don a hat or I should have sun trouble. I was hard pressed with deckwork and other jobs, and even by six that evening, when I was due to call the BBC, I had not got my sun sights worked out. I had got fidgety with impatience which made things worse. First I had had a muddle over the stop-watch I was using; I had noted down two different times for when I had started it at zero. Then I could not remember which was the right one. Then I made some mistake in reducing the noon shot for latitude. So I threw out the calculating method and went back to the old rule of thumb method which I had used a couple of days earlier and which was possible because I knew that I had taken the sight at exactly local noon. This cleared up the second mistake. In the end the position lines from the three different sights all met in a point. No navigator fails to utter (mentally if not actually) a sigh of satisfied relief when that happens. But what now puzzled me was the 16·9 miles dis-crepancy between the day's run sailed and the run made good fix-to-fix. The sailing had been pretty well in a straight line. How could there possibly be that discrepancy between 196·9 miles sailed and 180 miles made good? If it was due to the log over-reading, it made it almost certain that my project must be a failure. Or was there a consistent mistake in working out the sun sights? For example, an error of exactly 1 minute in the times used for the three position lines would account for 15 miles of the discrepancy which would then leave only a difference of under 3 miles be-tween the DR position and the sun fix, which was reasonable. Or had I sailed into an eddy of the Atlantic current which had set me back 15 miles? Later I believed this was the correct answer.

The wind was strengthening slowly but steadily. It fluctuated in long waves of three or four hours between crests, but each crest was a knot or so stronger than the last. At 1900 the true wind was E by N, 25 knots. With *Gipsy Moth* running before it, the relative wind as it appeared on board was NE by N, 17 knots. *Gipsy Moth* averaged 9 knots for a short period at that time under the big runner with the No. 1 jib, the main stays'l, the mizen stays'l, the tops'l and the mizen.

By 2200 I could hardly stand in the cabin. *Gipsy Moth* was lurching from side to side with all the deck gear banging, clanking and overstraining. This did not seem right, so I went on deck and first dropped the tops'l which was causing most of the trouble and does little or else unwanted work when there is enough wind to heel the boat well over. Then I re-trimmed the other sails, hardened in the boom vangs—the handy-billies which I used to downhaul the stays'l and mizen booms to eyes in the deck— eased the heading off the wind so that the wind would be coming in aft of the beam, and then hardened in the sheet of the big runner to bring the clew and pole somewhat farther aft. As soon as I was satisfied with the set of the sail and the pole, I took up the guys of the pole to keep it quiet. The result was that when I went below it seemed like the quiet of a churchyard, though the speed had only dropped from 9·12 to 8·95 knots. By midnight *Gipsy Moth* had knocked up 104·9 miles in the previous twelve hours, which was promising; but I had had so many disappointments that I was not going to be carried away by enthusiasm this time.

I had been forced out of my sleep and bunk by cramp in an instep. It was a lovely night with a gibbous moon shining down on the boat from high astern. I put the hood up again over the companion because the decks were being washed a lot by following seas and I had had to close all the cabin skylights. As I emerged into the cockpit a flying fish hit the cabin top three feet away from me with a hard crack, bounced off and disappeared. Judging by the patches of scales on the deck there would have been dozens lying there if the sea had not washed them overboard. The scales stick on hard and fast as I found when I swished the deck down with bucketfuls of sea water.

After dawn my first act was as usual to tune in to WWV Fort Collins, Colorado, for a time signal to check my Rolex and the chronometer. Then I decided to try dropping the mizen as I thought the weather helm which was needed to counter its slueing effect might be slowing the boat down. I could easily hoist it again if necessary. An hour later I recorded that it seemed to have paid off. I then tried easing the No. 1 jib, but that was no good, so I put it back exactly as it had been before, having marked the sheet first for that purpose. Then I decided to have another go at the tops'l; its pull when running would be great, if only it could be harnessed without making the boat unmanageable. By 1030 I had set it, sheeting it farther forward than usual, but I soon came to the conclusion that it was doing little good and maybe some harm. So later I hardened it in and this seemed to pay off because the average speed over the following one and a quarter hours went up from 8·7 to 9 knots. However, the wind also had increased slightly during that period.

At noon the apparent or relative wind on board was up to 20 knots and coming in from 120° on the starboard quarter. With the yacht's speed of 9 knots and the heading of 281°, this made the true wind 25·5 knots from 059°, roughly NE by E.

> **Sixth day's run to noon fix Monday 18 January 1971.**
> **Position: 14°50′N 32°15′W.**
> **Distance fix-to-fix: 207 miles.**
> **Calculated distance to finish: 3,013 miles.**
> **Days remaining: 14.**

At last! *Gipsy Moth* had broken through the 200 miles per day barrier. While making good the 207 miles out of 210 logged, *Gipsy Moth* had only twice reached a speed of 9 knots and then only for a total distance of 16·9 miles. Therefore the 200 had been reached by sailing the whole twenty-four hours between 8·3 knots, the average hourly speed needed to reach 200, and the 9 knots reached for only two short periods. Seven miles excess was not much of a margin but the wind was freshening and I not only expected it to keep up but to freshen further as *Gipsy Moth* ran down her westing; if it freshened up only another 5 knots *Gipsy Moth* could easily make good daily runs of 10 to 20 miles in excess of the 200 target. With the remaining distance to San Juan calculated to be 3,013 miles, *Gipsy Moth* had made good 987 miles in a straight line from the Bissau starting point to the noon position that day, whereas the sum of the six daily point-to-point runs amounted to 1,012·5, a difference of 25·5 miles, accounted for by the noon fixes not being themselves in a straight line.

I logged that I must watch the mast because it was bending where the heel of the runner pole was hooked on to the lug on the mast.

All the afternoon the prospect continued rosy. For four periods

Gipsy Moth averaged 9 knots, or over, sailing speed, and for the whole eight hours the average was 9 knots. During this run the apparent wind had been mainly from the NE, with the actual wind between 21 and 28 knots. This really was exciting. At 2100 the apparent wind on board had risen to 22 knots from 150° to starboard, only 30° off dead astern. The true wind to produce this and the sailing speed of 9·2 knots which had been averaged for the last period, was E by N, 30·5 knots. 'I must say,' I logged, 'that wild rushing through the night, surfing at, I guess, 30 knots, was most exciting. The boil or seethe of a breaker filled the air level with my face when I was standing on the foredeck.'

The next entry in the log, at 2317, was difficult to read: 'Pole doubled up while big runner was up in a fresh breeze. I was just about to turn in, unable to keep eyes open and choc-à-bloc with flying fish and fried onions, when the big bang occurred. Now again I can't keep my eyes open so more anon. 'Tis a long tale.'

At intervals later when I could find the time I logged the story. I expect it was about 2130 or 2200 when the big bang occurred. I could see from the cabin that Big Brother had bellied out forward and was banging the air from side to side like a balloon forward of the stays from topmast to stemhead. I thought the outhaul or the clew had given way. When I got on deck I saw that the 640sq.ft sail was thrashing about in the air in a wind of up to 30 knots with one end of the boom still attached to it. At first I could not tell if the other end was attached to the mast or bumping about on the deck. Then I saw that the pole was doubled up in the middle into a sharp V. I was darting in to deal with the mêlée when I suddenly checked; if the boom halves separated and the one attached to the sail began flailing the air I could easily become a stupid victim. The outboard half could act as a huge, lethal club and I did not like the prospect of working under it.

My hopes had collapsed like a pack of cards but I could not help laughing—always something of this sort turned up if I had a drink. I had had a stiff pink gin before supper, or lunch as it really was, if one can call a meal three hours before midnight lunch —and then I had eaten heartily of flying fish and fried onions. I certainly had not expected to be on the foredeck tackling an emergency immediately afterwards.

The first thing to do was to hobble the pole before it became lethal. I felt immensely grateful for the good light shining down from the crosstrees, but at first with the midnight darkness all around it looked as if it was going to be a desperately difficult task. In the dark as the pole was at times, it seemed impossible to tell how the kinked metal would behave; but it turned out not so bad when once I had sorted it out. The outboard end of the pole was ten feet above the deck, and the bottom of the V was periodically smashing into the deck, the skylight, or the forward shroud. Should I go for the sail first or the pole first? I decided I must get the sail smothered and began taking in the slack of the sheet at the winch in the cockpit to bring the clew of the sail as far aft as I could without its breaking the pole at the kink. Then I went forward to the mast and let the halyard go handsomely until I had the sail smothered on the foredeck. The outboard end of the pole was now sticking high into the air, held there by its topping-lift. With the sail detached it was a much safer proposition to deal with. I hardened in the fore and aft guys to lock the outboard end of the pole in the air and then passed a rope round the barrel of the pole near the deck and rack-seized it to the forward lower shroud. I could have rigged the other pole, but when the first pole had collapsed, its heel or parrot-beak had twisted and distorted another snap-hook which was under it, attached to the lug on the mast. This had jammed the parrot-beak hard in the lug. It would be very difficult to free it in the dark with the lively movement, even with the spreader lights to help. In those rough conditions it was going to require great care handling a 25ft pole bent into a V. It appeared that in order to stow it, one end would have to stick out over the side of the hull. So I aimed to keep the pole 'asleep' where it was until daylight.

I went below and made my log entry, forty-three minutes before midnight.

The wind was increasing; an hour and a quarter after midnight a big wave came aboard with a thunderous crash and slued *Gipsy Moth* round head to wind. I woke drugged with sleep but by the time I had got to the cockpit *Gipsy Moth* had righted herself and the self-steering gear had brought her back on course, which I thought a remarkably fine performance. My arrangement for keeping the pole asleep till daylight seemed to be working all right. *Gipsy Moth* was still doing up to 10 knots without anything poled out, still now and then riding a breaker without the running sail. The wild rushing through the night, surfing at 20–30 knots, was most exciting. The four sails left up, the No. 1 jib, the main stays'l, the mizen stays'l and the tops'l, totalled 1,370sq.ft. During the sixteen hours from the time the pole broke until noon on the 19th *Gipsy Moth* averaged 8·5 knots. At 0620 in the morning when I started work on the broken pole, the relative wind had risen to 24 knots, and by a quarter-past nine when I knocked off for breakfast, it had risen still further to 26 knots. That meant a true wind of 31 knots, which was a hefty breeze.

> **Seventh day's run to noon fix Tuesday 19 January 1971.**
> **Position: 15°17′N 35°45′W.**
> **Distance fix-to-fix: 207 miles.**
> **Calculated distance to finish: 2,810 miles.**
> **Days remaining: 13.**

I was not surprised to find that the seventh day's run was again 207 miles between fixes. If I could get the second pole rigged without too much delay *Gipsy Moth* ought to show the speed which I had been hoping for all along.

By three o'clock in the afternoon I had the wreckage cleared away and the second boom rigged with the 300 jib boomed out. *Gipsy Moth* was going well with it; the sailing speed went up at once from 8⅓ knots to over 9. By five the speedometer was reading 12 knots at times during surfing surges in a 28-knot wind. Except for breakfast I had been working solidly for ten and a half hours. Periodically I trimmed the boomed sail or one of the others, keeping a watchful eye for any chance of getting more speed.

A log entry after some eighteen hours of drama with the pole now seems quaint: 'Great news, the bananas are ripening; I have eaten three today already and how delicious they are. The yacht cruising chroniclers say that one gets sick of them at sea because they all ripen at once. I shall be interested in the effect on this ship. Now I must eat, lunch is overdue [this was written at 1925]; gin fairly stuns one after a hard night and day—but it's a great feeling after troubles have ceased to boil.'

At midnight the sailing speed had averaged 9·4 knots with an apparent wind on board of 25 knots 120° to starboard. This made a true wind of NE 30·5 knots. The trim and sail balance was now just right; as a result the going was so quiet that I kept looking at the wind dial to see if it was falling calm. The boomed-out runner kept the headsails quiet by turning the wind on to them. I had thought earlier in the night that it was too much squared off and trimmed it farther aft by 10° or 15°.

Wednesday 20 January, 0210: 'I had a brilliant idea, while more asleep than not, of sheeting the tops'l out to the mizen boom end with the boom carrying no sail itself. Now I was awake, however, I wondered if it would back-wind the jib. It seems to pay to keep the lee side sails fairly well sheeted in. After all, one wants to deflect the wind direction so that the wind shoots sternwards after leaving the sail like a jet stream. Perhaps it might make more sense to set the big runner as a genoa instead of the No. 1 jib and lead its sheet to the mizen boom end. Three hours after midnight I tried paying the tops'l off well but it was a loss of speed instead of a gain. Either the sail did no work or else it back-winded both the top half of the big jib and the top half of the main stays'l. I think it would be better without it.'

At nine o'clock in the morning the speed averaged for the last period was 9·63 knots, the highest *Gipsy Moth* had ever reached for a period. I dropped the tops'l because conditions of sea and wind had freshened a lot and sail reduction was needed. As soon as the sail was down there seemed to be a lull and everything went as quiet as in the Beaulieu River, though when I looked at the wind-speed indicator I noted that the wind was still 27 knots. It just showed how the wrong sail, or just the wrong amount of sail, can cause turmoil and discord. I had a sore leg burn where I had scraped a stanchion when a wave sluiced me across the deck and I ended with my legs overboard. There is one area of *Gipsy Moth*'s lee deck amidships where one cannot get a hand or foothold when doing something like furling the tops'l. No harm was done, and it was a lesson always to fasten on in fresh conditions, when an all-powerful wave can come aboard and sweep the deck.

At eleven the speed was still up to 9·36 knots for the past two hours. The true wind was now NE, 36 knots, up and down 4 knots. I went on deck and studied the rig trim to see if *Gipsy Moth* could carry Big Brother instead of the 300 jib. I found it was much more lively up there than it had seemed below since I dropped the tops'l; I would have dearly loved an extra knot for a day or two, but I had to keep sensitive to gear strain; if piling on more sail bust the mast or caused any more gear failure it would have been poor judgment. A 450sq.ft sail boomed out could have been borne but I doubt if the gear would have stood up to the 640. The wind was a good, fresh Force 8.

Giving more thought to my idea of the small hours of using Big Brother as a genoa instead of the No. 1 jib on the lee side to make a running pair with the boomed out sail on the windward side, I came to the conclusion that it would be a mistake; when sailing from Plymouth to Bissau, all the best speeds were with the No. 1 jib set and none when I had the big runner set as a genoa.

> **Eighth day's run to noon fix Wednesday 20 January 1971.**
> **Position 15°56½′N 39°27½′W.**
> **Distance fix-to-fix: 219 miles.**
> **Running total: 1,438·5 miles**
> **Calculated distance to finish: 2,595 miles.**
> **Days remaining: 12.**

It was a pretty rough sea running and I had to wash my sextant in fresh water after shooting the sun; but this was what I had come for and I felt that there was a good chance to catch up in the remaining twelve days. There were 2,595 miles to go, which demanded an average of 216·25mpd to make up for my 195 miles deficit. It was going to be tough but the winds in the second half of the crossing should be fresher than in the first half and also there should be a favourable current. *Gipsy Moth* had rattled off 633 miles point-to-point in the past three days. My hopes certainly were lively but the margin over the 200 was not great as a reserve. I went on deck to see if there was anything that could be done but there was a great deal more wind on the stern than one would think when down below. I thought it would be folly to hoist a bigger runner, but I'd have been the death of a hundred quid if I could have had a 450 runner right there with a pole strong enough to take the compression. I believe the mast would have carried it and it would have given me another ¼ knot.

Just before 2.30 p.m. I logged that the speed had dropped to 9 knots. The wind had eased and was now averaging ENE 30·5 knots. An hour later the speed had dropped again to 8·9 knots; I decided to hoist the 640. Everything went smoothly with the operation, although there was a rain shower as I finished setting it. At seven o'clock that evening the wind seemed to have changed after a rain shower and the heading improved from 295° to 275°. Then came another rain shower but fortunately it did not seem to have any vice in it. My remaining boom was only 22ft long, but the big runner seemed to be setting perfectly with it. In spite of that the speed average had dropped to 8·5 knots. I rigged the boom as far aft as it would go, until it touched the forward lower shroud. I slacked off the No. 1 jib, which was being filled with strong overflow by the big runner, and logged: 'If the gear holds, I could not wish for a better set-up. I reckon it is no use setting any more sail than now because the tops'l and the mizen would only take the wind out of the sails forward of them or back-wind their flow. I see that I am a good deal more than half way across to the Windward Isles of the Caribbean. I only wish this exciting sail could last a long, long time. Now for some lunch with a good brandy, hot.'

I think that last log entry shows how one can get in tune with the gear on a long voyage. 'If the gear holds, I could not wish for a better set-up'; I knew I was over-driving *Gipsy Moth*. An hour before midnight I logged: 'I am thrilled in the cockpit when *Gipsy Moth* is riding the breakers. The pick-up by the wave with the bows pointing downwards, the surge forward, the bows still pointing down a little, the boiling, seething cascade rising above the deck on each side if going straight with the wave or, if *Gipsy Moth* is taking the wave a little across it or has been slued sideways by it, the sudden, immensely powerful, irresistible lurch sideways followed by the surf raging all along the lee deck.' And ten minutes later calamity struck the project.

Thursday 21 January, 0330: 'Just back from the big schemozzle but too tired to describe it now. Pole bust in half, came unhooked at mast, flogged about with sail. Sail sailed under keel by *Gipsy Moth* etc. I have cleared up the mess but it has taken from after 11 p.m. till now, say four hours hard. Now we jog along.'

My thrilling sail, reaching at last the speed I had been aiming at was, to coin a phrase, up the pole. Two hours before midnight the speed was $9\frac{1}{2}$ knots, now it was $7\frac{1}{3}$ knots, and both poles were bust. What a lesson in life! My prospects were bright, *Gipsy Moth* had been sailing as I dreamed she would. Four hours later my chances of hitting the target shattered. I could hardly write eight lines in the log; my head kept dropping off to sleep and my pen wriggled on the paper before stopping.

A great amount of power can be harnessed by sails and occasionally one is reminded forcibly of this, as when the big runner began beating its neighbours savagely with the V-shaped pole, lifting and swinging it as if it were a cane, held in mid-air by the clew of the sail. The heel of the pole had wrenched itself out of its lug on the mast, but by the grace of Providence had jammed on a now jagged metal mast cleat a foot or two below it. I was staggered at my good fortune when I looked at the small amount of damage done; the deck was scoured a little here and there, the glass of the forehatch skylight deeply scarred—what amazing good luck that it was not broken! Even the foredeck net, which looked a tattered ruin, was only worked loose from its lashings—or perhaps some of those which were missing had been torn free. The clew outhaul rope, speckled red from the anti-fouling paint on the hull bottom, was undamaged. But most impressive of all to my eyes was how elegantly, firmly but without fuss, the big self-steering windvane was handling the situation, keeping *Gipsy Moth* steadily on her course despite the commotion at the bows.

This time it seemed much easier to hobble the pole without getting clocked by it; I seemed to be getting to know the drill. Then I had to recover the big runner from under the keel. I thought hard before acting. Although *Gipsy Moth*'s speed was drastically reduced she was still going at more than 7 knots. First I let the sheets fly through the sheaves at the side of the cockpit and when they were streaming free alongside the hull, clear of the keel, the rudder and the self-steering skeg, the sail stood under the keel to the lee side. I then recovered the sail and the sheets by hauling the sail in at the foredeck. It was virtually undamaged, although streaked with anti-fouling paint.

The next entry in the log at 0830 was short but sweet: 'Reckon I could make a pole up by lashing together the two ends of the two poles. One piece is 15ft and the other long end 18ft long. These would give a 22ft pole with an overlap of 11ft. By God! I'll give it a try. But first some breakfast.'

Ninth day's run to noon fix Thursday 21 January 1971.
Position: 16°40′N 42°43′W.
Distance fix-to-fix: 193·5 miles.
Calculated distance to finish: 2,408·5 miles.
Days remaining: 11.

So in spite of the collapse of my last pole before midnight,

Gipsy Moth had knocked out 193·5 miles between noon fixes. Up to an hour before midnight she had been over 9 knots for five and a half hours and had averaged 8·6 knots from noon to then. After that she averaged 7·7 knots sailing speed, or 185mpd until the next noon. The wind had actually strengthened so the accident had so far cost not less than 13 miles.

At 1700: 'Hard work to get everything done. Gybe necessary for the wind having veered to 110°. So long since *Gipsy Moth* was on the other gybe that much sorting of vang tails, sheets, sheet-horse slides, etc. needed. Booms pretty well ready for lashing up now.'

I had had to think carefully how best to do the repair, and I had turned for help to the invaluable *Admiralty Manual of Seamanship*. It sounds so easy just to lash two poles together. The difficulty is that the very heavy compression load ought to pass straight down the centre of the pole to its seating on the mast, otherwise the pole will start to bend and then bust out to the side. So a repair of two poles lashed together must aim to prevent that bend. And if you can solve that, another difficulty is that the poles must be lashed in such a way that they do not start scissoring.

I had searched out a dozen lengths of cordage most suitable as to thickness, strength and non-stretch quality. It was surprisingly difficult to locate enough pieces just right for the job. I chocked up the boom lengths so that they would not roll on the deck, then hunted out a length of anti-skid strip, which is like coarse sand-paper 3in wide used to prevent slipping on wet skylight glass. I passed two turns of this round each broken pole end, hoping the friction would help prevent the poles from moving against each other, and then lashed one of my boathooks into the little valley between the poles on one side and on the other side a length of plastic pipe about 1¼in in diameter. I hoped these would check the scissoring. A number of rack-seizings at intervals, figure-of-eight bindings with a dozen or so turns seized together, were the only kind of lashings to stand a chance of success.

An hour before midnight I decided to stop work and sleep; I was getting clumsy and terribly slow. I had been at the job for thirteen hours non-stop except for sailing the boat, navigating and eating. It was disappointing; I had hoped to have a boom up that night. Two hours after midnight the log read: 'Getting up to work on the boom, which is badly needed.'

The next entry, at 0515: 'Finished off the boom. Will it work? Changed No. 1 jib over to the starboard stay but ran into trouble. The starboard halyard had been in use with the big runner at the time of the crack-up and was hopelessly fouled aloft at the mast-head. I could not see by the torchlight what was the matter; so meanwhile borrowed the starboard pole topping-lift for re-hoisting the jib. The heading had fallen off to W by S. This made me think that I should have to gybe again soon; which, combined with the fact that I was now fagged out and my balance bad, decided me to flop down for some sleep until daylight could show me what the halyard trouble was.'

0800: 'The heading is now 40° off the required course (to the southwards) so I must gybe again and transfer the jib back to the port stay. My fingertips are so sore after the boom repairing that it hurts to use them.' But at 1050 I could write: 'Do-it-yourself boom up at long last with big runner attached. Seems O.K. but pretty heavy and clumsy to handle.' And at 1125, with great relief: 'Pole still looks O.K. Set mizen to balance leeward turning movement of big runner. Now for breakfast. Now and then (after a drama or such like) I have brandy for breakfast; this is one of the occasions.'

> **Tenth day's run to noon fix Friday 22 January 1971.**
> Position: 16°15½'N 45°03½'W.
> Distance fix-to-fix: 138 miles.
> Calculated distance to finish: 2,272·5 miles.
> Days remaining: 10.

Good news, bad news! This fix-to-fix run of only 138 miles for 155 miles sailed was a depressing setback because the total of the five previous fix-to-fix runs had been 1,006·5 miles in spite of the first pole-break during the fifth day. With the second pole break-ing there had been no running sail up for twenty-three hours of the tenth day. The wind had eased as well, and the sailing speed had averaged less than 6·5 knots; the day's run had been knocked to hell.

In the afternoon I changed the self-steering vanes, rigging the very big one. It was a difficult job working on the end of the counter while sailing almost dead downwind with a swell over-riding the ocean. I had rigged two more backstays to the top of the vane at its after corner to strengthen it, and to complete a busy day I had at five o'clock a good talk with Frank Page of *The Observer* and then with Kevin Ruane of the BBC Foreign News Desk. I reckon they must both be good men at their jobs, simply judging by the way they drew me out, making me feel keen to tell them what they asked for.

Before midnight I woke to find myself sitting head on arm at the saloon table, halfway through eating a treacle sponge pudding. I wrote: 'Was I in a heavy sleep! Somehow oppressive with lurky, ominous, mastering kind of dreams. I cannot set any more sail than now, unless possibly to set the 600 runner as a genoa in place of the jib which is 90sq.ft smaller; but that would be foolish because the jib is a really good driving sail. So the rig stands at the 640 runner, the 510 jib, the mizen and two stays'ls, 750, and the tops'l 370, which I make in total 2,270sq.ft of sail. *Gipsy Moth* is sliding quietly through the water at 8 to 9 knots and sighing with enjoyment as one of the waves—small at present— lifts her a little and rustles her along. The big runner when I set it to the new made-up pole has a romantic look, pinkish with here and there mottled red, due to its strange adventure in another element under the bottom of the boat.'

Eleventh day's run to noon fix Saturday 23 January 1971.
Position: 16°47′N 48°13′W.
Distance fix-to-fix: 185·5 miles.
Calculated distance to finish: 2,093·25 miles.
Days remaining: 9.

So now *Gipsy Moth* would have to make daily fix-to-fix runs of 232·6 miles for the remaining nine days of the 20-day target. It was a depressing prospect. The wind had eased too; at one time it was down to 6 knots. I got fed up with ambling along and altered course 20° to windward for more speed, but it meant that I was driving too far north of the track I wanted to follow.

'I am getting worried about the wind. First, of course, that it is not strong enough to give me a chance for my project, secondly that it keeps in the east and is driving *Gipsy Moth* continually north of the course. The farther north *Gipsy Moth* is driven the more southerly will the heading have to be later in order to reach Nicaragua. Worst of all, this heading if continued too long will push me out of the Trade Wind belt. Already I feel I would have stronger wind if farther south. The present heading is 31·5° off course. If the wind has not backed by tomorrow I must set to and gybe first thing. The actual wind is half a point N of E, almost exactly the reciprocal of the course required so that one gybe is as good as another. Gybing is a lousy job though because I must not only unrig the pole and re-rig it to port, but must drop both the No. 1 jib and the big runner, unhank them and transfer them to the other stay before re-hoisting.'

I wanted to sleep and not eat supper, so I turned in at half-past eight. But I only had a couple of hours before a small squall overpowered the self-steering gear and began pushing *Gipsy Moth*'s head to wind. Fortunately I had rigged a new tackle to the tiller which would be easier to work from my bunk; the lead-ins from the cockpit were now better placed so that there was less friction and the hard pull needed at the bunk was reduced. I was anxious not to have *Gipsy Moth* come up to the wind and put the running sail aback because of the strain on the mended pole, but after twice using the tackle from my bunk to bring *Gipsy Moth*'s head back on course, I gave in and went on deck to drop the tops'l.

At 0520: 'I had nightmares of Christopher Doll being aboard and chasing me with a cine camera to film the pole drama. I was wildly racking my brain how to hide from him and find some hide-out where I could sleep. In the end I woke fully because of hideous boom clankings, and I imagined the worst had happened, only to find that the spliced boom was apparently staunch and unmoved by the rough treatment.

'I am sure I need to gybe and search for better winds farther south, but I cannot bear to do it because at present *Gipsy Moth* is only 10° off her required course. I keep on saying this and have been steadily pushed farther and farther north as a result. Oh! for a north-easter instead of the continued easterly wind. I can hear a poor, silly flying fish beating the cabin top with its tail; but should one feel sorry for these fish which are fierce, merciless hunters in their own place?'

Twelfth day's run to noon fix Sunday 24 January 1971.
Position: 16°59⅓'N 51°42½'W.
Distance fix-to-fix: 201·3 miles.
Calculated distance to finish: 1,894·5 miles.
Days remaining: 8.

The speed had improved although the wind speed was still low, down to 8 knots at one time in the past twenty-four hours. After noon it perked up to between 12 and 16 knots.

I was trying to assess the tactical situation. On her present heading, *Gipsy Moth* was only 8·5° off course to the northward. A gybe to the other side of the wind would have her pointing some hundreds of miles south of Trinidad to British Guiana, and so it was just not on except in desperation. The best thing to do might be to pray for the wind to back. What was so tantalizing was that a north-east wind was a 50–60 per cent expectation in this area of the Atlantic, whereas easterly winds from which I was suffering were to be expected for only 35 per cent of the time. I wished I were 150 miles to the south where I had planned to be; there the wind expectation was even more favourable—75 per cent north-easterly. However, it was no good moaning about what might have been; I had got to wriggle out of this situation the best way I could.

In spite of the lighter winds, the speed rose to 9 knots for a short period in the evening. Squally rain showers were passing through and I had to be on the alert because there was a bit of a to-do with each one, and I had always to be ready to drop the tops'l in a hurry. At 1920, at the end of the 9-knot period, I decided to drop the tops'l without waiting for the next crisis. There was enough in these rain squirts to make the heel uncomfortable, but my chief concern was to avoid risking or over-taxing the mended boom. The powerful compression load it had to bear, even in fair weather, was shown by the difficulty in out-hauling the clew of Big Brother to the end of the boom, even when using a tackle with double sheave-blocks on the outhaul. With the tops'l down there was comparative peace but the speed dropped a knot.

By the evening I had had only one normal meal during the day —breakfast. However, that was a proper blow-out: wheat germ and Muesli with an orange squeezed into it plus some lemon juice plus raisins and grated nuts, followed by about 10 oz of potato fried with two eggs, plus two cuts of my newly baked 100 per cent wholemeal loaf with honey and marmalade, and a banana and coffee to top up. Otherwise I had had only four bananas in the morning and, after the evening radio session, a salad sandwich made from a cut of the new loaf, buttered and Barmened, with a layer of mustard from the garden, grated carrot, garlic and raisins;

also another cut of the loaf with cherry jam and two cuts of the Christmas cake with its delicious marzipan coating, given me by the makers in Plymouth. I didn't want another meal but I did want some sleep.

An hour and a half later, at nine o'clock, I woke to such bangings on deck that I was convinced the boom repair had come apart; I rushed up, but as soon as I was in the cockpit the row stopped and I could see that the boom was quite unmoved. What caused the noise I could not think, because I could see nothing wrong anywhere. Once in the cockpit, I could not leave it. The balmy air flowing over my naked body was deliciously cooling after the heat of the cabin. The diamond-bright stars were set in a black sky. Occasionally I shrank from the side of the cockpit when a wave broke over the counter and boiled alongside, but nothing came over the coaming while I was there, and I gave myself over to the romantic pleasure of sliding fast through the seas into the night in my slim, powerful craft.

An hour after midnight I tried to coax the self-steering gear to hold a better course more downwind, but the speed was cut down at once. It was tantalizing to have the wind astern if *Gipsy Moth* was headed for San Juan—tantalizing, because it was so pleasant and comfortable to sail, but the devil for speed.

At 0750: 'I was lying on my berth writing up the log when there was a tremendous bang, followed by the usual flapping and flogging. I was out on deck p.d.q. with no time for any clothes or safety harness. It was not the boom at all; that was banging against the topmast forestay but apparently still quite staunch. It was the metal clew ring of the big runner sail which had collapsed and let the sail fly out forward like a giant flag. I dealt with the situation, the only difficulty being to muzzle the flogging sail with only one hand while holding the halyard downhaul with the other. If I had let go of the halyard, the sail would have come down with a run and *Gipsy Moth* would have sailed over it again. That damn sail is already pink with anti-fouling paint. It was an hour before I had the big runner hobbled, dropped and bagged, and the tops'l hoisted again. Then I rigged the pole rest on the stem pulpit (it needed the vice to straighten the locking-pin which had been bent in the previous pole-break), and dropped the pole to inspect it. The repair job, however, looked absolutely unshaken and unmoved and I decided not to touch it. Feel feeble, will have small breakfast.'

That was the first of the day's troubles. What had happened was that a large sector of the big stainless steel clew ring, about $\frac{3}{8}$in thick and 4in across, of which a piece was sewn into the corner of the sail, had broken clean away. The break released the sheet and the outhaul bowlines which let the sail fly. I had to drop the outboard end of the boom on to the pulpit in order to recover the end of the outhaul. This was when the second schemozzle of the day occurred. One of the broken boom ends had a jagged point protruding beyond the diameter of the pole where the metal sides had been crunched together when the boom collapsed in a V and I had afterwards broken it in two. The boom was resting on the stem pulpit at one end and secured to the lug on the mast at the other end. While I was crawling under it, doubled up, I hooked this razor sharp jag into my scalp. Blood seemed to be everywhere; some running across my spectacles put one eye out of action, and decks, ropes and all were showered with it. When I got below I could not see what had happened because I could not get into a position in front of one of the mirrors where the light was strong enough to see by if I held another mirror in my hand above my head. Then I could not find any disinfectant except iodine, which I believe is out of fashion and anyway hurts like hell. Then I couldn't find a suitable piece of plaster for the top of my head. When at last I did find a piece in Sheila's first-aid drawer, I had trouble manipulating it, and could not see where to put it, because as soon as I took away the wad of paper I was using to staunch the flow, there was such a mess that I could not see where the wound was. In the end I used the more positive but surprisingly effective method of feeling for the cut with a finger and placing the plaster on by touch.

Thirteenth day's run to noon fix Monday 25 January 1971.
Position: 17°12'N 54°50'W.
Distance fix-to-fix: 180 miles.
Calculated distance to finish: 1,718·75 miles.
Days remaining: 7.

I bagged the clewless Big Brother and set the 600 instead. Then I worked out the position and the run from the sun sights. I felt thoroughly depressed; the fix-to-fix run of 180 miles was bad enough, but also I was worrying about driving into an impossible situation where the winds would grow progressively lighter and more variable the farther north I sailed. I must gybe at any cost. This meant a big operation and I had only an hour and a half before I had to call up the BBC. I had made a bad blunder in not gybing when the big runner blew out and I had had the pole down on the deck. I had been convinced then that I ought to gybe but I had acted instead on mathematics and reasoning which had made me re-rig the boom on the same side as before. I dropped the 600 runner, dropped the pole and unshipped it completely on the starboard side, dropped the No. 1 jib and gybed. The gybe was a pretty good botch-up. *Gipsy Moth* had been so long on the other tack that sheets, ropes and vangtails had been overlaid or tangled with other ropes.

I was just getting these sorted out when, glancing up at the self-steering gear, I saw what I took to be a big shark following close astern. I hopped on to the counter. It was no shark, but it looked like a 30ft sea-serpent or sea-snake twisting sinuously from side to side, too deep in the water to see clearly. I went to the end of the counter and then noticed a yellowish object two-thirds of the way along it. Those might be horns sticking out from it. Was it a mine? No, not big enough. I thought it might be a collapsed met balloon with a container caught up in it. Anyway, whatever it might be, it was hooked up on the rudder and cutting the speed in half. It must be got away. I sorted out and rigged my grapnel but *Gipsy Moth* had too much way on her for the grapnel to go down; it was swept astern by the slipstream. I must stop the boat, but with this rig *Gipsy Moth* cannot be stopped simply by putting her aback. The three boom sails keep her moving. I thought the best thing I could do was to drop all the sails and stop dead. I dropped the mizen stays'l and the tops'l, but then thought I could manage by leaving the mizen and main stays'l up if I came hard to the wind. This slowed *Gipsy Moth* down enough for the grapnel to sink in the water and I hooked the 'thing'. It was a big-meshed net of heavy, coarse netting. I began hauling it in and was astonished to find that the object half way along it was a turtle, hopelessly entangled. He was heavy and I had to tug and heave to get him aboard. Finally I worked the net heave-by-heave up and over the life-line until I could grab the turtle and haul him over too. He was an attractive pale brown, weighed some 40 or

50lb, and was very handsome. I was astonished to find he was alive. Since he could not have drifted against the Equatorial Current in the net, he must have come from Africa, 2,300 miles away, and could have been in that net for a year. (Later, I found that the net, 60ft long, was indeed made in Africa.) He never would have got free because each leg and his neck were through different meshes of the net. He looked like being a handful if I cut him free so I decided to photograph him first. To keep him from being awkward and perhaps damaging something, I turned him over on his back. Then I cut him loose. He evidently could not recognize a fairy godfather when he saw one because he at once snapped at me.

Finally I slid him back into the ocean where he flipped off gaily, as if he regularly made year-long voyages across the Atlantic imprisoned in a net. I wondered what the cumulative odds must have been against his being released. First of all there were the odds against his being caught in the net, then the longer odds against the net breaking away, further odds against being swept out to sea, further odds against entering the Guinea current to be carried into the Atlantic, incredibly long odds against the net being caught in the keel of a yacht 2,300 miles out in the Atlantic, almost as long odds against the net being hauled on board—and finally I would think it was a pretty lone chance that the skipper of the yacht should be vegetarian by preference.

I suddenly remembered my date with the R/T. I felt bustled; already I was late, the sails were mostly down and the deck seemed to be littered with untidy heaps of gear. Immediately I had finished talking, I set to work once again with urgency. First I re-hoisted the tops'l and the mizen stays'l, sheeted the mizen and the main stays'l properly, and hoisted the 600 runner to starboard as a genoa. By 5 p.m. I was ready for the tough job of moving the repaired boom across the deck. First it had to be worked aft along the deck until it would pass between the main mast and the main stays'l; then forward again to the stem pulpit. Although only 22ft long, its weight was now that of a boom 33ft long, plus the boathook, plastic piping and the long row of lashings. Besides that, the jagged edges of the two broken ends had to be treated with great respect. They seemed to catch up in every item of deck gear as I worked the boom across. I got the outboard end on to the pulpit pole rest, but the boom was now so heavy and clumsy to handle that I had to use a topping-lift to raise the gooseneck end off the deck to the lug on the mast. Then the belly of the joint wanted to hang downwards, twisting the boom round so that it was difficult to connect the gooseneck snaphook at the heel of the boom to the lug. Everything seemed to get fouled up, the boom lift was twisted round itself and had to be re-rigged, the aft guy had passed under the top life-line instead of over it and needed re-reeving, and then I found that one of the jumper stays had parted halfway up the mast and was fouled by the tops'l halyard. So down that halyard had to come. Next I had to drop the big genoa because *its* halyard was fouled. The whole enterprise seemed desperately hopeless, with no speed, and darkness and a rain squall about to catch me. However, I kept at it and in the end the tops'l was up, the genoa was up, the pole was up and the No. 1 jib was boomed out. The jib set perfectly and turned out to be much better for booming out than the 600 runner. It is true that it was 90sq.ft smaller but I think that was outweighed by the efficient lead-in of the wind to the genoa on the other side. At last all the sails were set and drawing to my satisfaction, and I returned to a brandy I had poured out at the time of the R/T session some three hours earlier. 'I certainly have enjoyed that brandy now,' I logged, 'and it is only a snifter compared with what I plan to have follow it.'

> Fourteenth day's run to noon fix Tuesday 26 January 1971.
> Position: 15°55'N 57°11½'W.
> Distance fix-to-fix: 157·5 miles.
> Calculated distance to finish: 1,574 miles.
> Days remaining: 6.

The bust sail, my bloodied pate, the turtle and his net, had between them wrecked the day's run. Distance was lost by sailing off course when the turtle net was hooked up on the keel, because at 173·5 the distance sailed was considerably more than the fix-to-fix line. The day before the speed had dropped 0·6 knot from 7·8 knots to 7·2 knots—8·4 per cent—when the big runner was put out of action at 0724. There was no boomed out sail for just over twelve hours and I think that 8 miles were lost to the run because of that, while a further 10 miles were lost by the disorganization of the sails and sailing while I was playing with the turtle. Altogether I would put the total loss at 24 miles or 1 knot over the day, and that is a conservative estimated rate.

With only six days of the twenty left, the remaining 1,574 miles would demand a daily run of 262·3 miles per day to reach my target, which was quite impossible. However, I thought I had the consolation of having achieved my original aim of 200 miles per day for a 1,000-mile run point-to-point. *Gipsy Moth* had totalled 1,006·5 miles, the total of the five days' fix-to-fix runs of 180, 207, 207, 219 and 193·5 miles between the noon fixes of 16 and 21 January. But when I calculated the five-day run, point to point, it was 995·5 miles. I had failed to reach the 1,000-mile mark in five days by a miserable 4·5 miles.

An hour after noon I climbed the mast to seek out the cause of the broken jumper stay. One of the screws of the bottlescrew, about halfway up the mast, had snapped. I could not find another of that size on board, so I secured the end as well as I could with cordage. The actual wind was now E by S. *Gipsy Moth* was headed for the Martinique Passage, 240 miles ahead, between Dominica and Martinique. I should probably need a star fix at dusk the next night if approaching the islands in the dark afterwards.

At nine o'clock the next morning, the 27th, I payed off both the mizen and the mizen stays'l as a speed experiment. The sailing speed during the hour before checking the sheets was 7·1–7·2 knots. During two hours with the sails payed off, the speeds were 7·9–8 knots. Then I hardened them in again and in the next hour the speed dropped again to 7·25. The relative wind was coming in on the port quarter.

At intervals during the night it had kept coming back to my mind: the original target I had set my heart on was a point-to-point run of 1,000 miles in five days, and a log entry later that morning reads: 'Thanks be to God for the world's most enjoyed breakfast, during which I worked out the route (which I like very much) for two five-day-1,000-mile speed attempts on the way home.' It would not be such a favourable time of year for them as I originally planned, but I would at least have the sport of making them.

Fifteenth day's run to noon fix Wednesday 27 January 1971.
Position: 14°33½'N 59°58'W.
Distance fix-to-fix: 181 miles.

Calculated distance to finish: 1,405·75 miles.
Days remaining: 5.

The passage between Martinique and Dominica was now 77
miles WNW, and the St Lucia Channel between Martinique and
St Lucia Islands lay ahead, WSW 55 miles off. The St Lucia
Passage looked the more desirable if *Gipsy Moth* could make it,
but it might be too much of a squeeze on that gybe. I thought I
must try to make it, however.

By six that evening I was getting restless at not having sighted
Martinique. Always after a long ocean passage without a position
check I am apprehensive of some awful blunder in the navigation.
Then suddenly, a few minutes afterwards, I could see land with a
high peak, a cone bearing 300°. 'I think this peak is Vauclin
Mountain,' I logged. 'I got quite excited at first, thinking it might
be Mont Pelée, the most romantic mountain in the world for me
as a boy because of a story in the *Boys' Own Paper* about the great
eruption of 1902 and the strong portraits of the characters in
the story, particularly of the old crone, the Sibyl, who foretold
the coming eruption.' On that terrible day the whole city of
St Pierre, with its 30,000 inhabitants, was wiped out within a few
minutes. In the harbour the ships burst into flame and sank in the
boiling sea. Then I noted that Pelée would be 22 miles behind Mt
Vauclin as seen from *Gipsy Moth*'s position, so I feared my romantic surge had been groundless. Later I decided it was Pelée after
all because it had the right bearing and the chart gave its height
as 4,400ft. When it comes to seeing a peak that high from seaward, what is 40 miles of distance?

Night fell as I was approaching the St Lucia Channel between
Martinique and St Lucia, with the swell livening up and rolling
in from the east. The log records a long series of bearings of the
Pointe d'Enfer light. It was a tricky passage because at first *Gipsy
Moth* would not point north of the middle of St Lucia. I was very
reluctant to gybe, however, both because of the hours of hard
work involved and because I suspected that the wind was being
temporarily deflected by the islands and would improve in direction. Meanwhile the heavy rain showers blotted out all the lights
on the land, and this I did not like. I knew there were strong
currents between the islands. The list of observed bearings
lengthened, but presently, at 2120, *Gipsy Moth* was far enough

into the channel for the Pointe Castries light at the north-western end of St Lucia to open up from behind the land.

2021½   Castries 200°; d'Enfer 020°
2135   d'Enfer 035°
2144½   Castries 200°; d'Enfer 045°

At ten o'clock I reckoned that *Gipsy Moth* was past the middle of the channel and into the Caribbean Sea. I celebrated with a glass of delicious Courvoisier and sank the empty bottle carefully and respectfully to the bottom of the channel which, I reflected, was appropriately French.

Before daybreak the calm, lake-like gliding through the water was quite different from what I had expected from the Caribbean. It intensified the feeling growing on me that I was being shut in. Although the Caribbean stretched 1,350 miles ahead of me, to leave the broad Atlantic gave me a feeling of claustrophobia, of being encompassed by menacing land.

The feeling of sailing in inland waters was soon shattered by a fierce, short rain and wind squall which came literally 'out of the blue' with the sun shining during it. *Gipsy Moth* got out of control broadside to the wind, even though I had the tiller tackle rigged; I think the rudder was too much out of the water or too near the horizontal to bite or be effective. At one moment I thought she would not come upright again without some more drastic action, such as letting all the sheets fly. It seemed very cold in the driving rain. I had had no time to put anything on as I rushed into the cockpit, but I grabbed a moonweave blanket which wanted a wash anyway and put that round me like a shawl. It was very effective besides being the quickest way of getting some covering. Maybe one needs some form of cloak in such emergencies.

'I have thought about this squall as there are others about. I must have a drill ready and I shall try having both the mizen and the mizen stays'l at the ready for dropping as far as topping-lifts, vangs and halyards are concerned. I could let them fly at the first sign of trouble and let them lie, to re-hoist easily afterwards. With the remaining sail area forward I should then have much more control. I would prefer to get rid of the tops'l but that has to be eased down its track and the halyard needs careful watching. What about some breakfast; it is 9.30?'

Sixteenth day's run to noon fix Thursday 28 January 1971.
Position: 13°45′N 62°36′W.
Distance fix-to-fix: 161 miles.
Calculated distance to finish: 1,249 miles.
Days remaining: 4.

The fix-to-fix was as much as I had expected through the St Lucia Channel.

At midnight 'I hoisted that damn tops'l again, this time sheeting it to the end of the mizen boom. I must say the boat seems more lively since but it does make much woe when a squall strikes. The set-up is so involved and the tops'l always causes trouble because it is set so high and therefore has a big heeling moment.' But it was a successful move and in the freshening wind *Gipsy Moth* was going well.

Seventeenth day's run to noon fix Friday 29 January 1971.
Position: 12°18½′N 65°28′W.
Distance fix-to-fix: 190 miles.
Calculated distance to finish: 1,077·25 miles.
Days remaining: 3.

In the afternoon I finished making up a makeshift clew for Big Brother. I pierced the strengthened corner of the sail behind the broken clew ring in three places with 1½in intervals between the holes, drove a shackle-pin through each hole to fasten a shackle there, then gathered these together by passing a fourth through them, to which I attached the bowline of the sheet. It turned out a strong makeshift repair which did not fail me. Immediately afterwards I had to gybe because I was headed for a group of islands, Islas Los Roques, belonging to Venezuela. Nine minutes later Isla La Orchila was abeam 10 miles to port. These islands caught me unprepared. I hurriedly studied them on the chart and referred to the Admiralty Sailing Directions, but I was definitely caught out and in a bustle. Then halfway through the gybe the time came for me to call the BBC. I asked them to defer my call, which they did.

I still had a lot to do and the islands kept cropping up and going by at what seemed a terrific pace for a yacht, which made me think there must be the father of all currents there. I had approached the islands to take advantage of the Equatorial Current on its way to the Gulf of Mexico to become the Gulf Stream.

However, *Gipsy Moth* was sailing faster than the speedometer showed; I was to discover later that the axles of the tiny propellers which measure the sailing speed of the yacht had worn out during the voyage and I had not realized it. As a result the log was not registering at all at low speeds and under-registering by about ½ knot at high speeds. I had thought that the distance made good was more than the distance sailed because of a strong current, whereas the difference was mostly due to the log failure. I was due again at the infernal wireless and felt jumpy at having to leave off keeping watch with so many islets close on hand.

At midnight I raised myself from my drowsy sleep to go and rig the pole for Big Brother, but when I got on deck I voted against it. The breeze had freshened up considerably—I saw the wind speed indicator at 24 knots—and *Gipsy Moth* could well do without the running sail at present. Perhaps my real reason was that with the end of the race in sight I was nursing the pole. I wanted in any case to put one more lashing at each end of the join before I used it again. It is very difficult with two large diameter poles lashed together to prevent the butt of one from slueing sideways in the join and it was already a few degrees awry: and as soon as they are not exactly parallel the compression load must set up a tremendous strain. So I secured the pole on deck again and dumped the big runner back in the forepeak.

'I am suffering from a complaint quite new to me tonight. My bottom is sore with sunburn. I was working for an hour or two on the clew of the big runner and I must have got burnt then. But I am not moaning about it because it is such a wonderful thing for a Briton to be able to get a burnt bottom in January. I dabbed calamine lotion on. I had a long talk on the R/T with Frank Page of the *Observer*. He seemed sympathetic and I am only too willing to be drawn out. He asked if I had done 1,000 miles in five days during this passage as, he said, I had told Captain Newman of the *Cutty Sark* I hoped to do. I said "No". . . . I feel there is a current fairly whisking *Gipsy Moth* along here and the run might be up to 200 miles tomorrow. The disadvantage is that I have had to come close to the string of islands along the coast to get full advantage of the current, and I could soon be in trouble if the wind backed when I was asleep. The heading is O.K. up to now, one hour after midnight.'

At 0400: 'It always tweeks a romantic chord to see the Southern

Cross again. Brilliant stars in a darkish sky; one or two tiny black clouds. Sea surprisingly pobbly.' At daybreak I suddenly thought I must try a star fix because I would almost certainly be needing one when running down on to the lee shore of Nicaragua. It was a dismal failure; by the time I had found the star volume and worked out the value of Aries, it was too light in the sky and I could not pick up in the sextant any of the three stars I wanted. It was a good lesson; I had not needed a star fix for a long time and I determined to smarten up the drill.

'The boom mend seen as it lies on deck has a bend in it and I must doctor it up before hoisting. It is now needed. The speedometer is recording only 7 knots though the wind is 17 knots. I suppose the speedometer *is* O.K?'

By eleven that morning—'At long last!'—the boom mend had been strengthened, the shackle clew for Big Brother strengthened, and he himself was boomed out to starboard. It was a long and at times tricky operation to shift the heavy, murderously jagged pole from one side of the deck to the other before even the hoisting could start, and I noticed that the mast was bending where the heel of the pole pressed against it, and that a whip had developed at the top of the mast. I hoped that the remaining jumper stay was strong enough. I hate jumper struts; I think them old-fashioned for offshore work and more likely to cause a mast-break than to prevent it.

> Eighteenth day's run to noon fix Saturday 30 January 1971.
> Position: 12°54′N 69°04′W.
> Distance fix-to-fix: 215·5 miles.
> Calculated distance to finish: 868·5 miles.
> Days remaining: 2.

By mid-afternoon *Gipsy Moth* was going well with a fresh breeze, but I was concerned to get still more speed out of her. I dropped the mizen stays'l experimentally. *Gipsy Moth* then seemed to sail less heeled and to be more efficient as well as making much less effort. She also tended to gripe up to windward less and I eased off the No. 1 jib as well. This gave fractionally better speed and more comfortable, less anxious sailing. I wondered if the 600 running sail with its lower cut and 90sq.ft more area would be better as a running genoa than the No. 1 jib, and I determined to try it when the wind eased at night as seemed usual in those parts.

Since noon *Gipsy Moth* had been sailing at a high speed, averaging between 8·7 and 9 knots during eight periods logged. (Later, I concluded that the speedometer was under-registering by about half a knot and that *Gipsy Moth* was belting out the fastest speed of the passage.)

At dusk I shot Capella, Procyon and Sirius for a three-star fix to improve my drill, and at 0635 the next morning I got a planet fix from Jupiter and Venus.

At 0955 on Sunday 31 January: 'I have been looking hard into the tactics and think it would be best to hold this gybe until after the R/T session which I arranged to make at 2.0 p.m. I reckon that to gybe now would entail taking 200 miles to pass across the main shipping lanes to Panama and that of this 200 miles 100 would be in the dark; whereas if I leave the gybe till 3.0 p.m. I shall then be about 75 miles past this morning's planet fix and will cut across the first three main lanes in daylight. These first three lanes are from the Mediterranean, the English Channel, and New York via Puerto Rico. That will leave me with only two more lanes to cross, New York via Windward Passage (Cuba–Haiti) 325 miles farther on and the last big lane from Mexico, Florida and the east coast of the U.S.A. to be crossed 215 miles from San Juan del Norte. Another reason for holding on as at present is that the longer *Gipsy Moth* stays on this gybe, the faster the speed she will make on the port gybe when she changes over.

'Now I must bake. I had no bread yesterday and this morning I missed it when I had only one potato ready for my breakfast fry-up.'

> Nineteenth day's run to noon fix Sunday 31 January 1971.
> Position: 14°15′N 72°49′W.
> Distance fix-to-fix: 231·5 miles.
> Calculated distance to finish: 665·5 miles.
> Days remaining: 1.

The nineteenth day's run of 231·5 miles between fixes was *Gipsy Moth*'s best day's run to date. At last I had got the sort of daily run which I had hoped for every day of the passage. The total of the fix-to-fix runs for the last three days was 637 miles.

At 1515 I wrote: 'The confounded R/T upsets everything. I held off gybing or starting any deckwork which I might not have had time to finish before the R/T session booked for 1405; but the operator, after I had spent an exasperating half-hour trying to contact him, said that he could not handle me at the time and that it would throw Portishead out of gear if he took the call then. He asked me to call again at 5 p.m. which is in one and a half hours time.* I ought to eat something, having had nothing but breakfast; so the R/T will chop right into the gybe or else I'll have to do that in the dark.'

Later, probably after nightfall, but no time is given in the log, I wrote: 'I started the gybe act an hour before the second R/T meeting arranged. (It's no go; I keep on falling asleep. I have put on a large saucepan full of spuds and onions. God knows why because all I can do now is to sleep for a while.) More anon.' And an hour after midnight on 1 February: 'I was quite upset—no, that's not quite the right word, perhaps "thrown" is better—by the R/T affair yesterday. I think it upset my "cool" and made me insufficiently aware of what was going on around me such as the wind and the weather. I just dug in to the job of the moment and paid no attention to the scene. I record this because it illustrates what a great drag and handicap is a daily R/T session, especially for long distance transmitting. If one considers the added fatigue and nervous strain caused by it, I reckon it can cost a racer anything up to 10 miles a day. However, this also shows how silly one can be to let trivial things disturb one.'

That morning, at 0616, I got another star and planet fix, using Vega, Jupiter and Venus. This gave a speed for the past $18\frac{1}{4}$ hours of 201·5 miles per day. When it came to the noon position of this, the last of the twenty days in which I had hoped to sail my point-to-point distance of 4,000 miles:

> **Twentieth day's run to noon fix Monday 1 February 1971.**
> **Position: 13°11′N 76°06′W.**
> **Distance fix-to-fix: 203·5 miles.**
> **Calculated distance to finish: 464.5 miles.**
> **Days remaining: None.**

So there it was. The flag had come down when *Gipsy Moth* and I still had 464·5 miles to go to the finishing point, a percentage of 11·6.

---

*The exasperation was excessive in the circumstances. The Post Office staff was on strike and it was sporting of Portishead to take my call at all.

I had not hit the target; but I do not recall any feelings of great disappointment as I completed my calculations on that twentieth day, probably because I had in my heart accepted on the tenth day that the daily average required from the remaining ten days—227·25 miles—was hopelessly beyond *Gipsy Moth*'s capabilities. I was more excited than depressed. The total of the past four noon-to-noon runs was 840·5 miles, an average of 210 per day, and I had high hopes of 'breaking the barrier' of 1,000 miles in five days.

In the afternoon the wind at last worked round to NE by E; but this time I wished it could have stayed where it was; 'I must gybe again, dammit', and just after six o'clock that evening, 'it has taken me all this time (1 hour 14 minutes) just to get the poled-out sail down, get the pole down, unrig it and nobble it on deck, plus coiling the ropes afterwards and unfouling the various of them twisted round each other. That heavy repaired pole is an awkward customer in this fresh breeze. Now to continue.' Fatigue was all through me and slowing up my reactions. I did not realize it, but it had been building up slowly over twenty days and nights of continuous racing. An hour later I was 'Trying to make up my mind what rig to wear. It is a pretty fresh breeze up forward.' The wind on board was 24 knots which made the true wind 29 knots from NE by N. 'The mizen and tops'l are doing all the driving at the moment. The only other sail up is the main stays'l. A pole-out is not wanted, thank heaven. Shall I hoist the No. 1 jib? I will a brandy sip which will the think-box clear (maybe). Later: I'll have a wee snooze meanwhile.'

I had a good sleep until I was awakened by a loud cannon bang at 2015. That noise always sends a shock-wave through me, and my instinctive reaction is one of dread that something has crashed or smashed. But a rapid casing of the joint this time showed that it was only the tops'l gybing. It could not stand doing that many times, so I changed the big windvane for a smaller, less sensitive one—a tricky job, especially at night. The big vane, meant for light airs, had behaved wonderfully after I had strengthened it; it had taken endless punishment without failing, but in the lively wind it was now banging the helm constantly and rapidly from side to side, which in turn put the tops'l at risk. While on deck I did some other jobs, outhauling the tops'l sheet to the mizen boom end, trimming the main stays'l, bagging up Big Brother and so on. It was quite a list. As so often happens, however, the sea had the last word. A souser wave swept aboard and some of the water shot through the cabin sky-light, which I had raised a few inches. One of its victims was a jar of peanut butter which I had left open in the galley when I dashed on deck and this was now filled with sea water. I had not had time for a meal since breakfast, but could not be miserable about that with *Gipsy Moth* 'going like a witch with this cut-down rig of only 850sq.ft—the mizen, tops'l and main stays'l; but the tops'l is a powerful puller if its wind is not interfered with by the other sails, and now I have the wind I had hoped for right across the Atlantic —30 knots from the NE.'

Shortly after four o'clock the next morning 'I woke with a feeling that *Gipsy Moth* was being dragged back by something though the wind was registering up to 25 knots and she ought to have been going merrily. I hoisted the mizen stays'l but still felt that something was not quite right. I'll try hoisting No. 1 jib after an infusion (into me) of tea. Perhaps the wind is losing its drive though still clocking up to 25 knots.' This entry in the log shows clearly that I was losing efficiency through fatigue: I ought to have boomed out a running sail there and then. As it was I hoisted the No. 1 jib then, but did not tackle the boom and the 300 until a quarter-past ten, when it took me nearly two-and-a-half hours to get it set out to starboard. 'Pole wouldn't stand big runner again I fear. Now must change vanes again. This one cannot control downwind in light wind.' Of course routine jobs, such as observing the sun and navigating, interfered with the act, but I would have taken much less time if I had not been fagged out.

> **Twenty-first day's run to noon fix Tuesday 2 February 1971.**
> **Position: 12°16′N 79°20′W.**
> **Distance fix-to-fix: 199 miles.**
> **Calculated distance to finish: 268 miles.**

This made a total for the last five daily runs fix-to-fix of 1,039·5 miles. It really looked as if I would have my 1,000 miles in five days this time. I calculated the Great Circle distance between the noon fixes at the start and finish of the five days. The distance was 982·25 miles. I was taken aback; it was like a blow in the face and at first I couldn't believe it. When I studied the chart I could see that the track over the past five days had two dog-legs in it; first, on the port gybe *Gipsy Moth* had borne down on the islands off Venezuela, then she had to gybe away to avoid the Curacao and Aruba Islands and the peninsula projecting into the Caribbean from Colombia. Finally I had gybed again and headed S of W for San Juan del Norte. The six noon positions were not in a straight line and the fix-to-fix straight line over the five days was 57¼ miles less than the total of the five daily point-to-point straight lines. The Spanish Main had done me down; I had lost distance by gybing away from it.

I was not moping. I had all the time a feeling of excitement, as though I were treading lighter. This 200 miles a day for a single-hander instead of the traditional 100 miles a day average was something new and exciting in small boat sailing. Since I entered the Caribbean I had had a feeling of excitement, of being hard-pressed because of the speed. There always seemed to be a rush to complete the sun or planet sights and to navigate accurately. Islands and land seemed to rush up, and it was difficult to get through all the routine work and yet sail the ship at its fastest and navigate accurately, even with time spent on eating and sleeping cut to a minimum.

At 1935 I made the distance to my finishing point 207 miles; course 251°. *Gipsy Moth* was sailing fast, having averaged 8·4 knots for the 7½ hours since noon. (The ½ knot underreading would have made the average 8·9 knots.) At dusk I tried for a star fix as more practice for the next night when I would be racing up to a lee shore, but cloud came up and hid all until it was too dark to see the horizon sharply enough for an altitude. Even if the sky had been clear, I would probably have failed to get the fix because I had not prepared thoroughly for it. For the star fix to be a success the stars must be picked up in daylight and the sights completed before the horizon becomes obscured by darkness.

My do-it-yourself pole was not going to last much longer; the concertina-ing compression effect on the lashings had moved one pole against the other a little and so shortened the total length by a few inches. I thought it amazing how it had survived being up continuously—except for the last night—from when I first hoisted it. But it was hell to shift it from one side of the boat to the other and then lift the heel ten feet up the mast to the lug. On that morning, while I was shifting the pole across, *Gipsy Moth* took charge and came up to the wind at about 10 knots with a big heel and the sea invading the lee deck. I feared I might lose the pole overboard but managed to hand on until I had it in a safe position and could leave it to set *Gipsy Moth* back on course again.

At 0634 on the morning of Wednesday 3 February a four-star fix, using stars Rigel and Vega and planets Venus and Jupiter, put *Gipsy Moth* 117·5 miles off the finishing line after a speed made good since the previous noon of 202mpd. At 1054 I took the first sun sight in preparation for working out the position for the final noon of the passage.

Shortly after eleven o'clock I got a clear R/T link with a man whom I understood to be speaking from Managua, the capital of Nicaragua. Managua is about 200 miles inland. When he said that he could not contact Christopher Doll, who was supposed to be waiting for me at San Juan, because there was no communication with that town, I was somewhat taken aback. My contact, whom I at first took to be 'Captain of the Port', said that the 50ft ship *Junior* was coming out to meet me from San Juan del Norte. That was kind, but with the craft manned by sailors perhaps unused to yachts, would not this be fraught with bash-up possibilities? Towards the end of our talk I discovered that I was actually speaking to a Captain Bartlett of a firm called Caribbean Marine, and that he was not at Managua, but at El Bluff, a port farther up the coast from San Juan. He asked me to give him my noon position and I arranged to call him back. All these arrangements struck home to me that I must set hard to work and clean up below—especially the galley and primus cooker—before I arrived.

It is extraordinary how easily one can get rattled when fresh contact with the land is fast approaching after several weeks alone at sea. I hurried through the calculations for the sun fix and was shaken when it put *Gipsy Moth* 20 miles south of the DR position worked up from the planet fix at dawn. Sure that there was an error somewhere I hurriedly took a third check shot of the sun. As soon as I started working it out I spotted the silly mistake I had made—using the Ephemerides for the sun's position for 2 February instead of 3 February. Was I relieved to find it!

A fix-to-fix distance of 209 miles for the day made the sum total of the last five fix-to-fix runs 1,058·5 miles, nineteen miles more than the five runs to noon on 2 February; but there would still be the same kink in the track where I was avoiding the Spanish Main and I thought it was scarcely worthwhile calculating the point-to-point distance. When I did, though, I was astonished and delighted to find that the straight line distance between the noon positions on 29 January and 3 February was 1,017·75. *Gipsy Moth* had done it! She had broken through the 200mpd barrier at last! Her average speed over the five days was 203·5 miles per day. I had given up all hope of her doing it and was taken completely by surprise.

Twenty-second day's run to noon fix
                        Wednesday 3 February 1971.
Position: 11°34′N 82°47½′W.
Distance fix-to-fix: 209 miles.
Total of fix-to-fix runs over past five days: 1,058·5 miles.
Distance made good over past five days: 1,017·75 miles.
Calculated distance to finish: 59.5 miles.

Now I was hard-pressed; I had to clean up the boat, navigate, plan for carrying all sail until the last moment and then dropping it as quickly as possible, feed, sleep, charge batteries, and make another call to Captain Bartlett at 1600.

First, the R/T; this time it was a triangular call, with Christopher Doll taking the third part. When Captain Bartlett asked me about my plans and I told him that I would be unable to enter the estuary or cross the coastline at San Juan del Norte because the entrance was too shallow for *Gipsy Moth*'s draught, he asked if I would come up to El Bluff where I could enter the port easily. I told him that I should be turning round as soon as possible and making for Panama; he sounded disappointed but said nothing more. He was clear, intelligible, and his voice gave the immediate impression that he was practical and reliable. I was very impressed by him and felt sorry when he seemed disappointed.

At 1600 I had less than 38 miles to go. I could not carry the poled-out runner after the R/T talk. I had kept it up longer than I should have done because I knew that Christopher Doll wanted a helicopter shot of *Gipsy Moth* sailing in, and he might have appeared at any time, but he was with the British Ambassador from Managua, staying the night a considerable distance northwards along the coast from San Juan in a house on a banana plantation belonging to an Englishman who had a radiotelephone. He began to unroll the most unexpected information for me. San Juan, which over the months had become a sort of

El Dorado for me, was like an almost deserted mining town with rows of empty wooden houses from which the paint had all peeled off, facing dirt streets ankle-deep in boggy mud. There were no navigation lights anywhere at the harbour entrance or near it. The chart showed a big hospital on the shore to the north of San Juan, so I asked if he could get the hospital authorities to put a bright light in one of their seaward facing rooms. He replied, 'There's no hospital now and even if there were, it would be too late for me to get there.' There was the silence of a hurried consultation. 'We could arrange a light for you forty miles north of San Juan.' I did not think that much good.

I should have to do the best I could without any shore lights and I did not like the prospect. I had already run 30 miles since the noon fix, which only left another 30 to go to the finish. With a 22·5 knot NE by E tail wind *Gipsy Moth* was driving fast on to a lee shore. The coast waters were described as having strong, unpredictable currents. There were no radio beacons or radio aids of any sort, nor any navigational aids of any kind other than my echo-sounder. Even that would be an uncertain protection; the sea bottom was so shallow off the coast that a depth of only 23 fathoms was charted 21 miles offshore and 12 fathoms only $2\frac{1}{2}$ miles off the beach. Besides that, the chart survey had been made in 1836 and with the strong eddying currents for which this coast is notorious, God only knew what the sea bottom would be like now. With this tail wind *Gipsy Moth* was fairly belting out the miles; I must drop the pole and running sail at once. But there was so much to do and I must not have anything interfering with the star fix, which was now vitally important.

Nightfall was at 1800 and I shot the first star, Sirius, one minute before, followed by Capella. The sky was clouding up and I could not snap Procyon until seventeen minutes later. When I worked out the sights and plotted the position lines they did not meet in a point. I had a cold feeling; it was fear. *Gipsy Moth* was racing at over 8 knots towards an unknown, unlit shore in the dark, and I did not know for certain where I was. 'This,' I told myself, 'is where you keep your "cool" or you will have had it.' I was not going to turn until I was definitely over my finishing line but the prospect of driving on to the beach was a chilling one. I started to re-check my workings. It was no use hurrying. It must be done thoroughly. In the seventh line of the Sirius calcu-

88

lation I found the mistake; this time I had taken the value of the Greenwich Hour Angle of Aries for 4 February instead of the 3rd. This had made an error of 52 miles. After correcting it, the three-star position lines intersected to form a "cocked hat" which, though not as small as I would have liked even on a large-scale chart, was small enough to be convincing.

It showed the danger clearly; on her present heading *Gipsy Moth* was 8·5 miles east of the finishing line, and this in turn was 5·3 miles from the shore at the entrance to the Corn River, where the chart read "Breaks across when little swell". By the time I had finished working out the three sights, finding the error in the Sirius calculation, then plotting the position lines, it was a quarter-to seven and *Gipsy Moth*, sailing fast, was only 4·5 miles from the finishing line. I had thirty-five minutes before she reached the finishing line and eighty minutes before she hit the beach.

The depth had already shallowed to 18 fathoms. I was up on deck as fast as I could get there. I had to drop the tops'l and big jib to ensure easy control of the yacht and quick manœuvrability so that I could spin *Gipsy Moth* round if she was suddenly in danger of grounding. The bottom here was mud and sand and the depth would be always changing with the scouring of the strong currents. I was thankful for the bright pools of light on the deck from the spreader lights above, though they seemed to intensify the thick darkness around. There was nothing visible anywhere, either on the sea, in the direction of the land or even in the sky above, clouded with heavy overcast. There was something ominous and threatening about the night. Was this the fore-runner of one of the fierce northerly 'busters' which the Admiralty Sailing Directions described as a serious menace at this western end of the Caribbean Sea?

By 1919, one hour and four minutes after the star fix, *Gipsy Moth* had run 8 miles and I reckoned she was half a mile short of the finishing line.

It was nervy work driving towards the shore in the pitch dark with not a glimmer of light from land or sea, or in the sky. I held to the same course for six minutes, when I reckoned *Gipsy Moth* was a quarter mile over the line. I cannot describe the immense surge of relief which I felt when I put *Gipsy Moth* about on to the port tack, close-hauled and headed SE by E away from that unseen shore.

Twenty-third day's run from noon fix to 1925
Wednesday 3 February 1971.
Position: 11°18′ N 83°47′W (finish).
Distance fix to fix: 59.5 miles.

The course would take *Gipsy Moth* away from the coast north of
San Juan, provided she was far enough north of San Juan to clear
a cape east of it. A northerly current could have been carrying her
south all this time. It was an uncanny feeling with not a single light
along the coast and no sign whatever of the shore. Yet I knew it
was there, close at hand, invisible because of its low-lying terrain.
Time after time I scanned to the west and the south with the night
glasses. The deck was an untidy mess with sails and ropes everywhere, but I dared not take the time from my anxious watch to tidy
it up. I wished I could stop work; I had a feeling of helplessness
and could have done with a good strong drink, but I would not
have anything because I should need to stay awake all night and
keep my wits sharp, or at least not to make them duller than they
seemed to be already. *Gipsy Moth* was sailing close-winded to an E
by N wind of 17 knots. At 2230 I suddenly noticed that the heading had been pushed round to south in a heavy rain squall. Was
Gipsy Moth clear of the point or headed straight for it on this
southerly course? The depth was 26 fathoms. I put her about to
make sure that she was headed away from the land.

The wind backed steadily and pushed *Gipsy Moth*'s heading
round to the north-west, so that now she was headed in to the
shore on the other tack, and half an hour before midnight I found
her headed south-west right for the beach, the wind having backed
to NW.

For the third time I tacked away from the land. It was not
long before I noticed that the heading had swung round from
north to north-west and once again *Gipsy Moth* was headed into
the land. I felt as if I were being hunted on to the shore. This time,
before putting about again, I took advantage of being on the starboard tack to stow the mizen more snugly on its boom, being
able to get at it better while standing on the side of the cockpit
on that tack. The new heading was 110°. It could not have been
a safer one for heading away from the land. Twenty minutes later
there was a 35-knot rain squall. The log entry reads: 'Pretty
weird goings-on here I call them. *Gipsy Moth* is plunging madly

in a 35-knot squall in a very rough sea indeed.' However the depth was now 60 fathoms, which was a great relief.

Shortly after midnight another nasty squall came in, a 40-knotter from the NNE, and I turned *Gipsy Moth* off the wind while I dropped the mizen stays'l; forty minutes later I had to re-hoist it and come up close-hauled to claw off the coast. An hour after midnight: 'A pretty how-de-do; heavy squalls with winds shifting from SE to N. Each time I have tacked away from the shore the wind has shifted and headed *Gipsy Moth* into land again. At present she is heading 25° E of S but the worry is that the coast for 60 miles from the San Juan Point runs 30° E of S. Must risk a sleep; beginning to totter.' By the echo-sounder the depth was more than 60 fathoms so that it seemed safe enough for a short sleep. The risk was that being fagged to the bone, I might fall into a heavy sleep, and at one place the chart gives a 60-fathom depth only 7 miles offshore. It was a horrible sea and I was feeling seasick, which never made anyone optimistic. But I had to sleep.

At 3 a.m. I woke to find *Gipsy Moth* becalmed. At last came the dawn to find me bleary-eyed and weary-skinned, having difficulty in concentrating sufficiently to decide the best course of action. I hadn't a clue as to where I was. There was nothing in sight and the sky was overcast so there was no chance of any star fix. It was not until 0915 that I was lucky enough to get a sun shot and this I combined with a rough DR of the night's complicated wanderings, which I forced myself to work out from the few entries I had in the log for the night before and my memory of the rest. As soon as I had crossed the finishing line I had found it difficult and irksome to make myself enter up log data. The project was finished and I resented having to do anything more. The DR position put *Gipsy Moth* 11·5 miles north of the beach at San Juan del Norte at the entrance to the estuary. At 1003 I got another shot of the sun which gave me a fix and put *Gipsy Moth* 9 miles from the San Juan entrance, NE by E of it. This was 9·3 miles south-east of my position worked out by DR since the star sight. I was well satisfied because this discrepancy was to be expected with a south-east going current as predicted for this part of the coast.

Shortly afterwards a helicopter clattered on to the scene, I guessed with Christopher Doll and Paul Berriff on board. I thought

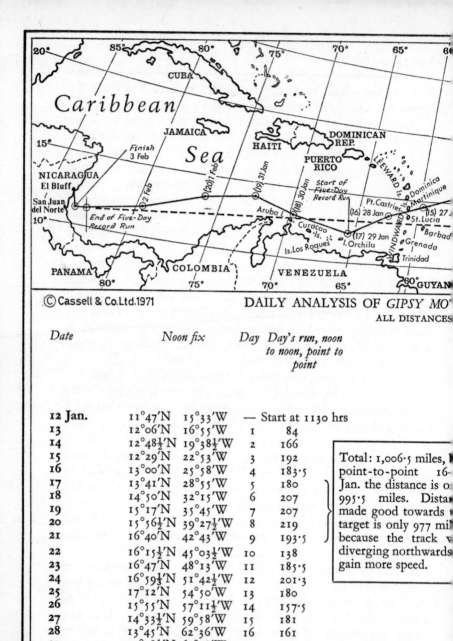

© Cassell & Co. Ltd. 1971

DAILY ANALYSIS OF *GIPSY MO*

ALL DISTANCES

Date	Noon fix		Day	Day's run, noon to noon, point to point
12 Jan.	11°47'N	15°33'W	—	Start at 1130 hrs
13	12°06'N	16°55'W	1	84
14	12°48½'N	19°38½'W	2	166
15	12°29'N	22°53'W	3	192
16	13°00'N	25°58'W	4	183·5
17	13°41'N	28°55'W	5	180
18	14°50'N	32°15'W	6	207
19	15°17'N	35°45'W	7	207
20	15°56½'N	39°27½'W	8	219
21	16°40'N	42°43'W	9	193·5
22	16°15½'N	45°03½'W	10	138
23	16°47'N	48°13'W	11	185·5
24	16°59¼'N	51°42½'W	12	201·3
25	17°12'N	54°50'W	13	180
26	15°55'N	57°11½'W	14	157·5
27	14°33½'N	59°58'W	15	181
28	13°45'N	62°36'W	16	161
29	12°18½'N	65°28'W	17	190
30	12°54'N	69°04'W	18	215·5
31	14°15'N	72°49'W	19	231·5
1 Feb.	13°11'N	76°06'W	20	203·5
2	12°16'N	79°20'W	21	199
3	11°34'N	82°47½'W	22	209
3 (1925 hrs)	11°18'N	83°47'W	22	59·5

Total: 1,006·5 miles, l
point-to-point 16-
Jan. the distance is o
995·5 miles. Dista
made good towards
target is only 977 mil
because the track v
diverging northwards
gain more speed.

Total 1,058·5 miles

Point-to-point, 29 J
to 3 Feb.:1,017·75 mi

Finish

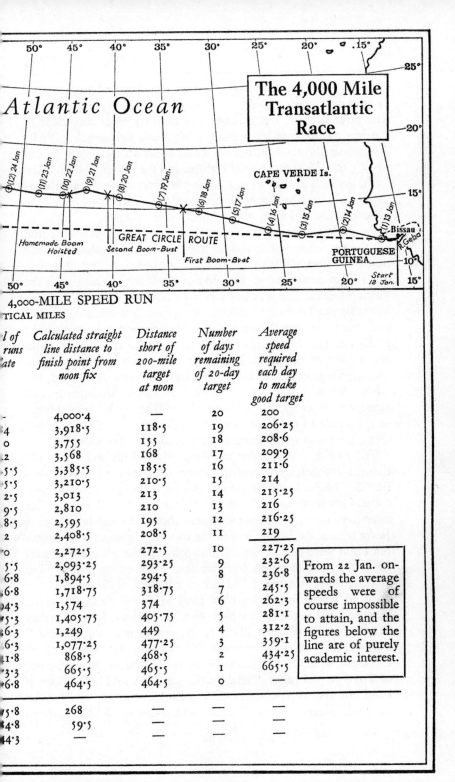

The 4,000 Mile Transatlantic Race

Atlantic Ocean

CAPE VERDE Is.

GREAT CIRCLE ROUTE

Homemade Boom Hoisted
Second Boom-Bust
First Boom-Bust

PORTUGUESE GUINEA

Bissau
R. Geba
Start 12 Jan.

4,000-MILE SPEED RUN

NAUTICAL MILES

Total of runs date	Calculated straight line distance to finish point from noon fix	Distance short of 200-mile target at noon	Number of days remaining of 20-day target	Average speed required each day to make good target
—	4,000·4	—	20	200
4	3,918·5	118·5	19	206·25
0	3,755	155	18	208·6
2	3,568	168	17	209·9
5·5	3,385·5	185·5	16	211·6
5·5	3,210·5	210·5	15	214
2·5	3,013	213	14	215·25
9·5	2,810	210	13	216
8·5	2,595	195	12	216·25
2	2,408·5	208·5	11	219
0	2,272·5	272·5	10	227·25
5·5	2,093·25	293·25	9	232·6
6·8	1,894·5	294·5	8	236·8
6·8	1,718·75	318·75	7	245·5
04·3	1,574	374	6	262·3
5·3	1,405·75	405·75	5	281·1
6·3	1,249	449	4	312·2
6·3	1,077·25	477·25	3	359·1
1·8	868·5	468·5	2	434·25
3·3	665·5	465·5	1	665·5
6·8	464·5	464·5	0	—
5·8	268	—	—	—
4·8	59·5	—	—	—
4·3	—	—	—	—

From 22 Jan. onwards the average speeds were of course impossible to attain, and the figures below the line are of purely academic interest.

they must be great optimists to have expected to find me, and then to be equally lucky to do so. I was feeling in a ghastly, bleary state after the past thirty hours, but the helicopter succeeded in rousing me to rage by putting *Gipsy Moth* first aback with its downwash and then into irons. I had to let all the sheets fly and work *Gipsy Moth* downwind right round the compass so that she could get sailing again. I said some very uncomplimentary things indeed about Christopher's knowledge of seamanship as the helicopter backed away and headed for the shore.

Presently a large, cumbersome craft showed up. At last I could see the shoreline but it was so low and indistinct that it would have been impossible to identify it. I seemed to be full of worry, due I suppose to fatigue. I could not think how to cope with the visiting vessel. The weather was now fine, but there was a considerable swell running from the north-east. If this big, top-heavy craft tried to come alongside *Gipsy Moth* there would be trouble. I sailed on slowly towards the estuary entrance at San Juan, turning it over in my mind. I dropped the mizen and after downhauling the main stays'l and mizen stays'l booms to leeward, put *Gipsy Moth* about so that the sails were aback. She then jogged along with steerage way at about a knot. This enabled the skipper of the *Junior* to come within hailing distance—and he remained there. He was a good seaman and I need not have worried.

The British Ambassador to Nicaragua and his wife, Ivor and Patricia Vincent, were aboard, as were Christopher Doll and Paul Berriff. The Ambassador gamely started making a speech of welcome. I felt sorry to be the cause of his having to suffer from what must have been a horrible movement aboard the nearly stationary *Junior* in that swell. He invited me to visit Managua, the capital, but I said there was not sufficient depth over the bar at the estuary for *Gipsy Moth* to enter, and therefore I was going to leave immediately for Panama. I had had a gruelling night and did not want to repeat it. Christopher Doll knew all this, of course, because I had explained my plans to him at Bissau. However, they pressed me to visit El Bluff, at the entrance to the Bluefields Lagoon, sixty miles to the north. It was an excellent harbour with a safe entrance. Christopher told me that the Nicaraguan Minister of Tourism and other officials at the capital would be unhappy if I did not visit their country after sailing all the way there. I felt pretty desperate about it. Then he added that at El Bluff, Captain

94

Bartlett was operating a shrimp fishing factory with workshops and every facility for making repairs. That gave me food for thought. *Gipsy Moth* could certainly do with some maintenance and repair, and I had been deeply impressed by Captain Bartlett on the R/T. So I changed my mind and accepted the invitation to visit El Bluff—and I never regretted it.

It was then 1130. At 1138 I set course for El Bluff. It was sunny with only a faint breeze, so it would be impossible to reach El Bluff before dark and I arranged to arrive after daylight.

Gipsy Moth ghosted along through the peaceful afternoon in the faintest of breezes. For a while I sat in the cockpit, musing in the sun and thinking over the Transatlantic run. The 4,000 miles had taken 22·3 days instead of 20. This was an average speed of 179·1 miles instead of 200 miles per day, a drop of 20·9 miles per day. Looked at another way *Gipsy Moth* had been short of the target after 20 days by 417·9, say 418 miles, of which 150 miles had been lost in the first two days. It was a failure, but on the other hand it was 38·6 per cent faster than my previous fastest straight 4,000-mile run in *Gipsy Moth IV* in September 1966 when sailing round the world. This was from 47°04½'N 08°40'W to 18°87'S 24°06'W. This run averaged 128·78 miles per day and took thirty-one days one and a half hours. As far as I could discover it was the fastest solo run of that length at the time. Then in 1969 Eric Tabarly, the great French yachtsman, made a solo passage from San Francisco to Tokyo covering approximately 5,700 miles in 39·6 days at an average speed of 144 miles per day, though at the time of writing I do not know if this was a point-to-point distance.

But there was one great, glorious consolation. With the five-day speed-burst of 1,017·75 miles in five days, *Gipsy Moth* had broken through the 200 miles a day solo barrier, exceeding *Gipsy Moth IV*'s 1967 run by 133 miles or 15 per cent. And with that to give me pleasure, I prepared for the approaching night.

IV

NICARAGUA

I need not have worried about arriving at El Bluff too soon; seven hours after I had set course *Gipsy Moth* was becalmed only 17½ miles NNE of the old lighthouse at San Juan del Norte, and seven hours after that she had apparently moved on only another 8½ miles. I had noticed that she was moving quietly through the water several times when the log was registering nil. Foolishly I paid no attention; I was in a state of mild euphoria after completing my Transatlantic project. The second half of the day had been lovely, fine weather, and I had got in some good sleep while *Gipsy Moth* ambled along. In the evening I went to sleep with *Gipsy Moth* sailing gently along NNE. I woke at 0130 to find her headed due west for the shore at a speed of 4 knots on the log; how far had she sailed on this heading? On that depended how close she was to the beach. I could see nothing, hear nothing. Assuming that she was in the worst possible position based on the depth and the distance logged, it would still be safe to keep going NNE until Paxaro Bovo Island was reached this side of Monkey Point, and that was 17½ miles ahead, so that it would be dawn before *Gipsy Moth* reached it at 4 knots and I would be better able to fix my position. I set her back on course, reckoning that I could sleep in peace for two hours at least, and probably four, but at 0420 the noise of a boom banging or a sail slatting woke me. The wind had backed 90° to NW and *Gipsy Moth* was once again headed west. What *was* going on in Providence's office? Another 3¼ miles of sleep and *Gipsy Moth* would have been on the beach.

I tacked and once again set off on the right course, but presently in the dark I could hear a rustling noise like a wide river running shallow over a stony bed. I listened intently. I could see nothing. It must be a tide race but the chart showed that there could not be anything of that sort there. Suddenly in the lightening darkness before dawn I was aware of an islet abeam. It was Paxaro Bovo and it looked to be only half a mile away. It gave me the cold creeps. According to the log it was not due for another 5 miles. Then I remembered how in the sunshine of the previous afternoon *Gipsy Moth* had been ghosting along in the zephyr at $\frac{1}{2}-\frac{3}{4}$ knot and I had been surprised that the log-impellers had registered nil speed. I found out next day that the log-impeller axles were worn, and the old navigational maxim was once more driven home like a nail hammered into my brain: 'Never trust yourself to only one method of checking the navigation; get an independent second check.'

Gipsy Moth arrived at El Bluff at the mouth of the estuary on 5 February and had a friendly, warm welcome when she tied up at the side of the Customs Wharf. The Ambassador was there and the Director-General of the Nicaraguan Tourist Board, Dr Ernesto Reyes, who presented me with a Nicaraguan flag to hoist to the starboard crosstree arm: I did not have a 'courtesy flag' because I had not expected to land in Nicaragua. Dr Reyes was one of the most optimistic 'pressers-on' I have ever met; he hoped that a result of my passage would be an international yacht race organized along my 4,000 mile course which would bring in its wake an invasion of prosperity-sprinkling tourists. Christopher Doll shepherded and shooed away invading spectators like a hen protecting its chick. Perhaps chick is the wrong word considering that the Nicaraguan press labelled me 'El Viejo Lobo del Mar'— 'The Old Wolf of the Sea'.

I looked round for my radio contact, Captain Bartlett, but there was no sign of him until the hubbub had died down, when he emerged unobtrusively from the background. 'Bart', as everyone calls him, the Captain from Connecticut, has a pointed greying beard and would need no make-up at all to play the part of a pirate captain of two centuries or more ago. In the days of Henry Morgan his tremendous personality alone would surely have made him the most successful—and certainly the most efficient— privateer cruising the Spanish Main. But at Bluff in 1971 he was manager of a shrimp packing factory with eighty-five trawlers fishing shrimp on contract. *Gipsy Moth* was indeed fortunate to be here because of Bart's willingness—in fact, determination—to help re-fit her in the factory workshops, which had to be both well-equipped and well-run to keep eighty-five trawlers at sea.

In the end Bart himself did most of the repair work on board *Gipsy Moth*, often working all day at it. I think that as boss of the works he missed the practical work and the little problems and challenges such as arise on a small craft, like correcting faults of rigging or thinking up and making replacements for broken gear. I never found out how old he was. When I asked him, he dodged the question. I thought he could be anything between fifty and seventy.

Every day we all, including the Ambassadorial party as long as it remained at Bluff, went off to lunch at Bart's house. Other visitors used to turn up, a steady trickle of men on business, and one day no less than five Ambassadors from neighbouring countries. I do not know why they were there but it was no wonder that their visits coincided with lunchtime because Donata, Bart's imperturbable Nicaraguan cook-housekeeper, unendingly produced great platters of the most delicious seafood; lobster, crayfish, giant prawns and excellent local fish—all fresh from the sea—with salads and a huge supply of the local favourite—a smallish red bean. I always had to retire after the feast for a ten-minute snooze before starting work again in the afternoon. Bart would join me later as soon as he had dealt with his office business.

Gipsy Moth needed many repairs after being driven so hard. Bart loaded the two broken booms on to his jeep and trundled them down the rough dirt track to his workshops, where the fractures were mended with lengths of irrigation pipe. Fortunately this pipe, which was used for supplying well-water to the houses of the little community, had the same diameter and thickness as the booms, and the aluminium alloy was similar, if not the same.

What could have been impossible to replace without long delay was the big lower insulator at the bottom of the backstay, which also served as the R/T aerial. This insulator had been crushed, but I had not noticed it before because the pieces were still held in place by the wire. I wondered when this had occurred and whether it was responsible for some of the difficulties I had had in making contact. It must have been caused by too heavy a load on the backstay, which not only stayed the mizen mast from the stern, but also the main mast by means of the triatic stay between the two mastheads. The main mast in turn carried the load of the stays from masthead to stem. The load on the backstay would therefore be greater when Big Brother or the running sail was pulling hard in a strong wind.

I did not think it would be possible to replace the insulator in Nicaragua, but Bart disappeared one day on a mission and in a direction which he declined to discuss, and next morning calmly turned up with exactly the right insulator for the job in his pocket. To fit it, all the rigging had first to be slacked off—topmast stays, forestays, and twelve main and mizen shrouds. Afterwards, all these had to be set up again. Bart carried out the whole job, and in the end I was satisfied that the rigging could not have been better tuned, with all the stays and shrouds set up to just the right tension—which goes to show that neither Bart nor I were adept at the rigger's art, because when I got back to the high seas all went slack and I had to set up afresh every stay and shroud.

Besides the boom and insulator, there was a long list of repairs, small jobs and large, such as the broken jumper stay bottlescrew, the boom rest, the big runner clew thimble, the main stays'l boom fitting, the inspection lamp, the leaking galley water pump, the damage to the cine-camera housing, and even the cabin vacuum cleaner, all of which needed repair, new parts, or overhaul. The self-steering skeg and oar had to be dismantled, cleaned of barnacles and weed, and repainted with anti-fouling paint. Bart also had a wooden toolbox made for me and some lead weights for the collision mat to make it sink under the hull in the event of a leak there. Cords at the corners of the mat then drew it against the hull. There were stores to be rounded up, such as fruit, water, paraffin and fuel, and the other food stocks had to be replenished.

I wanted to keep at the job until *Gipsy Moth* was ready to sail again, so reluctantly I had to refuse all invitations by the friendly Nicaraguans to visit Managua, their capital. Then one day I was told that the President, General Debayle, wished to present me with a gold medal. This put me on an awkward spot because it would be too churlish not to visit the capital to receive it. So an aircraft flew us off from the short airstrip on the rise behind Bart's house. For the first hundred miles the country was rough and wooded, very green and scarcely inhabited. It looked like the rough back country of New Zealand fifty years ago. The river which emptied into the lagoon inland of El Bluff twisted its way below, with an occasional steamer leaving a wake on the smooth water. For the second hundred miles there were roads, of which one looked like a new motorway and had a few cars on it.

At Managua I stayed with the Vincents in their bungalow. Ivor gave a big cocktail party to which many Ambassadors, Government Ministers and officials came. I had never before seen so many Ambassadors together. It was a geography lesson in how many States and Republics there are in Central and South America.

General Debayle was most amiable when I was taken to meet him in his Palace. I had wondered what suitable present I could give him from *Gipsy Moth*, and plumped for the burgee of the Royal Cork Yacht Club. This Club, founded 250 years ago, is the oldest in the world, and as *Gipsy Moth* was built four hundred yards from the Clubhouse, and I have the honour to be a Life Member, I thought it would be a suitable present. The burgee is an attractive dark blue with a golden harp. The general seemed delighted with this and said he would hang it on the wall of his bedroom. After this formal presentation we passed through a number of impressive staterooms and settled on the huge patio-balcony where we sipped Flor de Cana, the local rum, while talking. In the distance through the darkness we could see the giant pall of dust from the active volcano, Cerro Negro, which spread for 50 miles in every direction above the land, threatening to obliterate everything living under it. When the audience ended, we left after shaking hands all round, and I flew back to El Bluff. I never did get my gold medal.

On my return Bart and I set to work in earnest on *Gipsy Moth*. After nightfall he used to come back and have supper with me on board. We would settle down to yarning, but towards the end of a bottle of brandy or gin, the talking would give way to Bart's stentorian sea songs. When he was in full song he made the welkin ring and it felt as if *Gipsy Moth*'s hull were quivering, the warehouses along the wharf shaking as if in an earthquake.

V

ESCAPE FROM THE CARIBBEAN SEA

During the twelve days *Gipsy Moth* spent at El Bluff, I was planning the next move, pondering over charts, sailing directions, and hydrographic–meteorological charts. *Gipsy Moth* had achieved my principal ambition, to break through the 200 miles per day solo barrier, so there was no longer that excuse for a dart down to the Equator and back. But I wanted more adventure, and above all I wanted to be free, as free as a wild sea bird like the stormy petrel, to sail where I liked as long as I liked on the great ocean. This longing was strengthened by my feeling of being trapped in the Caribbean. I was enclosed by land, shut in with islands, cays, reefs and shoals—on a sea 1,550 miles from east to west and 700 miles from north to south. I had already made up my mind to sail down to the Equator before returning to England, but to give substance to my plan I thought that with the experience I now had of sailing for speed, I could coax *Gipsy Moth* to put up a much faster five-day run. I would try for one on the way down to the Equator and again on the way north from it.

I sailed out of Bluff on 17 February. I felt queasy and clumsy, truly 'at sea', and I don't suppose that having only three and a half hours sleep after my last party with Bart and his friends improved either my resistance to seasickness or my efficiency. My guests were invited aboard for a drink at six o'clock and I assumed that the party would end at seven because I could not speak any Spanish. At least I hoped so because I had so much still to do on board. However, at eleven I was still following the example of the Colonel in drinking Flor de Cana with lemon juice and ice. The Major was drinking whisky, Bart brandy, and Bart's boss, who was there too, gin. I fear they did not get a very sympathetic reception when they came aboard in the morning. After being tied up to the coastguard cutter for nearly a fortnight there was quite a lot to do to cast off in the strong tide pressing abeam on *Gipsy Moth* and I did not want to be distracted by anything. I wanted to be able to concentrate on working my passage alone

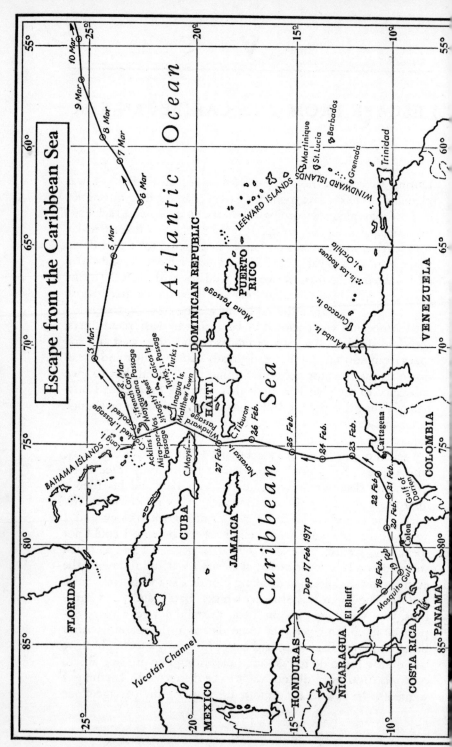

Escape from the Caribbean Sea

Atlantic Ocean

Caribbean Sea

FLORIDA

BAHAMA ISLANDS

CUBA

JAMAICA

HAITI

DOMINICAN REPUBLIC

PUERTO RICO

LEEWARD ISLANDS

WINDWARD ISLANDS

Martinique
St. Lucia
Barbados
Grenada
Trinidad

VENEZUELA

COLOMBIA

PANAMA

COSTA RICA

NICARAGUA

HONDURAS

MEXICO

Yucatán Channel

Mona Passage

Windward Passage

Mayaguana Reef

French Coys

Caicos Is

Turks I. Passage

Turks Is.
Turks I.

Inagua Is.

Matthew Town

Mira-por-vos
Passage

Acklins I.

Crooked I.

Long I.

Red I. Passage

Mayaguana I.

C. Maysi

C. Tiburon

Navassa I.

Aruba Is.
Curaçao Is.
Is. Los Roques
Is. La Orchila

El Bluff
Colon
Mosquito Gulf
Cartagena
Gulf of Darien

Dep 17 Feb 1971
18. Feb.
19. Feb.
20 Feb.
21 Feb.
22 Feb.
23 Feb.
24 Feb.
25 Feb.
26 Feb.
27 Feb.
2. Mar.
3. Mar.
5 Mar
6 Mar
7 Mar
8 Mar
9 Mar
10 Mar

25°
20°
15°
10°
55°
60°
65°
70°
75°
80°
85°

102

out of Bluff without ramming anything, going aground or what not, as well as waving goodbye to all my friends.

My agony could not have been as prolonged as it seemed because, although I did not leave the jetty until nine o'clock and then had to motor down the channel out of the harbour before hoisting sail, my log records that five sails were set by 0930. At 1030 my very good friend Bart shouted and waved goodbye and the landing craft in which he had been seeing me off returned to El Bluff. I was in 13·5 fathoms and felt seasick due to the strong head-on swell running on to the coast from the east. The movement was horrible. 'This boat', I logged miserably, 'is hellish on the wind.'

All the afternoon I dozed or slept or read Simenon's *Maigret et les Vieillards*, lying on my bunk and thanking God that I could do so because I wasn't racing and there were no hazards about. The sea was empty and there was plenty of sea-space ahead. What a relief to be able to do nothing when feeling seasick!

I felt depressed and lonely, however. I missed Bart's company and my beloveds in England seemed a long, long way away in time and distance. But it was no good giving in to this sentiment so I pushed myself into preparing and taking a star fix. It was useful in getting me a good fix, but perhaps its chief value was in the satisfaction of doing a job well, and I began to feel better.

I was rather bitten by this star fix business. I used to scorn it because only a little cloud is needed to prevent one from finding a star during the short period of a few minutes at twilight when both it and the horizon can be seen, whereas the sun can usually be glimpsed through light clouds or, if not, is likely to show through almost any cloud after a few minutes or at worst a few hours. This means that the sun can still be valuable when the weather is foul, stars are useless, and a sight is badly needed. On the other hand, two big advantages of a four-star fix are that a double check is obtained and the whole operation is completed in a comparatively short time; with the sun it is necessary to make at least two separate observations with an hour or more interval between them in order to get a fix, and wait another similar interval for the third observation, if a check of the first two is needed.

I had always expected a trouncing when it came to escaping from the Caribbean. There are only three outlets from the western half, the Yucatán Channel between Cuba and Mexico, the Windward Passage between Cuba and Haiti, and the Mona Passage between the Dominican Republic and Puerto Rico. The eastern half of the Caribbean is ringed by a string of smaller islands curving round from Puerto Rico eastwards and then south to Trinidad and mainland Venezuela. Passages can be made between most of these islands, but it would be sheer folly to beat 1,350 miles into a 20–30 knot wind against an Equatorial Current of up to a knot making its way to the north-west end of the Caribbean to pass round the west end of Cuba and become the Gulf Stream between Cuba and Florida. Escaping at the west end was formidable enough. The Mona Passage lay ENE a thousand miles from Bluff and the Windward Passage NE, 750 miles. Both were a beat to windward. In that fine Admiralty volume, *Ocean Passages of the World*, sailing-ships, squareriggers and clippers of a hundred years ago which had business on the Spanish Main were advised to wait if possible until the summer months, when the wind was likely to be south of east, in order to sail out of the Caribbean by way of the Windward or Mona Passages.

The easy way out would have been to take the same route as the current, but at that time of year it would entail running the gauntlet of the formidable northerly busters. I considered this too risky for a single-hander sailing through comparatively close waters for 750 miles, first of all among the unlighted cays and sandbanks at the north-west end of the Caribbean, then through the Yucatán Channel between Mexico and Cuba, followed by the Straits of Florida with the Bahamas crowding the water to the east of Florida. As I was not going to wait for the summer, my best tactics were to follow the coast south-east from Nicaragua, past Costa Rica, and along the coast of Panama to Colombia, until I reached Cartagena when I would beat across the Caribbean north-east to the Mona Passage, 650 miles, and from there into the open Atlantic. At first *Gipsy Moth* ought to keep in a favourable current eddy by hugging the coast some fifty or a hundred miles off for 570 miles in the Mosquito Gulf, along the Isthmus of Panama, and in the Gulf of Darien. At least there ought not to be a contrary current there, according to the Admiralty Routeing Chart for February. The trouble was that near the coast the wind was likely to be patchy, with calms interspersing squalls.

Before *Gipsy Moth* was a day out of Bluff, I was beginning to have trouble with the rigging. In the morning I found the main topmast stay slack and hardened it up; in the afternoon the mizen stays'l stay was slopping about and I had to harden that up; the same thing happened with the main stays'l stay; then I noted that the top of the main mast was curving forward above the cross-trees although the backstay was taut, so taut that I felt it would be unwise to harden it up any more to straighten the main mast. I would try slacking off the main lower after shrouds and taking up the forward ones to straighten the curve, and this was partly successful. I decided that Bart and I would never become tycoons in the yacht rigging business.

Nothing is more exasperating for a singlehander than calms alternating with squalls. At midnight, with the spreader lights shining down in the darkness the water looked like oil and at first I thought it was coated with oil. It had that dead slap on the hull and bubbles in the bow wavelets which happen with an oil-covered surface.

How I dislike the slatting of sails, the banging of sheets, and clinking of booms that go with near-calms. It is hard on the gear, but that was not the reason why I should soon be sewing for hours to repair a row of seams at the foot of the No. 1 jib. There was no chafe on that sail along the foot. These seams had opened up simply through bad sewing where the stitches were not in any way anchored at the end of the seams.

On the afternoon of the 19th I thought *Gipsy Moth* was in the Trade Wind at last and set the No. 2 jib in place of the 600. I expected the wind to freshen and *Gipsy Moth* would sail closer and more comfortably to the wind with the flatter, smaller jib. I did not relish a week's solid hard pounding into the Trade Wind, its seas and swell. I wanted to make life as painless as possible, compatible with efficiency. But at 0725 the next morning I logged: 'This is a very weary man writing. The going is so rough that it is difficult to stand without being thrown, difficult to focus on small things like the latitude scale at the chart margin, difficult to rest. On top of that I am dopey with lack of sleep.' *Gipsy Moth* was plugging close-hauled into a north-east wind of up to 30 knots. She had sailed through the steamer lanes converging on Panama from the north-east but I had seen only three steamers.

It was not always rough going. On 21 February I woke at 0300 to calm, peaceful sailing at 6 knots hard on the wind; an extra-

ordinary change from the rough riding which seemed interminable when sailing against the wind in the Caribbean. At noon I
was able to write: 'It's good to feel fit again and I certainly am
grateful for a quieter sea. I shall be on the wind continuously for
another 770 miles before I get out of the Caribbean—120 more in
the Gulf of Darien and then 650 to the Mona Passage. Although it
is comparatively quiet today, *Gipsy Moth* has jumped twice off wave
crests this morning; the tin of butter was jumped off the saloon
table and other mop-ups were required.' The noon fix had shown
that *Gipsy Moth* had been in a strong current which had set her
21 miles southwards into the Gulf of Darien in eighteen hours.

In the evening: 'It has been quite a livestock day. First, that
tarantula has turned up again. He scuttled out a couple of inches
from under the tier of drawers below the liquor locker in the
main cabin. When he saw me he stood defiantly with his two
claws held in the air before him like a scorpion's, then bolted up
the face of the bottom drawer and hid behind the bow-shaped
drawer handle. He thought himself safely hidden but I could see
his back and the two claws raised above his head. A nice thing if
I had gripped the handle to open the drawer! I darted for my
death-ray gun and aimed the deadly beam at him. He turned and
ran for it, scuttling back under the framework. He did not seem
worried or affected. He seemed to be a survivor and I began to
admire him for it. If he survived this he was a member of the
crew.

'Then a horrible new creature turned up. At first I thought it
was a giant flying ant. There was a touch of the praying mantis,
which eats the fore-half of her mate while he is making love to
her, about its looks. I thought of the invasion of the earth by
the Triffids and again rushed for my death-ray of insecticide. This
time I aimed the death-dealing jet with positive success for later
I found the creature on its back with its knees all drawn up. I felt
sorry for it then but there just is not room for a horrible-looking
creature like that on a singlehanded yacht.

'Later, when I was sewing the seams of the No. 1 jib on deck,
a moth appeared, a handsome, beautifully mannered creature
sitting on the sail where I would need to be sewing later. I did
not want to frighten or disturb him—no, I am sure now that it
was "her"—so I worked on as quietly as possible so that she
could fly away if she wished. But where could the poor creature

go, thirty odd miles from land? So when the time came to work at the seam near her pitch, I fetched an empty honey jar and induced her to enter this where, after a short flutter, she settled down as if she was enjoying the honey. (Tasmanian honey with an aroma almost as if scented.) After I had finished sewing I took her into the cabin and removed the lid so that she could please herself. At present she is perched on the beam above my berth and looking very contented. I do hope she will survive but boat life is full of hazards for fluttering creatures. They will hide in out-of-the-way spots like a furled sail or coil of rope, which sooner or later will be brought into violent or sudden action.'

At 2040 on Monday 22 February *Gipsy Moth* was 40 miles WNW of Cartagena. The sails had been banging and slatting incessantly all day. Now a faint breeze put them to sleep. The currents in that area are tricky and treacherous and of course near the coast must be more or less unpredictable. According to the current and wind chart for February, *Gipsy Moth* should have been in a favourable $\frac{1}{2}$-knot ENE current in this area, instead of which she had been set in the opposite direction by what appeared to be 3 knots for the past seven hours. I wondered if that was partly due to a tidal current. It is a worry for a solo sailor near land needing to sleep six or seven hours a day.

What I wanted was a good breeze to get clear of the Spanish Main, and in the end a freshet of wind had me out of my berth at 2200. The wind steadily veered until *Gipsy Moth* was headed E by S. With the likelihood of more calms to follow I did not at all like heading in to the coast at night in case the very strong on-shore current was still at work, so I decided to abandon my coast crawl with its calms and squalls and strike out across the sea where I hoped to find a steadier wind. So I tacked to the north. All night *Gipsy Moth* was plugging into a strong wind and a bouncing sea. There is nearly always a big swell running in the Caribbean Sea; with the night glasses I watched a long steamer pitching to the swell and periodically disappearing completely from view behind it. *Gipsy Moth* behaves excellently in this sort of rough, hard going, provided she is precisely set up for it. A degree or two more off the wind and she pounds and bashes, due mostly to the extra speed. A few degrees closer to the wind she slows right up and nearly stops. The amount of sail set is critical. She must have no more than the right amount or she makes life a hell below. In this case she was sailing between 27·5° and 35° off the relative wind of 25–32 knots. I dropped sail after sail until only the mizen stays'l and the main stays'l were set. In eleven hours throughout the night *Gipsy Moth* sailed 53 miles at an average of 4·8 knots.

There is one thing about rough weather—and things were rough outside—nothing is to be done on deck. If the boat is trimmed to sail comfortably and safely, the crew can sit back and relax. One obvious reason for stopping maintenance and deck-work in a gale is because it becomes dangerous to move about, particularly in a boat at speed. I have to be careful, above deck and below, not to be thrown between handgrips. I always try to make sure that one handgrip is sound and firm so that if the boat suddenly jumps off the top of a wave, or lurches madly to one side, I shall not be twisted away from the grip. However, in spite of this fine theory, I am often caught between grips and knocked about. Also I always intend not to be caught out with something in each hand, such as a plate in one and a mug in the other, when moving from the galley to the cabin. Sometimes it seems so quiet that nothing can go wrong and I make a dash for it. Then *Gipsy Moth* gives a big jump, everything comes to grief, there is tea all over the cabin and I am left the mug.

At 1600 on the 23rd the wind began veering right round the clock from south, through west and north, to finish up in the north-east six hours later. First *Gipsy Moth* changed over to the port gybe and gradually came hard on the wind on the port tack to end up as close to the wind as she could lay on the starboard tack. The heading then was between N by E and NNE, about 45° off the heading I required to make the Mona Passage. It was dreary going, and by the next afternoon I had dropped the No. 2 jib and was not far off needing the mizen stays'l down as well. The foredeck was taking a lot of water green and the wind was 35 knots up to 40 in a clear sky. I thought it must be associated with one of the northerly busters. I must have hit one of those two days in a hundred on which gales of Force 8 or more were predicted by the U.S. Hydrographic Office for this 5° rectangle of latitude and longitude.

One of my chief blessings was not having to do anything I didn't want to. *Gipsy Moth* was headed away from land and there was no racing urgency to carry all sail possible regardless of discomfort. I slept that night from about 8.30 p.m. until 7.30 a.m., except for a couple of hours at midnight—the longest sleep I had at sea on the voyage. At midnight I at last dropped the mizen stays'l (the wind was up to 43 knots), then I had a meal after filling the primus stove, the bottle of meths, and the meths priming can. After that I watered the garden and wound the chronometer before turning in again. I was fagged out; it had been a constant strain since I left Bluff with the strong unpredictable currents and a succession of calms and gale squalls, often with the wind swinging right round through 180°, seeming bent on sailing the boat into the breakers.

When I woke, the wind had dropped to 27 knots; but it was not the wind that was important but the sea. Just as I was entering in the log that the sea had quietened down, a wave slammed the side of the boat and cascaded into the cockpit, and the wind, which had seemed to have lost its driving, forceful, get-out-of-my-way note, piped up again. I thought the reefed mizen would be worth while in giving a better heading into the wind. Without the main stays'l *Gipsy Moth* would not come up closer to the wind than 70°–75°, however much the tiller was put down to leeward, and the large amount of rudder needed to keep her to that acted as a brake.

Wednesday 24 February, 0957: 'Mizen reefed at last. It takes longer to do any job in a gale and of course the mizen is damn awkward with the boom high above the cockpit and the tiller knocking one's knees, doubling them up, as one straddles it with a foot on each side on a cockpit seat. However, I am bursting with pride at the result. As I had made a botch-up of the job last time, I ran through the operation step by step in my mind. The result now looked neater and the reefing had been an easier job. It made all the difference to the sailing; first it got rid of the lee helm which was braking the forward movement severely. Secondly it enabled the heading to be pointed up 40° nearer to the wind. Thirdly it put the speed up from 3·5 to 5·25 knots.' I came up on deck to see a small trawler cross close ahead amid cloudbursts of white water as her bows ploughed into the waves.

At noon, the day's run made good was only 104 miles; the position 13°44′N 75°52′W. That was fair enough in a gale when not racing, but I was concerned about the leeway and the track made good. The fix was no less than 35 miles to leeward and the track made good, roughly north, was 20° to leeward of the heading sailed. I was puzzled by this. I felt sure there had been nothing like as much current when I was running down to Nicaragua (the noon DR position was almost on top of my dawn fix of 1 February). The Admiralty chart gave the current as west-going, 1 knot. From the islands north of Venezuela to here, the current was the strongest in the Caribbean. That would account for 24 of the 35 miles, but what about the remaining eleven? I could not account for them.

The course for Mona Island in the Mona Passage was 061°, distance 540 miles. To reach it *Gipsy Moth* must keep on her present tack for 225 miles until near Jamaica, where the adverse current was only half a knot; then on the port tack for 470 miles until south of Mona, and finally a starboard tack into the Passage. Or could I make a quicker escape from the Caribbean? Instead of tacking when near Jamaica, another 200 miles on the present tack would fetch the Windward Passage, and most of that 200 would be in the lee of Haiti; winds would be light and the current variable there. It would be a tough task for a singlehander afterwards, breaking out through the cays and islands of the Bahamas and I would have to mug up the information about the various passages; for 320 miles I should be lucky if I got a few short snatches of sleep. On the other hand *Gipsy Moth* would be moving steadily north to lighter winds. I decided to make for the Windward Passage.

Noon, 25 February: 'Today another poor run of only 94 miles between fixes and *Gipsy Moth* sailed 123·5 miles to make good that distance. She was set 41 miles to the WSW by the current and the leeway in the gale. The track made good showed nearly the same angle of leeway as yesterday, 18°.' I would have to keep *Gipsy Moth* close-hauled hard on the wind if she was to make Cape Tiburon, the south-west point of Haiti, at the approach to the Windward Passage.

'Today, the 25th, is the anniversary of our wedding 34 years ago. I opened up one of the bottles of Veuve Cliquot which Gilo had given me before I left Plymouth. Before I could start to draw the cork it went off like a gun trying to blow a hole through the cabin roof. I tried to say a toast to Sheila's and my happiness together, but a gulp stuck in my throat. Thirty-four years is a very large slice of life. Well, I drank the toast anyway, and another to Gilo's happiness.'

After the Champagne I tried to call up Portishead to congratulate Sheila on having survived a third of a century of married life, but it was a wash-out; there was not a peep out of Portishead. I was not surprised, with a huge mountainous lump of land like Haiti in between. I needed cheering up; the going was hellish rough with *Gipsy Moth* knocking out 6½ knots hard on a Force 6 wind in a rough sea, 35° off a wind of 25–35 knots. Day after day of this did not make for a joyful spirit.

From the 0603 planet fix on the 26th, the course for Cape Tiburon, 114 miles away, was 007·5°. The chart gives a west-going current prediction in this area of half a knot but I added an allowance for a 2-knot current. The leeway for the past eighteen hours had been 17·5°, nearly the same as for the preceding two days, and it would take a 2 knot current to cause that. This gave a steering course of 27·5°, but I could not ease my heading of 45° because a reserve was needed above 27° in case of a wind shift backing northwards.

At 1400 I reckoned that *Gipsy Moth* was now far enough upwind to permit altering course 20° off the wind and I eased the sheets of the mizen and the mizen stays'l accordingly. Blessed, blessed peace! My new course was no promenade stroll but it was a heavenly amble by comparison.

The fatigue due to pounding hard on the wind is well known and I can well understand that people went mad after a long period of it. I find tenseness and uncertainty about the navigation, or any strain, tiring too. I should have to make Cape Tiburon in the dark and there were no lights there. If I allowed for the leeway *Gipsy Moth* had had all the way across and it lessened, *Gipsy Moth* would be charging towards the land in the dark. If I did not allow for it, there was a low-lying island, Navassa, 31 miles to the west of Cape Tiburon. This was shown on the chart to have a light flashing at two- and fifteen-second intervals, but was it working? If not, a set to the west might push *Gipsy Moth* on to Navassa. I was concentrating tensely on the best way to deal with this.

I badly needed a fix but this was impossible. There were no radio beacons or radio aids and I could not get a star fix till nightfall. However, I could use the sun to make sure I was on the right heading. I used part of the same navigation system I devised to find Lord Howe Island when flying alone in a seaplane from New Zealand to Australia in 1931. I wanted to sail to the middle of the passage between south-west Haiti and Navassa Island, say Point H. The principle of what I did is as follows: Supposing that I was where I thought I was, call it Point X. I waited until the sun's direction was at right angles to a line joining H and X. In astro-navigation terms both H and X were then on the same circle of equal altitude of the sun. The circle was so large that part of it could be regarded as a straight line. I worked out what the sun's altitude would be from anywhere on that circle or line. Then I observed the altitude with the sextant. If the sextant reading was greater, say 30', than the calculated one, *Gipsy Moth* must be correspondingly nearer, by 30', to the sun. That is, she must be that amount, 30' or 30 nautical miles, off course on the sun side of the line between X and H.

My sun position line at 1700 showed that *Gipsy Moth* was only 1½ miles west of the course for H; the leeway had almost completely stopped. This was very strange, though it did agree with my feeling that it had eased. How could the current suddenly cease to flow? I acted on it, changing course accordingly; but could there be some mistake in the sights? How *could* the current vanish almost suddenly? I would have been less anxious had the sights shown that the current was persisting. An hour and a half later, at nightfall, I took a three-star fix with great care. This confirmed it: no leeway. From having too much current I seemed to have passed abruptly to not having any.

By the star fix *Gipsy Moth* was 19½ miles south-west of the nearest land, Gravois Point in south-west Haiti. There was a light on this point but tantalizingly its range was only 9 miles. Point H, halfway between Cape Tiburon and Navassa Island, was 53 miles to the north-west. The track to it would be roughly parallel with the coast and within 10 miles of it at Cape Tiburon. The required heading was 310° and *Gipsy Moth* would run into land if the heading changed 18° or more northwards.

At 2100 I could see the mountain range on Haiti silhouetted against the night sky; the range runs east–west from 2 to 20 miles inland with a highest peak of 7,400ft. I could not see any of the land to seaward of it or identify any peak. For hour after hour I periodically swept the northern horizon with the night glasses but could pick nothing up. At 0123 the DR position was logged at 11 miles WSW of Cape Tiburon—and sometime about then

I fell asleep on the chart table and woke an hour and a half later to find *Gipsy Moth* headed 340° instead of 310°; she had changed her heading while I slept. I felt guilty at placing myself in the hands of Fate like that at a critical time; only twenty-five minutes later I saw a weak wink of light. It showed intermittently, but after watching it for some time I decided the blinks fitted a ten-second period framework. Although the chart gave the Navassa Island light as flashing at two- and fifteen-second intervals, there was no other light within 36 miles so I accepted the ten-second light as being Navassa. It was also where I expected the Navassa light to be according to my DR. Every flash fitted into a ten-second framework and exactly ten seconds, although some of the flashes were missing. This might have been due to waves in between obscuring it, but I doubted that; the island is low-lying, but the light itself is on a hill of 395ft. Its bearing was due west of *Gipsy Moth* and as it was also due west of Cape Tiburon on Haiti it meant that I was clear of Haiti and could turn north. To give *Gipsy Moth* her due she had been trying to turn north every time my back was turned for the past two hours. The next land, Cuba, was 90 miles to the north so I could have a sleep; I found I was tottering and I am apt to make stupid mistakes through lack of sleep.

The Trade Wind lost its bite after *Gipsy Moth* had rounded the south-west corner of Haiti and she was becalmed or merely ghosting to a faint breeze, often in the wrong direction, all day. The calm sea surface under the hazy sunshine gave me a feeling of unreality after the violent movement of the past few days. But *Gipsy Moth* was not to escape so easily from the Caribbean. The same conditions persisted through the night, with *Gipsy Moth* sometimes ghosting at 2 knots to a zephyr from the south. If the expected 2-knot south-going current was running, she would be nearly stationary in the darkness. The distance from the Navassa Passage to Cape Maysí on the Cuban side of the Windward Passage is 120 miles, and by 0600 the next day the distance made good was only 47·5 miles of it.

Even the Windward Passage would not mark escape into the open Atlantic. There were still 180 miles to go to be free of the great barrier of the Bahamas, a thick ring of thousands of islands, reefs, rocks, sandspits and cays, most of them unbuoyed and un-lighted. There were five likely passages through the Bahamas. The most desirable was the Turks Island Passage to the NE by E, between Turks Island and the Caicos Islands, the most favoured passage for steamers. I would like to have made it because near the end of the 1960 Singlehanded Transatlantic race from Plymouth to New York, I dropped a Plymouth Gin bottle overboard from *Gipsy Moth III* at George's Sound, Nantucket, with a message inside. Two years later, possibly after a tour round the ocean in the Gulf Stream and the Portugal currents, the bottle landed up on the beach at Turks Island. However, after thinking about it, I was sure it would be crazy to attempt reaching the Turks Island Passage, however much more desirable, unless it could be done without a tack. The Admiralty Routeing Chart gave the average current between Haiti and the East Bahamas as half a knot. Tacking against Trade Wind and current, with Haiti to the south and a whole string of islands, cays and banks to the north, was not for me if I could avoid it.

The next passage to consider, working anti-clockwise, was the Caicos, to the NE by N; then the Mayaguana, N by E; the Acklins Island–French Cays to the north and the Mira-por-Vos Passage leading to the Crooked Island Passage, which was also 180 miles from the Windward Passage and lying N by W from it.

The Caicos was unlighted both on the Caicos side and the Mayaguana Island side and to reach it would mean sailing past the unlighted sides of Great Inagua and Little Inagua Islands. I ruled it out.

The Mayaguana was the one I liked best. If *Gipsy Moth* could hold to her present heading she should fetch up to the leeward side of Great Inagua Island on the way to Mayaguana Island. The distance from Cape Maysí to Matthew Town at the south-west corner of Great Inagua is 45 miles. At 6 knots *Gipsy Moth* should arrive there at 0245. There is a light at Matthew Town and also a radio beacon, though I had not been able to pick that up. From there a track N by E would take *Gipsy Moth* through the centre of the Mayaguana Passage, 87 miles distant, where she should arrive at 1715. That seemed the best prospect. It would be important to arrive in the daylight so as to see the land, because there is no light at the south-west end of Mayaguana.

As *Gipsy Moth* approached Cuba, the land looked sombre and savage, as if a storm was all over the near end of it, while the sun was shining in a summery sky 15 miles off the land to the east.

At 1636 a fresh breeze was coming in and I reefed the mizen. At 1755 two shore bearings put *Gipsy Moth*'s position 6½ miles offshore, but not yet abeam of Cape Maysí. The sea was exceptionally rough, with short, steep, and high-breaking seas. It was somewhat like passing Portland Bill in rough conditions except that the Bill is 4 miles long and Cuba 600, with its tip, Cape Maysí, 15 miles across, compared with the Bill's ¼ mile. The wind was heading *Gipsy Moth* in towards the land and the closer she came to the shore the rougher it would be. If I tacked to the east, away from the land, it would still continue rough for several miles before *Gipsy Moth* was out of the turbulence. If I could hold the present heading *Gipsy Moth* might scrape past the cape without a tack, in which case, although it would get rougher still it would not last for so long. I ought to tack, but I thought it would be exciting to see if *Gipsy Moth* could get by.

Considering there were no great waves, the seas were the most violent I have ever seen. The wind had got up to 40 knots and *Gipsy Moth* was thrown, bounced, slammed. It was exhilarating, because she was going through it all like a witch. She never would have got past the cape without tacking but that the sails were exactly balanced; this was due to the reefed mizen which seemed to act like the feather of an arrow, and improved the heading I could hold by about 20°. It was at this point that I discovered why the leeway had amounted to between 17·5° and 20° during three days of the Caribbean Sea crossing. I was standing on deck hanging on to the mainmast weather cap shroud and watching the main stays'l, the mast top and the running gear to satisfy myself that they were standing up to the terrific snatching strains they were being subjected to, and I could clearly see *Gipsy Moth* being cast to leeward at every big sea and sliding away on the leeward slope of waves. It would add up to a lot of leeway in a day, when pinched up hard on the wind as she was. The leeway had eased when approaching Haiti not because the current eased but because *Gipsy Moth* turned off the wind. I was not used to this because the previous *Gipsy Moth*s had a lot more keel and made very little leeway.

Gipsy Moth was still not round the cape when darkness fell, but I seemed to be through the area of turbulence, although the wind was still up to 40 knots.

At 1830 the Maysí light, flashing every twenty seconds, was

bearing WNW, but the north coast of Cuba was beginning to open up to view.

On her heading at midnight, *Gipsy Moth* would pass west of Great Inagua by 3½ miles. In any case the strong current of about a knot would have been setting her W by N since Cape Maysí. That meant a 6-mile set to the west so far, and as it would take another six hours before the island was abeam, I reckoned that *Gipsy Moth* would be giving it a handsome miss. Therefore I could turn in and have a sleep without any worry except for going over the Clarion Bank off the SW point of Great Inagua, where the depth shallows from 1,700 fathoms to 230. I imagined it would be very rough water there but on consideration I thought it would be negligible compared with the seas off Cape Maysí. I would look up the Clarion Bank in the Admiralty Pilot: 'Lord, how I would love to be deep asleep instead of just dropping off all the time as I write. Later, I read up the Clarion Bank; no one seems to worry about it so why should I? Goodnight.'

At 0600 on 1 March I got a fix from Jupiter and Arcturus. This put *Gipsy Moth* 20 miles west of Great Inagua and also 20 miles W by N of the DR position, so that for twelve hours the leeway had been at 1·6 knots.

I had to review my escape tactics. The Mayaguana Passage was bearing 27°, distant 101 miles; 27° had been *Gipsy Moth*'s heading (more or less) since Cape Maysí but she had only made good a track of due north. Therefore she would have to beat up to Mayaguana and spend another night on the way. There were no lights on French Cays or on the south-west corner of Mayaguana. There was a light on the Hogsty Reef which had to be avoided on the way, but the east coast of Acklins Island was unlighted for 45 miles. I decided that I would like to avoid both the Mayaguana and the Acklins Island Passages. That left Mira-por-Vos Passage followed by the Crooked Island Passage north of it. The Mira-por-Vos was bearing 347°, distant 68 miles. It was lighted and appeared to be a shipping lane for traffic to the U.S.A. If I went for that I should reach it at about dusk but would then have another hop of some 50 miles to the Crooked Island Passage without a chance of any sleep. I decided to think about it while setting more sail. That was at 0700 and at 0745 I altered course for the Mira-por-Vos. *Gipsy Moth* would not be hard on the wind as until now, and so although the passage would be longer, it would be much faster.

At noon *Gipsy Moth* was 32 miles off Castle Island, the eastern portal of the Mira-por-Vos Passage. At her speed of over 8 knots she should arrive there at 1540. This was exciting navigation. Castle Island and Acklins Island behind it were low-lying, while there were low rocks on the other side of the Mira-por-Vos Passage, eight miles to the west of Castle Island. Eight miles sounds like a wide target but always there were those unpredictable currents and eddies. However, it was a lovely, fine, sunny day and the sailing fast and joyous.

It could have been a dangerous approach, but for the sun; I was able to use the same trick which had put *Gipsy Moth* on the right heading for the Haiti–Navassa Island Passage. I waited patiently until the sun was on the right bearing, which was at 1421, and then took a sight which showed that *Gipsy Moth* was off course 5° to the westward. I altered course accordingly and at 1535 I sighted the lighthouse ahead. There was no land visible anywhere, nor any buildings, just a mottled brown pin sticking up out of the sea four miles off. Without the position line from the sun I think it could have been very difficult to find it in daytime without radar.

At night *Gipsy Moth* sailed into smooth water in the lee of the cays, rocks and sandbanks stretching for 27 miles from Castle Rock at the south-west end of Acklins Island to the south end of Long Island. Here there was another light, visible 8 miles. It was very weak and erratic but I picked it up at 1909 and from there it was an easy sail seventeen miles northwards to the Bird Rock light at the north-west end of Crooked Island, a good strong light, flashing every five seconds, with a range of 16 miles. This light was abeam at 2136.

With a great surge of relief and a wonderful feeling of achievement such as only comes rarely to one during a lifetime, when some difficult project ends positively and successfully and can be seen to have done just that, I dropped the mizen and trimmed the remaining sails to come hard on the wind, heading NE. *Gipsy Moth* was through the Crooked Island Passage and had escaped from the Caribbean into the broad Atlantic at last. Within five minutes of setting on the new course I was in my bunk, asleep. It was the end of a four-day marathon; I had been unable to relax for a hundred hours.

VI

AMBLING EASTWARDS

Tuesday 2 March, 0852: 'I'm lying in my berth, relaxed. It seems an age since I could rest or let go the tension, or allow myself to have a deep sleep. I am sipping nectar. Maybe it appears to be the same old brew of tea, except for having a slice of Nicaraguan lime in it instead of lemon, and sugar chipped off a round brick with an ice pick; but to me this morning it is nectar. And the biscuit I am eating reminds me of when dear wonderful old Jane Beer used to bring me in a cup of tea and two wine biscuits to wake me up when, as a boy, in 1909, I was staying with my great-aunt in Devon. Where does all this tension come from, you may well wonder. Why couldn't I just drop the sails and sleep as long as I wanted to while working the Passages out of the Caribbean? I think the currents are the chief bandits. . . . In the open ocean they may be inconvenient but they are seldom dangerous . . . but among these islands and sandbanks they are strong and unpredictable. Maybe at X the current will be west-going and 1·5 knots or sometimes 2·5 knots, but also maybe it will be east-going at 3 knots in certain conditions, which can be expected or is sometimes quite unpredictable. For safe navigation in these waters a sailing vessel needs a constant lookout and plenty of time so that dangerous approaches can be made in daylight.'

It seemed to me that the currents of the Caribbean are in league with the winds. If an onshore current was tolerable because there was a wind which would enable me to sail away from the breakers —then the wind fell dead calm. If I left the ship sailing safely along the coast while I had some sleep—and even two hours of sleep can seem a heavenly gift at times—as soon as I was oblivious, then the wind swung right round the compass until it was blowing from the opposite direction to try to put *Gipsy Moth* among the breakers before I awoke.

Now all that was past; I was at large at the edge of the ocean, in calm seas under the sunshine, and with a light, pleasant breeze.

I stood looking at the clumps of Sargasso weed, pale yellowy brown, the size of a lilypond, drifting past and opening briefly a straight path for *Gipsy Moth* to pass through.

There followed a delightful sail such as yachtsmen all hope for but in most cases only experience in their dreams. Smooth seas, moderate winds, sunshine and mostly fine weather. It is true that *Gipsy Moth* was on the wind nearly the whole time, sailing as close as she could towards her target, Point X, 20°N 40°W, 2,000 miles due east in the middle of the Atlantic, but I started off determined to enjoy myself. I was not in a hurry because for one thing I wanted time to carry out various repairs and experiments before making a speed dash down to the Equator. To start with I had to set up all the rigging afresh. I started a log so that I could keep a record of changes I made. This soon filled up with entries such as 'Took up backstay a further two turns [of the bottlescrew] trying to cure forward bend or curve in top half of main mast, also curve forward of mizen mast'; and 'I regret to say I shirked tautening up the topmast stays at the stem head because it is so damn wet there when close-hauled. The lifelines are festooned with Sargasso weed brought aboard in the green water.' (Actually the sea was a lovely blue, a tint of ultramarine, and 'green water', the water coming aboard solid and sweeping the deck, gives the wrong impression.)

Periodically—far too often—I am amazed at my stupidity. In *Gipsy Moth*'s cabin was a swinging table which used to make me swear. When she was heeled to starboard the table hit my knees and upset any glasses of water and such like that were on it. When she was heeled to port the table was at the level of my mouth and I could not see what I was cutting on my plate without standing up. The other side of the table cannot be used at all because it is too far from the settee. The stupidity in this case is that it had never occurred to me until three and a half months after leaving Plymouth that I had only to sit on two or three cushions when *Gipsy Moth* was heeled to port to bring me up high enough to eat comfortably.

On 5 March, after dark, *Gipsy Moth* was buzzed by a low-flying aircraft. This was a very unusual thing to happen out there, three hundred miles from land and in the dark and I thought the pilot might be having engine trouble or had lost his way, so I put on my spreader lights in case the poor fellow had to ditch. The aircraft turned, buzzing down again to a height of about 200ft above *Gipsy Moth*, then flew off to the north. I wondered what I would have done if he had ditched. I could stop *Gipsy Moth IV* in a few lengths but *Gipsy Moth V* will go on sailing if put aback because of her boomed sails. I thought I would make a first pass and drop a lighted buoy, then drop some sails and come back slowly to the buoy. Or, if I could see whoever it was I was aiming to pick up, I would approach him as if he were a buoy.

By 7 March *Gipsy Moth* had sailed 830 miles from Crooked Island. Every spare hour I had been absorbed in analysing the results of the 4,000-mile run and planning my 'Equator Dart'. Several points stood out which surprised and disappointed me. First, *Gipsy Moth* was not the flier I had hoped for. She was little or no faster than most other ocean racers of the same size. Vanished were my dreams of averaging 10 knots. I had never touched 10 knots in *Gipsy Moth* for any one-hour run since she was launched. Occasionally she had surfed up to speeds as high as 17 knots, but only while surfing on the crest of a wave, for a period of seconds.

It was clear that I should always have quite a task to squeeze 1,000 miles out of five days, however carefully I chose my 'racecourse'; during the 4,000 miles *Gipsy Moth* only sailed at 9 knots or more on twenty-two occasions worth recording, over distances which ranged from 2·87 miles to a longest of 41·48 miles. In face of that it seemed to me remarkable that she had made good 2,000 of the 4,000 in ten days—1,017·75 in the last five days and 995·5 in the five-day period during the first half of the passage: 2,013·25 in ten days is an average of 201·325 per day, or 8·388 knots.

On 9 March: '10.45 a.m. At a meeting of the Ship's Company this a.m., the M.O. and Chaplain in attendance, Captain presiding, it was unanimously agreed on the tactics for the first part of the coming speed trial, namely, to sail down the 40th Meridian from 20°N to the Equator. The Medical Officer said he was very relieved that the Captain had come out of his mental purdah and finished his cerebral ordeal with some result, whatever it might be, and apparently without losing his sanity. He said the whole crew had been worried about their master being immersed in calculations and rows of figures for day after day, to the—he wouldn't say neglect—to the delay in dealing with other matters which naturally seemed to them much more important. Some of the less understanding of the crew, such as himself, had wondered if the master was doing his nut or, in scientific medical language, going crackers. The Captain ordered an extra round of brandy for all hands and grunted his way below to the security of his cabin.'

I handled some of the 'other matters' the next day, when I adjusted the backstay and two forestays, the latter an awkward, niggly job at sea in a boat with a narrow, pointed stemhead. I also finished adjusting the starboard fore and aft lower shrouds, after which the main mast did not look too bad. It still had some curve forward at the top, but I dared not harden up the backstay any more. It was as tight as I cared to see it with the new insulator fitted by Bart at Bluff of uncertain compression resistance.

I also made myself a chart. The Admiralty chart I had for the area took in the whole Atlantic and was much too small in scale. Making a plotting chart is not difficult. The scale must be chosen carefully so that it is large enough to make plotting of DR and astro position lines easy to see and accurate, while being small enough for one sheet to cover a reasonable number of days' sailing. I use a sheet of graph paper, choose some meridians of longitude and label them at the bottom or top of the sheet, and then mark off the degrees of latitude at the side, according to their value in meridional parts given in navigation tables. The meridional parts of a parallel of latitude are its distance from the Equator in terms of the distance between meridians chosen for that sheet. For example, the meridional parts of 40°N are 2607·6 and 41°N, 2686·2. The length of that degree of latitude is 2686·2 minus 2607·6 = 78·6 minutes of longitude at the scale chosen at the bottom of the chart. I divide each degree of latitude into six parts equalling 10' or miles each, and divide one or two of those into five equal parts of 2 miles each. For 1 mile it is easiest to judge half of a 2-mile division. These charts I made were much the most convenient I had for plotting and gave the most accurate results.

Thursday 11 March, 0200: 'I do not know if all kinds of solitary living have the same effect. The solitary sea-life . . . makes me think and feel more than is comfortable for my peace of mind. I have dreadful attacks of remorse. My chief remorse is for unkind acts to friends in the past. Maybe something deeply wounding that I have said or done. Then I find myself stuck with such things for ever; they cannot be undone and the awful thing is that often they did not mean much to me, nor were even seriously believed, but were used as a cruel weapon to hurt. Thank heaven I have a lot of jobs and work waiting to be done; otherwise, if able to lay about with nothing to do but think and feel, I would soon get into a maudlin state and eventually I can imagine the possibility of finding life too hard and cruel to bear. This life makes one so sympathetic with others in trouble with their conscience or unable to cope with the overwhelming difficulties of their life. I often think of Donald Crowhurst with great sympathy. For me, to be nine months alone without aim, project, objective, challenge, would mean exposing my soul far too much. I can understand it being damaged or destroyed by continuous considering of it, relentless probing of it. I can only stand a very little peep of it now and then. Thank God for activity of body and mind to keep me away from my soul.'

There was certainly plenty to keep my mind occupied. I wanted to have my big 41-gallon tank of drinking water empty for racing as it was for the 4,000 miles. There was a misunderstanding some-where at El Bluff and my tanks, including the big one, were filled while I was away in Managua. There was no real problem, but in order to empty the 41-gallon tank by the time I started the speed run, I used fresh water as freely as if I had been in a house. I noticed the carpet in the galley/navigation cabin was wet and thought that was due to an overspill from the galley where the pump for the No. 1 tank squirts water into the galley sink unless I cork up the pump pipe when the yacht is heeled over. I had seen water jetting into the sink from this pump pipe, and also noticed that the pump itself was leaking. However, one fine day I took the carpet up to dry it on deck, and found water running from a loose pipe connection to a gauge which had been fitted at Buckler's Hard. Suddenly the big tank pumped dry, but I did not mind that, since I wanted it to be empty before I started my run. The trouble was that I had also been drawing freely from the No. 2 tank, which I had intended to top up from the big tank before I started. I sounded the No. 2 tank and found there were only nine gallons left, plus the full jerricans and Portuguese water bottles in the forepeak, to last me for about 9,000 miles of sailing back to Plymouth. I immediately rationed the water severely and limited it to drinking, baking, watering the mustard and two glassfuls every other day for shaving and washing. But I wanted more water than that otherwise I should have no pasta or rice, because I have found I cannot cook these in sea water as I do the potatoes (I steam the onions on top of the potatoes in a basket gadget which Sheila found for me). And although it is amazing how much washing of oneself one can do with two glassfuls if one tries—besides shaving they provide for an all-over wash with a flannel and a clean of the razor and basin—I like to have fresh water for frequent swab downs in the Tropics to get rid of the sea salt on my body, which can cause rashes and boils. I also like to wash my clothes in fresh water: I don't use clothes much in the Tropics but I was already running short of shirts, shorts and such like. So all my brain cells had to be put to work to devise how to provide fresh water.

Friday 12 March, noon: '600 miles to go to Point X. It looks as if a calm day is needed to finish off the chores which remain to be done before the speed trial: Inspecting the batteries for water, adjustments to the life-raft, sewing the mizen stays'l batten pocket, finishing the rigging adjustments and taking up the cap shrouds.' The next morning *Gipsy Moth* was still making heavy weather of it, hard on the wind with some hefty seas coming aboard forward. The jumper strut bottlescrew which Bart repaired for me came adrift and the wire began to flail about at the end of a jumper strut like a whip, with the bottlescrew attached. The bottlescrew weighs about half a pound and I feared it would damage the tops'l track and other gear attached to the mast, or jam up the halyards. When the bottlescrew first parted during the 4,000-mile run, only the broken screw-eye was attached to the jumper stay end. That was bad enough, but now the barrel of the bottlescrew, a solid lump of bronze, was thrashing about. I wished I had my bo'sun's chair tackle rigged up—I used it always in *Gipsy Moth III* and *Gipsy Moth IV*—but even that is no joke if the mast is pitching quickly. However I had not got it, so I would have to climb up the mast to the crosstrees or above to secure the bottlescrew, but I did not want to go up in this rough weather if I could help it. As the crosstrees on *Gipsy Moth* are reached, there is one place where it is decidedly tricky to hold on in a seaway. There is one narrow foothold just wide enough to take my toes, and a single handhold vertically above it. Rolling is not so bad, but at every pitch my whole body is wrenched forwards or aft from these holds.

That night the second jumper stay broke adrift and joined in the fun of flogging the mast, but conditions were too bad to attempt to climb up to them. I just had to bear the agony as best I could.

I was also worrying about Sargasso weed damaging the self-steering skeg and rudder. Although with *Gipsy Moth* clearing a path it was difficult to see how the skeg could get entangled in a clump, the fact remained that it was continually picking up small clumps of weed which straddled it and would not come off. Presumably more and more piled on until the heap overbalanced to one side or the other and pulled away. This strained the self-steering gear and of course interfered with the steering control.

By noon on 15 March Point X was to the south-east, nearly in the eye of the wind, with *Gipsy Moth* hard on the wind heading east, about 240 miles from the 40th meridian. The port tack to the south would be a little more favourable but I wanted rather to arrive north of Point X, from where *Gipsy Moth* would be on the southerly heading of the speed run and would be getting trimmed up for it. It was interesting how the hydrographers differ; the American pilot chart shows for this area averages of nearly the same amount of wind from every octant of the compass rose, whereas the British routeing chart shows wind from every point on the eastern half but either very little or a negligible amount from the western half. I usually go by the British chart nowadays, because it gives more details than the American charts. But let me pay tribute to that great American, Lieutenant Maury, USN, who conceived the idea of these wonderfully useful charts, and to the United States Hydrographic Office for collecting data for their charts for a hundred years longer than we have. It is always much easier to climb on a pioneer's back.

Shortly after noon I got ready a bag of tools, shackles, cordage, and so on to have a go at the jumper stays, but then a wide belt of rain squalls started going through. The stays were flailing about like cats-o'-nine-tails with a bottlescrew at the end of each, periodically twining together, but I had waited this long and was not going up in that sort of weather unless I had to.

In one squall I rigged the rain-catching gadget I had devised to the boom of the mizen, but it only rained for about a minute and was blowing so hard that with the heel the boom was sloping down to the water and all the water ran down it instead of towards the mast where I had planned to catch it. There was too much wind to top up the boom end and make the water run inboard. Once I got to the Doldrums at the Equator, there would be plenty of heavy rain with no wind—but 1,600 miles was a long way to go for a drink.

I noted at midnight that *Gipsy Moth* had sailed 3,540 miles since leaving Bluff, mostly on the wind, and 10,924 miles since leaving Plymouth. Also that the wind was back again at 22 knots and that it had that persistent whining note which says 'Take care, for I am a lot stronger than I seem to be!'

On the morning of 16 March, conditions for the ascent of Mt. Mast were about as good as I could expect. 'I reckon to drop the mizen stays'l, bowse down the main stays'l boom and the mizen boom to leeward, after sheeting them as hard as I can. Then I shall gybe and head up into the wind. With the sails aback *Gipsy Moth* should do little more than creep ahead, the pitching should be damped and the mast will be heeled a few degrees so that the ratlines are to windward, to make it easier for me balancing on top of them to work on the jumper stays. "Us'll zee loike", as the Devon lads used to say.'

When I got into position at the weather crosstree, I thought for a minute that I should have to climb down again. I had left the long broom handle on the deck attached to a long cord, of which I took one end up to the ratlines with me. I needed the pole to get one of the stays free; it had spiralled itself in and out around the two stays'l stays above and was out of reach. When I tried to haul the broom handle up, it had caught one end under the furled tops'l on deck. I tugged and tugged but could not get it free. The cord was attached near one end of the pole and it was the short pole-end above my clovehitch which was caught up. In the end I pulled so hard that I up-ended the long piece of pole on the other side of the knot and it came away. When I did get the jumper stay free it lashed round the other side of the mast and the bottlescrew at the end of it flew back and hit me on the cheek. Luckily it was not a serious blow. Once, while I was using both hands to make a loop out of the bottom end of one of the jumper stay wires, and using a racking seizing to bind the two parts of wire together, I got a scare which made my blood feel hot round my heart. *Gipsy Moth* suddenly pitched, jerking the mast forward and trying to catapult me away. I had my legs round the mast with my ankles locked together. Fortunately they stood the strain and I regained my balance.

I was lucky to be working at the crosstrees where I could sit astride one of them. If the job had been higher up I would have had to stand with a foot in a kind of stirrup step on one side of the mast, and the other in a similar step two feet higher on the other side. So most of my weight would have been on the ball of one foot and I could not have lasted out anything like the time it took me to do the job, one hour and thirteen minutes.

To me it always seems much higher up a mast than it is. Perhaps this is because I fear any height if it is possible to fall from it. I never had this fear strongly before my flying crash in Japan in 1931. Sitting astride the crosstree, my head was only 34ft above the sea, yet it felt like three times that height. The sun was shining in a clear sky and the deck laid out below on the vast expanse of ultramarine ocean was a fine sight. But what interested me most and greatly surprised me was the size of the pale yellow patches of Sargasso weed lying flat on the surface. These weed 'ponds' were far bigger than I had ever imagined from the deck where I suppose they appeared foreshortened. Some were as big as two tennis courts joined together.

For once, everything went well with this job and I could not find any damage to the tops'l track on the lee side of the mast. I was left without jumper struts, but when I came down I voted for a walloping brandy, sour and hot, as a treat for breakfast; I really enjoyed it.

At 1900 on 16 March *Gipsy Moth* was three hours from the 40th meridian and the turn south for the run down to the Equator. *Gipsy Moth*, ambling eastwards against wind and current from Crooked Island to 26°30′N 39°51′W, had logged 2,213·3 miles in fifteen days and eleven minutes, averaging 147·5mpd, and had made good 1,890·5 miles in a fix-to-fix straight line, averaging 125·6mpd.

I was excited, uneasy, reluctant. I had grown used to my holiday plug to windward and suddenly I had to turn at right-angles and charge down the middle of the ocean for 1,600 miles as fast as *Gipsy Moth* would go. It would be a joy to get a free wind as I sailed south, though that would not be until the wind backed from the present south-east to east or north-east. Surely that must be soon, or had Aeolus not heard that this was a north-east Trade Wind zone and not a south-east one?

VII

THE EQUATOR DART

....

I tacked to the south at 2212 on 16 March. My new adventure was on.

By noon of the 17th *Gipsy Moth* was plugging into a 20-knot wind. It was rough on deck forward with a lot of sea and spray coming aboard. According to the American pilot chart this was the edge of the Trade Wind belt and I imagined that the squalls of the past few days were turbulence created by the mixing of two different zones of air, but I was hoping for some milder weather before reaching the 20th parallel.

1800: 'There is still fairly rough weather about. A dirty big squall is just passing some miles astern and another passed ahead some time ago. I expect to catch another sooner or later.

'I am running the motors to charge the batteries, which are badly down. There was a heavy drain on current with the R/T session and I used a lot more with spreader lights and so on during a squall in the night. However, I am anxiously watching the inclinometer which measures the angle of heel, because I fear that too much heel will prevent the oil from circulating and the bearings will seize up. This happened with my charging motor in 1962. Occasionally *Gipsy Moth* slips upright and I hope that is sufficient to circulate the oil.'

At midnight a hefty squall with 40-knot gusts went through. I woke up just before it and noticed the heading had backed to SE. The wind started to freshen up so I reckoned a squall was on the way and got into a hard-weather suit to be ready for it. I had to use the tiller tackles to turn off the wind when *Gipsy Moth* would not answer the helm and for about a quarter of an hour we ran off south-west before the blast. Later, the wind dropped and freed, and had I been enthusiastic I would have set bigger sails, but I was content to hold to the south-east heading through the night and gain some valuable easting. I thought I would just pop up and hoist the mizen stays'l, but I left it down and the wind soon swung back to set *Gipsy Moth* close-hauled again, heading south, in a wind 27 knots from ESE.

If I stuck to my heading *Gipsy Moth* would take too much of a pounding, and if I payed off as I had just done, it would result in my being 60 miles downwind or west of the 40th meridian by the time I reached the starting line the next day. That I could ill afford, so I decided to hold on for an hour in the hope of it easing. That would cost 2·6 miles of leeway. The bigger worry was that my scheme would be euchred if the wind persisted from this direction. I thought the best tactics were to pinch up as much as tolerable for the present and then turn off the wind enough to increase the speed to the minimum needed for 200mpd. As it was *Gipsy Moth* was doing 7 knots. The wind was coming out of a fine, sunny sky, so I thought it was the true Trade Wind and would not now ease off. The direction, south of east, did worry me, but I could not believe that the wind would not back two and possibly four points to ENE during the next 200 miles.

I went to sleep about 1900 and, apart from the hourly stirrings to know that all was well, slept till half past midnight, when I found the weather fine and mild, with a nice breeze. Going to sleep soon after nightfall is quite a good move for the singlehander because he is nearly always up for a good chunk of the night, either on deckwork or crises, and it makes half-past two in the morning seem a good time to have dinner!

After noon the next day, the 19th, the wind veered instead of backing and the time came when *Gipsy Moth* was headed to the west of south with a south-easterly breeze. As she had not got up racing speed I felt this was squandering hard-gained easting so I tacked to the eastwards. The more easting I got the better; in fact, I had been regretting that I had not held on for another 500 miles when I was at 27°N. That would have given me more scope to sail between south and south-west on the speed run without running into South America or making it difficult to get another speed run on the way back from the Equator. After tacking I found it pleasant to be heading east again, with the westering sun streaming into the cabin through the companion. I had been headed east for so long that I had had a twinge of regret, like homesickness, at leaving the old route.

It was incredible how clumsy I had been all that day. It seemed to take an age to change jibs. At every step something got hitched up somewhere. To crown the non-performance, after I had bagged the No. 2 jib, dropped it down the hold, and hauled the No. 1 bag forward, when I opened the bag and pulled the jib out to start hanking it on, it was the same No. 2 jib that I had just bagged with such an effort—and made of heavy, stiff Terylene, very difficult to get into its bag. The bag I had dumped in the hold was the one I had just pulled out of it. That was the sort of clueless boob I made at every step.

I suddenly realized that I could not stand on deck without hanging on; also that I had lost my balance. This was a serious matter and a big worry. My legs felt as if I had just got out of hospital after being bedridden for a month. Whenever I had a job to do on deck, unless I had one hand free for a hold, I had to arrange so that a leg was bearing against something; otherwise I lost my balance. The loss of balance I accepted; it started with my big fall on the deck of *Gipsy Moth IV* in 1966. After I had improved it with exercises, I then slipped and had another fall on the Cornish coast, shooting about ten feet down a rockface and hitting the very same place on my left leg when I landed on the rock below.

I did some leg exercises and it was at once obvious that they were badly needed. I could not swing my left leg forward and back without the sole of the foot scraping the floor. I could not bend the foot upwards at all at the ankle and I hadn't enough strength in the left foot to move the toes in a circle, bending the foot at the ankle. I decided that I would have to exercise seriously several times a day until I got back to normal. It may seem absurd that a singlehander racing a 57ft, 29-ton yacht across the Atlantic could not have enough exercise, but it must be that only certain muscles are used in working the ship; other muscles and tendons are never needed and by nature's relentless law, what is not used wastes away.

At midnight *Gipsy Moth* was becalmed in a heavy shower of rain and I was hard at it rain-catching for a couple of hours. I had the mizen sailcover attached underneath the mizen boom, and the rain ran off the sail on to the boom and from there into the sailcover. Near the mast end of the boom I funnelled it down into a bucket in the cockpit. From that I syphoned it into a 20-litre jerrican which I hauled forward to the tank at the fore end of the

main cabin, there syphoning it out of the jerrican into the tank.
At the end of the shower there were 14 gallons in the tank.

At noon on the 20th *Gipsy Moth* was becalmed and the day's
run had been negligible, 73 miles sailed, due to the calms and
ghosty airs. But at 1400 a breeze came in from the north by east.
I rigged the pole out to port, boomed out the 300 and by nine
o'clock that evening *Gipsy Moth* was doing over 8 knots, but 10°
off the required track of my speed run. To make good 200mpd
when 10° off track, a yacht must average 8·46 knots; 20° off track,
8·86 knots; and 30° off track, 9·6 knots, to equal 8·3 knots on the
direct heading to the target.

Sunday 21 March, 1015: '*Gipsy Moth*'s sailing speed has averaged 7·75 knots since the four-star fix at 1815 last evening.
7·75 knots sailed would amount to 14 miles short of the 200mpd
rate, but the fix-to-fix would be even less. So I guess this lot is
not for the speed run unless I am desperate for mileage at the
other end to make up 1,000. The Trade Wind belt in which I can
expect enough wind is only about 1,200 miles thick at the best, and
if I put off starting until well inside it I may run out of distance. I
shall not be able to make up the 1,000 from the Doldrums at the
other end where 4 or 5 knots is good going. The best thing is to
keep the run to now up my sleeve for emergency at the Equator
end. . . .'

At noon on the 21st the fix-to-fix run was only 148 miles, the
position 17°50′N 38°34½′W. The wind kept on veering until the
heading was 25°W of S. It was very light, 6 knots, and useless
for racing. I could not see any sense in squandering valuable
easting so I decided to drop the boom sail and turn into the wind.
Gipsy Moth then headed nearly south-east. I felt depressed. She
was already 130 miles into the 1,200-mile wind belt. Every mile
of southing reduced the length of run possible. Though headed
south-east she was still making southing. I had got myself into
a bad position—what was best to do? It was no good squatting
on the north edge waiting for a change. I might wait weeks,
months; the Trade Winds plan their tactics months in advance. I
could start across the belt south-westwards to get a longer run in
the good wind belt, but it would almost certainly spoil the chance
of a fast run north later.

At five o'clock the next morning the wind had punched up in
strength and *Gipsy Moth*'s sailing speed was up to 8·5 knots. This

was on the fastest point of sailing without a poled-out running sail but not fast enough to allow for the percentage drop which must be reckoned on to arrive at a point-to-point speed. I was bursting with impatience; *Gipsy Moth* was now 250 miles into the 1,200-mile wide wind zone. I decided to start the speed run from the time of the first position fix I could get. Stars were off the menu at daybreak because of the cloud, but I glimpsed the moon through it, so thought I should be able to get a fix later from the sun and the moon and start the run at 0600.

Of course I wanted to get on to the best course, and pole out the 300 jib, and set the tops'l, and take sextant shots of the sun and moon, all at once. The moon gave me a lot of trouble because neither of its thin cusps or horns was long enough to make a sure tangent to the horizon. I had to follow the curve of the cusp round in my imagination to judge where the moon's edge would have touched the horizon if visible. To avoid an error here I shot the upper limb of the moon three times, that is by putting the moon under the horizon in the sextant's mirror, and then the lower limb five times (the moon was near its zenith and only climbing very slowly at 2' of arc in a minute of time). After adding or subtracting the semi-diameter of the moon for each shot to get the centre of the moon, I plotted the individual readings against time on graph paper for a check, and was astonished how accurate the individual shots were. None of the five shots I used was more than $1\frac{1}{2}'$ (representing $1\frac{1}{2}$ miles) from the line drawn among them. The sun-moon fix was at 0724, $16°01\frac{1}{3}'$N $37°35\frac{1}{2}'$W.

I stayed in an impatient, frustrated state all day, always fretting to finish one job and get on to the next while studying the effect of changes of heading and different sail trims. Most of the time there was not enough wind, 9 and 10 knots, and nothing a record is made with. The highest wind speed recorded all day had been only 15 knots, but I was sure that I should need that day's sailing to make up 1,000 miles and could only hope for extra speed in the middle of the zone to put up the average.

At noon on the 23rd the fix-to-fix run was 181 miles and *Gipsy Moth* had sailed 198.3 to achieve it. The fix-to-fix distance of 181 miles needed to be increased by 10.5 per cent to obtain 200mpd; therefore the sailing speed to produce this needed to be increased 10.5 per cent, from 8.3 to 9.4 knots. As *Gipsy Moth* had scarcely touched that speed on the whole voyage and had not a

The first spinnaker boom was bent into this shape by a wave breaking on deck. The port navigation light box can be seen on the corner of the cabin top in the foreground. The starboard box was later carried away in a storm

Working a wet foredeck—but the sea looks flat calm

Where the boom breaks; the jagged edge slit my scalp

Arranging the exact starting point in the estuary at Bissau with the
Portuguese Naval commander

Stowing the bust boom, lashed to a shroud at the V

The turtle enmeshed in his fishing net, part of which is on the right. He is studying where best to bite me when I cut him free

Working the two halves of the second boom to and fro to complete
the break and separate them and, below, preparing two ends
for lashing together. One of them can be seen on the deck, the
other beneath my chin

My proudest moment of the voyage. The makeshift 22ft boom, which I constructed from the two best pieces of the two broken booms, looks as if it will work. The 11ft 'splice' can be seen half-way out. With this boom up for more than three days, I achieved my ambition by sailing 1,017¾ miles in five days

Using the B. & G. D/F loop as a hand compass to take an ordinary land bearing

At El Bluff with all plain sail set

Bart brings me home for lunch at El Bluff

Leaving the Customs Wharf at El Bluff, the big light weather vane
set on the self-steering gear. One of the local shrimp boats is in
the background

Sheila's cabin, starboard side, eight days after the knockdown, seen from where her bunk would normally be on our voyages together. The mess on the paintwork is mostly 85% wholemeal flour!

In search of speed. *Gipsy Moth* is nearly too close-hauled for the tops'l, which is only half at work. Also, the leech of the mizen can be seen shaking where back-winded by the tops'l. But she is still going like a bat out of hell

hope in hell of keeping it up for five days on her then heading of 90°–95° off the relative wind, the only hope would be to bear away enough to set Big Brother instead of the 300 jib.

At 1835: 'I feel thoroughly punctured. This scheme has deflated suddenly today without a bang. I expect to abandon the run south tomorrow. I felt certain that today would be a 200-miler or very close to it. As *Gipsy Moth* only sailed 1·7 miles short of the 200 today and any current should be across the heading and not against it, it looks as if the log is over-reading. However, on further thought I believe there must have been an eddy against *Gipsy Moth* today. Putting that aside, the fact is that I have made a failure of today's run in the middle of the Trade Wind belt and now have only 750 miles left before reaching the Equator and the Doldrums. It is worse than that because there is a strong likelihood of running into the Doldrums or light airs some way north of the Equator. I cannot slant off south-west to get a longer run because that would ruin the chance of a run north and also I would expect great difficulty in getting away from the South American coast if I ended up too near it. . . .'

Wednesday 24 March, 0900: 'There is something unsatisfying and unpleasing about not sticking to one's original plan and I fear I must do that even if it dishes a chance of a fast run. Besides, there is a feeling of romance or something—perhaps adventure—about sailing down to the Line.

'I had to ease the jib sheet because the mast has more bend to leeward at the top than I like. *Gipsy Moth* is going well. Now I would like some breakfast—after my leg and feet exercises of course. Their lamentable weakness has improved already, also my balance.'

At noon on the 24th the fix-to-fix run was 202·5 miles and the distance sailed by the log 212·1. The R/T link with England that evening was terrible. I could hardly hear an intelligible sentence. I don't think that anything I wanted to say got through except maybe that I was sticking to my original plan and should be at the Line in three days. When the R/T does not work properly, it is an awful tyrant. I was sweating and dry-mouthed and my side was hurting where the lurching of the yacht caused the belt holding me into the seat to bite into my side, while the edge of the chart table cut into my ribs and I got cramp trying to keep in a position where I could listen, talk, and work the set.

But I soon cheered up and at 0245 on the 25th I recorded that I was again 'reclining in my berth like a Pasha, sipping a tin of, nay, a saucepan half full of, delicious pea soup. This is after setting the poor old tops'l which gets so abused but it is doing an excellent job at present. The speed I reached for the latest period is up ⅓ of a knot compared with the last period before setting the sail, 9·2 against 8·9 knots.'

At noon on the 25th the fix-to-fix run was 189 miles. This was most disappointing because *Gipsy Moth* had logged 214·28 miles and had been registering over 9 knots since six o'clock that morning, right through to noon. The total point-to-point run of the past three days, from 22 to 25 March, was only 569·5 miles, an average of 189·8 miles per day. The position at noon was 6°00'N 37°50'W.

'Flat! that's me, after that announcement by the Navigation Department. I really thought it was going to be a good run today. The log had been showing frequent touching of 10 knots and average speeds of 9 knots or over. But it was not to be. Conclusion: it confirms strongly that you cannot have a winner every time.'

Shortly afterwards, *Gipsy Moth* was becalmed for several hours in a heavy rain squall. At 3°50'N she reached the edge of the Doldrums. I had to face it; the run south had turned out a complete flop. *Gipsy Moth* needed at least 20 knots of wind for a straight line speed of 8·5 knots. With only a 1,200-mile belt where there was a fair chance of such a wind speed, *Gipsy Moth* had sailed through 600 miles of it, from 20°N to 10°N, before the wind had once touched 20 knots, and on that day, the 24th, I think she did well to make good a fix-to-fix run of 202·5 miles. But now that she had run into the edge of the Doldrums, the dart to the Equator was finished. At 1034 the log read: 'Been going round in circles for 2 hours.' The rain had been very heavy for four hours. I could have filled my tank ten times. As it was, buckets stood about overflowing, three pillowcases, a blanket and a sheet, also a pair of underpants, lay in the best places in the cockpit and on the doghouse where they would get a thorough freshwater rinsing. Periodically I went to wring them out.

I had arranged to call up England at eleven o'clock, which was just when I should be position fixing. It meant that I might not be able to get a noon sun fix because the sun passed almost directly

overhead and it was only possible to get a fix from it in the few
minutes when it was swinging from a bearing of due east to a
bearing of due west which it would hold for the rest of the day.
At 1155 I logged: 'Hurray! Blue sky ahead; but it must be reached
quickly if I am to get a position fix today. I will get the sextant
and the "doings" ready in case of luck. Later. Noon. A wash-out;
no fix possible.'

At noon on the 26th *Gipsy Moth* had sailed 185 miles in the past
24 hours, and my estimate of the position was 03°23′N 37°37′W;
if correct the run was only 159 miles. It was no use moaning; I
turned *Gipsy Moth* on to E by S and kept her as near east as
she would head without pinching up too close to the wind.
I wanted to make good a reserve of easting before turning round
on to north or north-west for a second speed attempt on the way
home.

I settled down the next day with charts and sailing directions to
work out the best tactics for the home run. After analysing the
winds which gave the fastest speed on the run down, I proposed
to sail on a heading to keep the wind three points, 35°, aft of the
beam on the starboard side. First, what was the expected wind
according to the Admiralty chart? On the run south the wind
ranged from NE to NE by E in the narrow belt where its strength
was of any value for speed. There was more north in it on the
fringe of the 1,200-mile belt. The answer was a sour lemon; I
could not start from here. The heading needed to have the
wind 35° aft of the beam would take *Gipsy Moth* up the River
Amazon! In order to start from close to the Equator and sail the
heading relative to the wind which I wanted for speed, I should
have to sail east right across the Atlantic to the Congo before
starting. The alternative was to work north before starting. I
wanted to start from as near the Equator as possible to take advantage of the current. Offshore, at the latitude of the mouth of the
River Amazon, and along the coast of Brazil and French Guiana,
fairly close inshore, the current was predicted at 1·5 knots in the
Admiralty chart for March: continuing past Surinam, Guyana and
Venezuela to Trinidad, it was predicted at 1 knot. It certainly was
a whale of a current, but I could not make use of it without fore-
going running with a poled-out sail; and the wind forecast was
not strong enough to give a hope of success without the running
sail set. The best tactics were to tack and head northwards for a

day. This would make a big difference to the angle of sailing off the wind and I should have a clear 1,500-mile run to Trinidad, with a good wind all the way. I would probably get involved in the Caribbean islands again and I did not want that to happen, but in search of speed I had no other choice. *Gipsy Moth* was still 120 miles north of the Equator, but I decided to proceed no farther either to the south or east. I would tack to the north and work northwards for at least a whole day; then start the speed run towards Trinidad.

So at 1420: 'Tacked for home and loved ones (I hope). A whacking great rain storm just to leeward and also I think another ahead. It looks like a big belt of them. I snapped a sight of the sun to get at least a longitude of the point of departure. These rain storms seem to last about four hours which means, if involved in this one, that I shall have no chance of a star fix at nightfall. I could not get a single star this morning because of cloud and was lucky to catch Jupiter and afterwards to find Venus in a clear patch in the daylight.'

But at 1725: 'I made a thorough bungle of today's operation. *Gipsy Moth* was chugging along quite happily to the ESE, making some hard-to-get easting, and I had promised myself an easy day or two's sailing. Then I fell like a real sucker for the opportunity of making easting and northing at the same time with a favourable tack; but landed almost at once in awful muck of torrential rain and fresh wind—backing steadily until *Gipsy Moth* was heading more or less for Trinidad, which was just what I did not want to do from a position so far south. I keep on plugging away in the hopes of getting through the belt of dirt and then back on to the right course.'

In the end I could no longer stand the north-westerly heading with its pounding and excessive heel, so I put on the spreader lights and went forward to drop and bag the No. 1 jib; then I re-hoisted the mizen stays'l and close-hauled *Gipsy Moth* again, still on the starboard tack. After that she plugged along at a modest 5 knots but at least it was in the right direction and without discomfort. By midnight the wind had backed nearly to the north and *Gipsy Moth* was again headed north-west. I was dead against using up westing by heading north-west until I had started on the speed run; so I went on deck again and tacked to the eastwards.

At dawn on the 28th *Gipsy Moth* was still plugging eastwards. I had a look at the main mast from different angles to see how it was taking the strain in the worst kind of conditions without jumper stays. Obviously there would be much more strain in a storm or even a strong gale, but otherwise, with a fresh of wind up to 30 knots, with the stays'l set but no heads'l set to the masthead, the conditions were the worst for strain on that upper part of the mast, which the jumper struts were designed to support. From the deck I could not see any movement in the mast and was relieved, although it was what I expected. The load I would be anxious about was when a big jib and also a big poled-out running sail were set in a strong wind. The compression load then must be formidable and the lack of effective jumper struts might cause the mast to bend forward.

I would also have to do something about the slide fastenings on the mizen before the whole sail broke away from the mast. They had been parting one by one. The sailmakers used a short length of broad tape to fasten the slides to the eyes in the luff of the sail and this tape seemed to chafe through easily.

All in all, I decided that I would be glad to get away from the Equator. It is a sort of no-man's-ocean with huge black-grey rain squalls appearing from nowhere, creeping up in a sinister way. It seemed barren of life. I saw only two birds, Mother Carey's Chickens, in three days, and few flying fish. The sun, being in the same latitude as *Gipsy Moth*, could not provide a fix, though it would, of course, give a longitude any time it was visible. There was no chance of a position fix until dusk and by then the rain had arrived and shut off the heavens from sight.

At 1300: 'Today is not one of my best: I feel jaded, depressed, with no vitality, energy or go in me. Of course everything seems to go wrong when feeling like that. So much so sometimes as to make me laugh. Item—I picked on six eggs one after the other which were bad. Item—On throwing one of the eggs out to sea through the companion, after getting bored with carrying them out for a ceremonial burial one by one, I jerked my head in the act of throwing, hit the roof and cut open my scalp. Item—It never stops raining with periodic deluges which would make Noah feel at home. With these squalls the wind mounts to 30 knots. Item—I have not been able to get a sun fix since 25 March, three days ago. I had the good luck, though, to snap a fix at 5 a.m. yesterday of two planets, Jupiter and Venus; I say lucky because

I only saw one star through the clouds all the time and that was gone before I could draw a bead on it. Item—The boom-end lug used to secure the clew of the loose-footed mizen stays'l has bust apart. It is in an awkward place because I must get the sail stretched out to the end of the boom somehow. Thanks be to Bart again for finding me a big hacksaw at El Bluff when I discovered that mine had walked off. I was left with only a tiddler with a 5-inch long blade. I was expecting a dirty job because the last piece of stainless steel which I had tried to hack off, the big runner clew ring on the 4,000-mile passage, had just laughed at this little hacksaw blade and bit lumps out of it. However, I hoped that this boom lug might be an aluminium alloy in which case it would be easy enough to cut. Item—Nearly all the mizen sail track slide fastenings have now parted and I shall have an hour or two's work fixing them. . . .

'I decided to do something about the deckwork but as soon as I emerged into the deluge it blew up to a gale squall of 40 knots and I was freshly amazed how cold it was. I could truly say I was wet to the skin since I had nothing on except a thin oilskin top and the water soon forced its way under that. The wind steadily veered until *Gipsy Moth* was headed south: I thought very poorly of that, so tacked, and headed north. After which only one slide still held the mizen to the mast track. All the others had gone from the line of reefing right up to the head of the sail. Fortunately it was the top slide which remained. I had re-fastened it at Bluff, using some of the tarred twine which the trawlermen drew from Bart's stores. If this top fastening had parted the slide might well have jammed at the top of the track and could have caused trouble; so I dropped the mizen. I felt as if Fate was having a laugh at me because immediately I had finished struggling with furling the loose mizen in the gale and deluge, it stopped raining and the wind eased. Meanwhile, with only one sail left set, *Gipsy Moth* was rolling like a permissive word and at 1½ knots not exactly dashing along. I dealt first with the jagged bust boom-end lug which sawed off easily. I then filed the remains smooth enough not to cut the cordage and made a complicated lash-up of the clew ring to the end of the boom, using the best anchorage I could find. It might not work but at least it is working at present. I felt I had finished all the extra chores which could be expected of me on my Sunday day of rest and went below to settle down; but I could not stand the thought of sitting there while *Gipsy Moth* made leeway westwards so I went back on deck and dug the No. 2 jib out of the hold to hank it on. Again I reckoned I had finished for the day but this time I could not bear wasting the rainwater sitting round in buckets; so I lifted it along the deck and poured it into No. 1 tank.'

On the 29th I found the source of the bilgewater which was sloshing to and fro in the main cabin in a trickle running down the mast. It was not coming through the mast coat which seals off the whole of the deck where the mast passes through, but through a hole in the mast itself which admits the bunch of electric cables to the interior of the mast. I guessed it was due to the cataracts of rain. There are two separate cables to the spreader lights, another to the masthead light, a fourth to the wind direction indicator and another to the propeller at the masthead which measures the wind speed. There was not much I could do about that, because if I plugged the hole the mast would fill gradually with rainwater and that would do no good at all.

In the late afternoon, I finished repairing the mizen and set it again. It increased the speed from 3 to 6¼ knots, a great relief, because the sailing of the past few days had been the most disagreeable I have known. The log read like a dirge: sails hoisted to be dropped an hour or two later, repeated bearing away in rain squalls, deluges of rain; tack, tack, tack, due to the wind shifting round the clock; and day after day failed attempts to get a fix.

I tipped nine more gallons of water, half of it fresh rainwater, into the big 41-gallon tank on the starboard side, making 12 gallons in that tank. I decided to keep on filling it if the opportunity offered because *Gipsy Moth* would be constantly on the starboard tack for several thousand miles and this would keep her more upright or, to put it another way, less unbalanced, and she would sail more efficiently. A boat heeled may look dramatic but its speed is cut down.

The position at noon on 29 March was 02°06'N 34°06½'W, 126 miles north of the Equator, with *Gipsy Moth* still headed east.

Getting the fix was quite a joke. The sun, or more properly the spot vertically below it, was moving north at the rate of 23 miles a day. That may not seem much, but it never stopped. It was rather like the tortoise and the hare with *Gipsy Moth* as the hare, making good northing of, say, 0–150 miles per day. The sun, tortoise-like, did not stop or slow down. On the 29th it was about 90 miles north of *Gipsy Moth*, so I took one sun sight and then went on working for only fifteen minutes, knowing that the sun was going to whip round quickly from east of *Gipsy Moth* to west. I had a good pitch for observing the sun before noon when it was in the east, sitting on top of the cabin roof and looking forward. I could just see the sun clear of the mast and rigging forward of my position. When I went up only fifteen minutes later for the second shot I could not get the sun into the sextant's mirrors at all. I scanned the sky through the sextant, across the mirror and up and down. 'This is absurd,' I thought, 'I must move all the sun shades and hunt for the sun glare in the naked mirrors.' It was then I found that it was now, only fifteen minutes after the first sight, on the other side of the yacht and over the stern. Although I had known in theory that it would be moving very rapidly at noon, it was astounding to be caught out like that.

On the 30th I was able to record that 'yesterday was a fine day with the sun shining all day. It was pleasant working in the cockpit in the sun and I was able to get a sun fix for the first time since 25 March. On the whole, though, I think this is a goddamned depressing dump of the world's unwanted weather, and the sooner I get out the better I'll be pleased. . . . Meanwhile, exercises and breakfast. I have worked out an excellent routine, taking about thirteen to fifteen minutes, which I can carry out while lying in my bunk no matter how much *Gipsy Moth* is rolling or pitching. These consist primarily of bending forward to bring my head between my knees, then twisting my torso first to the right and then to the left, then head between knees again, then back to lying flat on my back. Relax everything. Have a really good stretch, first of all with hands clasped behind my head, stretching one elbow behind my head and with legs held straight lifted off the bunk, stretch the toes of the corresponding foot upward with a good stretch. Then the same for the other foot and the other elbow. Relax everything. Draw in a full lungful of air and when the lungs are full, hold the position while counting ten, while keeping the throat open as if trying to get more air in. In other words not locking the air in the lung. Then breathing out as fully as possible and after that holding the lungs in the empty position, again with the throat open as if trying to get out more air while counting another ten. Then I circle the toes of each foot seven times with the leg held straight sticking up about 30° from the bunk. Circle the foot seven times for each leg.

'Repeat this sequence four times, at the end of the second time circling the feet in the opposite direction; at the end of the third time stretching both toes as far aft as they will go, followed by stretching them as far forward as they will go, and repeating this seven times. After the last sequence I twist the feet sideways at the ankle first outboard and then inboard seven times.

'I gradually developed a very complete second sequence of exercises when I was standing upright in the navigation galley space. About ten exercises. What a world of difference they have made both to my physique and to my outlook on yacht life.'

At 1130 on 30 March I again tacked for home and the loved ones, and on 31 March at 1409 I started the speed run. The odd time of the start was due to getting a longitude then from six shots of the sun. The position was 03°41′N 33°48′W.

I could only get a meridian longitude because here *Gipsy Moth* had again caught up with the tortoise sun and both were now 4° north of the Equator. However, an accurate longitude was the important starting line for this speed run westwards. For the latitude I depended on the dawn fix from Venus and the sun which I had been lucky to get then. I moved this fix forward to the 1409 time of the fresh longitude, working it up by dead reckoning, and from it obtained a satisfactory latitude for the start. The position put *Gipsy Moth* with the north-east corner of Trinidad bearing 285° and 1,670 miles distant. Therefore I considered 285° as *Gipsy Moth*'s limit of heading; she must head as much as possible to the northwards of it, which permitted a poled-out runner to be carried to the best advantage.

Then the line connecting the self-steering gear to the tiller suddenly parted, chafed through. I was expecting something of the sort to happen: I had actually said to myself 'I bet something will turn up because I am enjoying so much this damn good brandy sour after finishing all the deckwork.' I could not leave the tiller for more than a few seconds because when I did so *Gipsy Moth* either gybed or came up hard to the wind with the poled-out sail aback. I had to nurse the tiller with an elbow or knees while I found my lifeline and harness, then some suitable cordage for a new tiller line, some rope, a knife and some tape in order to fit the line through the various leads and four blocks to the self-steering gear.

I had poled out the No. 2 jib as a try-out; 50sq.ft smaller than the 300, its clew is much higher and I rigged a snatch block to its sheet to prevent the clew from bouncing the pole up into the air and straining it, but after a while I came to the conclusion that it was not as effective as the 300.

Gipsy Moth was going well with a relative wind of from 13 to 20 knots on the beam. The speedometer was registering 9 knots frequently. It looked promising for a good day's run, but at 2045: 'I have been wrestling with the tops'l for about an hour. Something is preventing it from being hoisted fully to the masthead. Unfortunately I cannot see by torchlight what this is. I tried all the tricks I could think of to shake it free of the obstruction but, whatever that was, it was not to be budged. The odd thing is that the tops'l goes up and down easily and freely to that same point where it always sticks. However, it seems to be pulling well though not fully hoisted and of course there is less heeling moment, the lower it is.' In daylight I could not see anything wrong with the tops'l halyard or track on the aft side of the mast. However, the sail was doing well where it was so I decided not to hurry to investigate further. Obviously something was jamming somewhere and I suspected that the tops'l halyard might have jumped off the sheave in the masthead.

At 1409 on 1 April the fix-to-fix run for the past twenty-four hours was 207 miles, distance logged 204·6, position 03°55½'N 37°14'W. This was decidedly encouraging for the first day because I knew that *Gipsy Moth* ought to be able to put up a greater speed as she worked her way into the core of the Trade Wind zone.

I changed the No. 2 jib for Big Brother, boomed out, which started pushing the boat's head to leeward. I wished I could have countered this by hoisting the tops'l to the masthead. I had several tries, and the tops'l went up like a bird, but it always stuck at the same place. In the end I fitted the big windvane. I was not going to get any sleep otherwise unless I put up the smaller jib for the big runner or something drastic like that. Every time *Gipsy Moth* griped up to windward until the wind was forward of the beam, the poled-out runner came aback, the tops'l thrashed, the speed dropped and I had to wake up, grab the safety control line to the tiller and pull hard. Even though I could do this from my bunk I still had to wake up. Similarly when she payed off downwind. As she approached the dead downwind heading the booms clanked, the sails flogged to and fro and the speed dropped to 7 knots. 'I had hoped to dodge fitting that vane before daytime because of feeling tired at the end of a long busy yesterday. It was not three hours since I was first woken up by steering trouble. How could I have used all that time for merely changing a windvane? To start with I was not going out there dopey with sleep so I made a big mug of tea with big lumps of Nicaraguan sugar brick in it. Also I did my leg and feet exercises which I was too tired to do before turning in at 8 p.m. I bet this sounds pansy but it was really worth while before tackling that acrobatic job. Then I had to service the big vane before rigging it; it needed two holes bored to take cord ties, and four other short lengths of cord attached; also a short strip of white tape sticking astride the leading edge to identify that in the dark. Finally, fitting it was a tricky job when perched astride the pulpit so as to have both hands free, bouncing up and down at the end of the stern with the vane, which is designed to catch the wind, needing great care in handling to avoid having it blown away out of one's hands. There were eight cords to unfasten on the one in position and of course the vane was on the jiggle the whole time, working the tiller, and the darkness did not help. The cockpit light shone somewhat weakly on one side of the vane but the other, like the moon's backside, was in darkness. I used one of those little handbag torches held between my teeth to see at the back of the vane. However, it was really worth while. Peace followed with a steady enough heading and much better speed. Incidentally, I blessed Tony Morris who made these vanes to my requirement (he makes the whole gear) for all the trouble he took.'

The second day's straight line run was 212 miles, but I had been unable to get a good fix due to the sun in transit passing so close to dead overhead. The distance sailed was 203·6 miles, the position 05°26½'N 40°26'W. I now had high hopes of an exceptionally good five-day run, but at 1409 the following afternoon the day's run fix-to-fix was 193·5, the distance sailed 192·2 miles, the position 05°33'N 43°40'W. The gloomy truth was driven home to me; winds of 16, 17, 18 knots were just not strong enough to get the speeds I wanted. Another 3–5 knots wind speed would just have done the trick, assuming that the gear would stand it—and I soon had the answer to that.

Sunday 4 April, 0400: 'It was at about 9.50 p.m. that the big crack sounded. The boom had bust in half with the big runner attached. . . . I am getting to know the drill for this schemozzle now. I was scared of that boom, though. The two halves were still attached by a small piece of the metal and they formed a sharp V with the point of the V downward and outboard of the boat.'

When I got below after nearly three hours of hard concentration and continuous deckwork, I could not keep awake while writing the log so turned in for a short sleep. Then I reviewed the situation. I had turned downwind at midnight to make everything as easy as possible when tackling Part One of the pole-bust mêlée. That and the slower speed through losing the big runner must have cost at least 10 miles in fix-to-fix distance made good. I could set-to right away to rig the other pole but I thought it was dangerous and an unjustifiable risk in the dark, even with the help from the spreader lights, to get the damaged pole down from the mast at one end and lower the other end successfully to the deck. The outboard end was sticking up nearly vertically in the air near the side of the deck and guyed in position. As soon as I slacked off the guys it would be tricky work lowering it, then working it backwards and forwards until the two halves were safely separated so that they could be stowed and lashed on deck. Squalls were going through one after the other, usually laying *Gipsy Moth* well over to leeward during the first blast, with a consequent steeply tilted deck. The seamanlike procedure was to wait three hours till daylight before tackling the job. Then of course there would be the other pole to work across the deck, rig, guy, and top up.

Up to the last entry before the pole-bust *Gipsy Moth* had averaged a steady speed of 7·7 knots that day. What was so tantalizing was that the wind had strengthened considerably after the pole-bust and indeed it was probably a first gust after the wind had speeded up which caused the pole to collapse. If the pole had lasted out for the remainder of that day I felt sure that *Gipsy Moth* would have well exceeded 200 miles for the day's run. But, as it was now, the fourth day's run was going to be well short of 200 and the first three days had only totalled 612·5 miles, which would be further reduced when the straight line distance between the starting and finishing fixes was computed.

If the fifth and final day's run was a good one, at, say, 210 miles, that would still only make the total for the five-day stretch a bare 1,000 miles. A thousand in five days was not what I was after; I had hoped to get it up to 1,100 to make a proper job of the 200mpd breakthrough. There hadn't been a hope of this on the way down to the Equator, and on the second run it was impossible without a lot more wind than I had had, though *Gipsy Moth* could have exceeded the rate right enough had the gear stood up to it. I nearly said it was an impossible target with *Gipsy Moth V*, but of course few things are impossible. I ought not to make excuses; someone else with the same tools would have succeeded. But I was interested in the technical cause of the failure; I think that the reason lay in the breakage and collapse of gear. *Gipsy Moth* seemed determined not to exceed a certain speed and would do everything she could to avoid doing so. She would go up to her 'theoretical maximum' of 9·282 knots but she jibbed at going above it, with the result that it was practically impossible to *average* that speed.

For example, there were only two occasions during the 4,000-mile run when she averaged that speed for more than a few minutes. Both ended with a boom breaking. There were other gear failures when I was pushing her hard and there were two periods when I was pushing her so hard that I feared for the main mast. The pole with its terrific compression load was bulging the mast out to leeward in a way which looked to me to put it on the edge of collapse. The other time was when there was an ominous bend right at the masthead. The scientific reason for the difficulty in holding the theoretical maximum speed over a period is shown by the way the sea was level with the counter, that is the deck at the stern, and seething there so as to make a flat continuation of the deck and the water when *Gipsy Moth* was hard pressed. This was caused by the crest of the bow wave which she had made forward, which left the hull fitting exactly into the trough of her own wave. Gigantic thrust was needed from the sails to get her to climb out of that trough.

Looking back at the speed attempt which had just come to an abrupt halt, it was extraordinary how I had been bedevilled by calculations. Morning, noon and evening these had gone on all

through the four days. It seemed as if I never got a straightfor-
ward fix and I was always working away like a fanatic to overcome the difficulties. The sky clouded over or it rained heavily
just before the morning and evening twilight which meant that I
could not use the stars. I cannot describe the oppressing and
depressing effect of those damned black squalls coming through
in endless succession with the sky being mostly invisible day and
night; the muggy heat, the deluges of rain. Once or twice I got a
measly fix from Venus and Jupiter because I could see them in
daylight after the overcast had cleared; or I got a fix from Venus
and the sun, but that would be of poor quality and reliability
because they were too close together. Then there was the trouble
caused by the sun being dead overhead. I would be crawling precariously round the deck with sextant, stopwatch and notebook
in hand, trying to decide which side of the boat the sun was. I
daresay it sounds as if I am joking, but I believe the difficulty
would be understood by someone marking with a pencil a point
on the ceiling of a room crowded with jostling people and then
trying to make another pencil point on the floor *exactly* vertically
below the first. It is funny that I should have come up against
navigation difficulties because navigation has always been my big
interest. The hours I spent trying to get results could have been
profitably spent in nursing the sailing, getting more speed by
endless tending of sails and general trimming. Another effect of
all the hours of tedious calculations which I had to make was that
I became prone to blunders which had to be detected and which
in turn caused further hours of brain twisting.

As I had expected, the fix-to-fix run at 1409 on 4 April, the
fourth day of the speed run, was only 185 miles. The distance
sailed was 195·5. This ought to have been less than the run made
good if there had been a favourable current. The position was
06°41′N 46°32′W.

It was not until the late afternoon that I finished tidying up the
deck, recovering the two pole halves without accident and getting
them safely on to the deck where I lashed them down, recovering
all the guys, blocks, outhaul and so on. The only casualty apart
from the pole and a sail which was getting pinker every time it
went under the ship's bottom, was a Swedish snaphook which I
had to cut from the end of the guy to allow the guy to pass
through a block and then away under water. It had been prevent-

ing the sail from going completely under. I had not been able to haul the sail in on the other side of the keel because of this guy and the outhaul and the sheet. I let fly both the sheet and the outhaul and later, because they were still attached to the sail, recovered them from the ocean.

'I fear this schemozzle has mucked up the day's run and maybe the whole speed run. I was lucky finishing the deckwork just before a big fella rainsquall arrived. As soon as it is through I must go and hoist more sails. The mizen stays'l is still down, also the tops'l, but there has been too much wind for them.' At 1830: 'Again no hope of a star fix. The sky is completely overcast. It must surely be a rainy season down here though I have never heard of there being one.' The next morning, 0545: 'No star fix again. Not a star or planet to be seen and also rain has now started so that there is no hope for this morning. However, there will be no trouble about a sun fix today if it is visible because *Gipsy Moth* has now overshot it in latitude, being near 9°N while the sun will be 6°N at the time of observing.' At 1409: 'Fix-to-fix run for the twenty-four hours, 188 miles. Position 8°58'N 48°30'W.'

Tuesday 6 April, 0930: 'Thank the Lord it is a fine day.'

VIII

THE HOMING RUN

It was a stirring thought, a quickening feeling, that *Gipsy Moth* was heading for home, sailing full and bye to a fresh ENE Trade Wind. I remember that when I changed the heading on 4 April after the pole-bust, *Gipsy Moth* seemed to spring to life like a spaniel when its owner turns for home after a long walk. And Lord! was I grateful to be shot of the endless calculating and brain-twisting about the speed run and the position fixing needed for it. My last two sums were to work out the distance along the Great Circle between the starting and finishing positions of the five-day run. The answer: 930 miles. Then I repeated the process for the first three days before the pole-bust. To my surprise the answer was 601 miles for daily fix-to-fix runs totalling 612·5, so that at least I did 200mpd for those three days, which was some consolation.

Were I anywhere else in the world I would have said that the sea was extremely rough, but because I was in the Trade Wind belt I pretended that it was fine weather water. I felt slightly seasick and had to be very careful where I moved. On the morning of the 7th, for instance, I was shaving and had braced myself against the edge of the basin sideboard to keep from being pitched into the mirror. Suddenly I was thrown backwards into the door of the heads. It was not bolted, flew open, and landed me in the passageway on the other side of it. Sailing like this *Gipsy Moth* could keep going fast in spite of the rough seas; and the fix-to-fix runs for the three days were 188, 182 and 189·6 miles. My tactics were to follow the clipper practice of sailing full and bye through the Trade Wind belt to the 300–500 mile stretch of variable winds in order to reach the westerlies as soon as possible and then have a favourable wind for the run to the Channel.

In my narrative log for 8 April I wrote: 'Today has been a lovely one, the most delightful of the voyage I think. Contrast is probably the key to it. After weeks of never wanting to emerge from below because of the foul weather, strong winds or rough seas sweeping the deck, today was sunny with a blue sky and a nice breeze and a sudden change from throwabout seas to something that certainly splashes aboard now and then but allows one to stand up down below. After I had finished the navigation at 3 p.m., I mixed a Squire's Gin and bitter lemon and sat in the cockpit in the sun to drink it. Then I wanted to settle down at ease with my head on a cushion, but as soon as I did so I dropped off to sleep, my muscles let go and my bottom slid between the seats into the well of the cockpit.

'I scouted round and found a splendid pitch on the side deck beside the cabin top, sheltered from wind and in the full westering sun's rays. It was not very wide and my behind overlapped the edge of the deck about 1½ft above the water, between two of the mizen shrouds which kept me from rolling overboard. I watched the bow ploughing white water and cascading it in an arch to the side. The swish and rush of the water swirling past soon put me to sleep. When I was half-awake I felt a little vulnerable and drew my hand inboard in case a shark took a fancy to it. And I wondered what I would do if the tentacle of a giant squid began feeling my leg. I thought it would be an awkward situation and that probably a girl would better know how to deal with that! When I woke I lay basking with the warm sun on my skin and daydreaming. How stupid to be always trying to do things. What wonderful thrills, excitements, longings, desires and, of course, successes to be had as often as you like by daydreaming. As I said, contrast is the key to these delights; suddenly I had no commitments, worries, frustrations, and my feelings opened like a flower on a sunny spring morning.

'I have an idea why Tarantula has not appeared for some weeks. I feared that his number was up, and that he had been trapped and drowned by a surge of bilgewater; but surely if he was able to survive my attempts to assassinate him he was too cunning in survival to be caught like that. Today he suddenly appeared from under a plastic bowl in which I keep the butter and cream cheese cool by constantly evaporating water from cloths draped round them. I thought he looked a bit small and timid and that his wits were not up to standard. In fact I could easily have kyboshed him under the bowl, whereas before he used to scuttle, to flee like the wind into some unassailable bolt-hole, like the space under the chest of drawers and above the cabin sole. He had shrunk. He was no longer the bold, truculent buccaneer. What was wrong? I wondered if he was saying to himself, 'But yes, I have no bananas.' Then tonight I think I began to get a clue to the situation. I am dashed if a little 'un didn't appear on my chart in the pool of light shining down from the electric bulb in the ceiling. Into this arena of light advanced to my amazement a little replica of Tarantula. It took short, dancing steps into the light centre, raised its claws to defend or attack, then finding no enemy danced round in a circle. It backed and it advanced. It really was a dance and I watched spellbound. Undoubtedly this was Son of Tarantula. I had to get on with my chart work and after watching him for a while I reluctantly but with great care shooed him off to the side of the chart table. He seemed petulant or hurt at being disturbed. But where was Dad? Then the stern truth dawned on me; the smaller size, the softer personality, earlier today. Of course, that was not Tarantula I had been looking at at all; it was Wife of Tarantula. The question now is, 'Where is Pa?' Is this one of the species of which the female eats the male after mating? It is very sinister. I could not bear the thought of Tarantula, after escaping my attempt to assassinate him, being devoured while mating with his soft-mannered, demure little madam, who looked as if she would be more at home in a boudoir than in an ocean racing yacht. Incidentally, they must be living it up in a big way, because when I was rooting for some onions, a cloud of fruit flies shot out of the onion net where one or two onions had started to grow and had rotted in the process with a high stink. I never saw Tarantula again and he left a lingering touch of nostalgia behind him.

'I am disappointed. I thought I could claim a day or two at 200mpd on the way down to the Equator, so I set-to to calculate the start to finish Great Circle distance for the three best days. I did not need to proceed far. I could see at a glance that the distance was nowhere near 600 for the three days 22–25 March. The best day only just scraped into the 200 class. It had a change of latitude from 12°32′N to 9°11′N, which is at least 200 miles.'

Good Friday, 9 April: 'During the night something unusual happened. I had a solid sleep of four and a half hours. This was after making a cup of peppermint tea at 3 a.m. when I decided to set more sail. However, I was sitting on the step in the galley section, looking for a piece of nylon cord, when something hit the side of the boat with a bang and knocked me sideways. At first I assumed it was a wave though nothing came aboard, but later decided it was a squall which had struck *Gipsy Moth* out of the blue. It blew up to 30 knots for a minute or two, then settled back to 23 knots. The upshot was that no more sail was set and back to the bunk I went with the peppermint tea.'

The days seemed so short. My Good Friday chores included making a plotting chart because I had nothing satisfactory for this area of the ocean; then I had to work out the distance home and forecast an ETA. There was a deck agenda to prepare and the time had come to jettison the remainder of my eggs. They had done me well with two visits to the Tropics during the four months since they were loaded on board. It was amazing how well they had kept considering they had only been greased with Vaseline and there was no refrigerator or even an icebox on board (a frig would use up too much fuel on a long voyage). Now a big proportion of the remaining eggs were 'off' and it turned me up opening them one by one until I found one which seemed good —and then only seemed good because it did not smell bad but just very doubtful. I had a remarkable supply of dried fruits and nuts left, thanks to Sheila's careful victualling, and these would give me ample protein.

There were still squalls about as we ran north; ugly-looking, darkish clouds, but small. It seemed that *Gipsy Moth* was running into a belt of turbulence at the edge of the Trade Wind zone where the Trade Wind overflows its banks, so to speak, and mixes with the colder air alongside. I wish we used that lovely French word for Trade Wind, 'L'Alize', which seems so well to express their nature when in one of their benevolent, fine light breeze moods. *Gipsy Moth*'s heading was slowly swinging round and veering eastwards for home; it was now NE by N. It is true that after deducting magnetic variation this became only 018°, but until recently the wind had been pushing *Gipsy Moth* west of north. Of course if it were not for the pounding, the heading could have been made much more easterly, but 60° off the wind created all the trouncing and heel that was tolerable, and by 10 April *Gipsy Moth* was at position 22°N 55°W, out of the squall zone, and I was able to head up to windward, changing course from 010° to 055°, which was 45° off the apparent wind.

The next day, Sunday 11 April, was Sheila's birthday, which

Gipsy Moth celebrated with a fix-to-fix run of 182 miles, from a distance sailed of 200. There were only 2,802 miles to Plymouth where Sheila would meet me, and after I had finished my navigation at about three o'clock I sat in the cockpit in the afternoon sun and drank a toast to her with a small bottle of Champagne. I also wished happiness to Edward and Belinda Montagu who were married on this same date, and they and Sheila have what is now almost a tradition of holding a party together. It was wonderful sitting in the sun in perfect sailing conditions, thinking of them and *Gipsy Moth*'s home in Edward's Beaulieu River, with *Gipsy Moth* herself gliding along at 7½ knots fairly close-hauled. This is the most lovely part of the oceans that I know; it has a peaceful, happy, relaxed atmosphere which I daresay is unique and would make it an ideal place for one's soul to take off if it wished to leave the earth. The only thing to mar my day was not being able to get through on the R/T to Sheila that evening to wish her 'many happy returns'. I had trouble throughout the voyage trying to make radio contact with the BBC, *The Observer*, and my family. I hated the necessity to make the calls (however worthy the object) because they always seemed to be booked for a time when navigation or *Gipsy Moth* desperately needed attention.

There was another serious aspect to it all in that because of the battery time spent in my abortive attempts to get through I had been using fuel for charging the batteries in a way I had never anticipated. I had stocked up at Bluff with what I thought would be sufficient for my usage, but I was making great inroads into it.

By 13 April the distance to Plymouth was 2,474 miles and I was reading up the sailing directions for the clippers, which were recommended to cross the 40th meridian at 40°N latitude in winter and 44°N from April on. I had been planning to cross it at 36°N and hoped that I was not trying to be too clever as I was when going round the world in *Gipsy Moth IV*. I had thought that in a modern yacht I could do better than the clippers by sailing closer to the wind than they could, but I flopped badly. Their lore on ocean passages was the result of thousands of voyages, and afterwards I read that the *Cutty Sark*'s fastest point of sailing was 45° off the apparent wind, which is closer winded than *Gipsy Moth V* can sail in a rough sea.

As we made our northing and the weather grew colder—or rather less hot—I dug out my sleeping-bag from the after-peak and hunted up some shirts and warm clothes. The wharfie's long oilskin coat which I was given in Sydney in 1966 came into its own again for the nights as well as the hard weather days. The fashionable short oilie smock is a genuine bum-freezer unless oilskin trousers are put on as well; whereas with the long coat I can sit or kneel on the cockpit seats to work the leeward winches, which I have to do because the seats are so broad, without getting my pyjama trousers wet, and it is a single piece of clothing I can slip on quickly instead of two I struggle into with difficulty. If only the long coat had a neck fastening to keep the rain and spray from going down my neck, I should use it even more than I do.

Three days later, on the 16th, my position was 32°56′N 43°35′W, and I had only 2,038 miles to sail to Plymouth. It was also the day on which my troubles started. During the afternoon I heard the motor cough and stop. It started again, but I checked how much fuel was left and the gauge showed empty. Owing to the heel there was likely to be some in the tank, but it could not be much. Of course my batteries only needed charging for the lights and the R/T but they were important. Sailing into the English Channel singlehanded, with only feeble oil lamps and no navigation light and more than a thousand steamers a day going to and fro is criminal, unless watch is kept all night. And I jibbed at staying on watch all night as well as working and watching all day. I decided to put in to Horta in the Azores for more fuel, and that evening one of the Portishead operators relayed a message to Sheila asking her to telegraph Peter Azvedo, who with his father runs the Café Sport at Horta, warning him of my arrival. Peter is a sort of nautical 'Kim', a friend to all the yacht cruising world.

I dug out paraffin bottles from the under-settee cubby-holes, hunted up hurricane lamps from the after peak, the cockpit bin, and a third one from beside the chart table, filled and cleaned the lamps and trimmed the wicks, and filled the bottles with reserve paraffin. I was depressed and at first quite taken aback that I should be so low on fuel through my carelessness. However, I got three lamps lighted, and felt I had had enough for the day, but it was not so. After the R/T session, on looking at the steering compass with a torch, I found that *Gipsy Moth* was not heading close enough to the wind and I changed the setting of the windvane. Presently I found that she was still not pointing high enough and I gave the vane a fresh twist. There was still no change in the heading and, on turning the torch on to the vane, I found that it was right over trying to put the self-steering rudder on. I thought at first it must be due to an exceptional load of Sargasso weed caught astride the self-steering rudder. When I went to the counter to examine it, I found the length of soft cord connecting the vane to the self-steering rudder had parted, the same cord that I had renewed for the same cause only recently. I cursed it and went to hunt for something tougher. *Gipsy Moth* began playing up, coming up to the eye of the wind with sails flogging, even when I tried to balance the ship's rudder with a piece of shockcord. I was scurrying to and fro like a fevered mouse hunting for crumbs. When I had a collection of cord together and went back to the counter, I found the real trouble. Something had pushed the skeg rudder unit astern and bent the pillar between it and the vane unit above. At the same time a screwed-in sleeve inside the pillar had become unscrewed or been forced out on to the gear below and was chewing up the steel parts of that, incidentally cutting the skeg rudder cord and at the same time being crushed, bent and cut about itself. I didn't know what this screwed-in sleeve was intended for, perhaps just for strengthening, and it looked as if the self-steering gear might still be made to work if I could cut or get rid of the protruding piece of sleeve. My extra large screwdriver would make no impression on it at all. I fetched the hacksaw from the fore cabin and tried to saw the sleeve off, but in the dark I could not see what was happening and the submerged parts of the skeg-rudder unit kept swinging in the slipstream and interfering with the hacksaw. After several failed attempts to saw or prise the protruding sleeve away, I decided it was not 'on' in the dark and that the whole skeg-rudder unit would have to be unshipped and brought aboard so that I could clearly assess what the total damage was and what could be done about it, if anything. I certainly would not be able to make good the 800 miles to Horta in my estimated five days if I could only keep *Gipsy Moth* sailing in the right direction when I was at the helm, and even achieving some sort of balance with a lashed helm would add two or perhaps more days to the voyage. I decided to turn in and sleep on it, after doing the best I could to set *Gipsy Moth* on a heading, but determined that after I had trimmed her as well as I could, I would leave her to do what she liked. It was more important to get some sleep so that I could start on the job in daylight with a fresh brain. By now I had been working at the self-steering gear for two hours and the cabin looked like a junk shop outhouse, strewn with tools, cordage, bottles of paraffin, hurricane lamps, oilskins, life-saving harness and, just to make the scene more dreary, a pile-up in the galley of about two days' washing-up. My sleeping-bag was a comfortable bolt-hole from it all. I did wake up a few times in the night when *Gipsy Moth* began to pay off downwind as I could tell by the sound of the sails, whereupon I gave the lee tiller line a pull from my bunk and went to sleep again. As it turned out at dawn, *Gipsy Moth* had kept a fairly good heading about 20° farther off the wind than was ideal, and at the cost of my having hardened in two of the sails to balance the trim, which slowed her down somewhat.

I was up at 0500 and started work at once dismantling all the lines and preventers so that I could get the skeg-rudder assembly on board. I drew the main axle by knocking it through its bearing with a big screwdriver and a maul, but then I found the rudder top frame jammed in its parent frame above. However, by hitching a line to the skeg shaft near the waterline and pulling on that I managed to free the skeg-rudder unit from the frame above. It dropped down and away astern with a rush in the slipstream. But after that, things went better. The unit was heavy and cumbersome and it was a tricky operation with the slipstream trying to wrench it from my grasp while I manhandled it up to the counter and struggled to work it up over the pulpit on to the deck. I only had one accident when I let one of my fingers get pinched between two moving parts. This spattered the deck considerably, but a plaster dressing and some surgical spirit applied externally, with a good shot of brandy applied internally, dealt with that. At last the 10ft-long unit was lying on the counter and lashed down. I sawed the extruded sleeve off, once again blessing Bart for getting me such a fine hacksaw. I marvelled at the way the steel frame had been chewed up by the extruded sleeve. It seemed miraculous that no essential, irreplaceable part had been smashed. The tube standard or pillar was considerably bent at the bottom and the rudder assembly cocked up, say 15°, but I thought it would work all right if it did not get another blow or load such as must have caused the damage. Later, I came to the conclusion that the cause of the trouble must have been an exceptionally heavy pile-up of Sargasso weed on the fore edge of the skeg. The pressure of a cartload of this stuff straddling the skeg with *Gipsy Moth* sailing at 7 knots would be destructive. I was lucky the damage was no worse. When I handled the skeg-rudder assembly back into the water, the slipstream again swept it out horizontally astern and I found it was as much as I could hold. I could see that I would never be able to coax it into position and hold it there while I refitted the axle unless I took way off *Gipsy Moth*. So I tacked, leaving the big jib aback which effectively stopped her, and then I got the unit into place and drove the axle through with my maul. The operation had taken three hours. I felt immensely relieved and lucky that things were no worse, collected all the tools and gear together, got *Gipsy Moth* sailing under the control of the self-steering once more and had the other half of the brandy, hot with lemon, for breakfast.

On the 23rd *Gipsy Moth* seemed to have the smell of the flesh-pots of Horta in her nostrils; I had been taunted by the winds ever since I gave my forecast of five days to Ilha Faial, but now she was galloping along. I only hoped it was in the right direction because the weather was too thick for any glimpse of the sun or chance of a sun fix. However, there is a radio beacon at Horta which I had picked up and that put *Gipsy Moth* to windward of Faial, which was what I wanted.

Soon I could see the mount 473ft high at the south end of Horta Harbour, behind which lies the whaling station, and I started reducing sail as I ran down towards the end of the mole. Presently along came the pilot launch, and a minute or two later João de Faria, the Chief Pilot and our friend of 1960, when Sheila and I sailed in from New York in *Gipsy Moth III* after the first Singlehanded Transatlantic race, was aboard, giving me a great hug. And there was Peter, the little friend of all yachtsmen, smiling on the pilot launch. It was like coming home after a long time away.

IX

KNOCKDOWN

I left Horta on 30 April. João took the helm until *Gipsy Moth* was in the Canal do Faial, the channel between Faial and Pico. Then he signalled to his pilot launch which came and took him off. I was sad to leave Horta, although I was longing to be home again.

All day it was slow going but in fine weather, with gentle breezes. For a while in the evening *Gipsy Moth* was becalmed and only sailed six miles over a four-hour period. In one way I was contented enough to go slowly because I was in a lazy, listless mood, but I could not clear the archipelago of islands before dawn next morning so I had very little sleep. I had the same trouble when leaving Horta in 1960 with Sheila—of not being able to settle down to a sleep until Graciosa was astern.

At 0630 the next morning I could see Praia, the town of Graciosa, on the north-east side of it, and at 0900 I noted that with the big runner boomed out to starboard 'Gipsy Moth had a businesslike press-on gait, with a slight roll to port, a gurgle of water along the hull as she rolled back which gave a feeling of power and speed.'

Sunday 2 May, noon. 'Run fix-to-fix 115 miles, sailed 121.25. Distance to Plymouth 1,091. Distance sailed since leaving Plymouth 17,400 miles.'

Nightfall came with heavy rain and poor visibility. I dropped the mizen stays'l, which was making a lot of noise, clanking and flapping, and seemed to be obstructing the airstream on to the heads'ls for the most of the time and only pulling periodically itself. *Gipsy Moth* was playing her devilish trick time after time of imitating a steamer's engine beat, which never fails to make me apprehensive and nervy. Half an hour after midnight I was woken by the change of movement of the boat and waves, to find *Gipsy Moth* heading south instead of north-east. The wind had veered, bang! from S to NW; so *Gipsy Moth* was now headed into the seas raised by the southerly wind which had been blowing all day. The movement was horrible, jumping, twisting, snatching and rolling. I could not stand, even in the cockpit, without holding on to something. I was faced with getting the runner down, then the pole, then gybing and coming up to the wind. However, I plugged away and it was not as bad as I had feared. I had to be very careful how I moved about and it was a long job because of having to hang on to something all the time. Going up the mast, working at the heel of the pole and then lowering the pole turned out the easiest part because I had things to hang on to there. I used the topping-lift to lower the pole off the mast after I had freed it. The whole operation took two and a half hours.

I changed the windvane down to a smaller one but it was decidedly not my night; by the time I had finished *Gipsy Moth* was becalmed and aback and I had the tiresome job of working her round to her proper heading as she bounced about on the old sea. When the wind came I expected it to go back to the south so that I should have the joy of rigging the boom and all that once more. However, I decided to turn in. *Gipsy Moth* could do what she bloody well liked. I was chilled, shivery and seasick, and above all I was fed-up with the extraordinary antics of the wind.

At 1100 on the 3rd I donned my harness to go and raise the tops'l, only to find that *Gipsy Moth* was on the wind and no tops'l could be used. I could not see anything wrong with the weather to account for the wind's odd behaviour. It seemed that a tiny secondary with wide open isobars giving near calm winds had passed through on a north-easterly track. The barometer was high and had scarcely moved. I had only recorded it twice in the past twenty-four hours, 1023mb at 1300 and 1022mb at 1825 on 2 May; the next reading given was not till 2000 of the 3rd.

Monday 3 May, noon. 'Run only 91 miles for 124·5 sailed. Position 40°51′N 23°21′W. Distance to the Hoe 994 miles.'

At 1733: 'A dull, dreary, grey sea, grey sky and grey light, with drizzly fog cutting visibility to about half a mile. I spent two hours on deck clearing up after last night. This included freeing the mizen topping-lift which was wound round the backstay insulator at the top. The wind is veering once more and I could do with a poled-out sail again but not today, thank you. I am grateful I am not racing and can take it easy if I want to. I am now looking forward to lunch; I am keenly hungry for once and have some sweet potatoes on the boil. I wish I had something appetising like Peter's red mullet to go with them. My remaining tinned fish is dreary, though I may have one tin of bonito left which is the best. However, the sweet potatoes fried after parboiling are delicious on their own. I slipped up in not looking for tinned fish at Horta; the Portuguese turn out good stuff.'

In the middle of lunch (at 6.30 p.m.) the wind began to veer considerably, so I dressed up again and gybed. The gybe was needed and it was better to do it before dark, which was just falling. The result was good, giving the heading required and a knot extra speed, though to be fair I think the extra knot was due to increased wind speed. The true wind now was from nearly west, speed 17 knots. I ought to have worked out the true wind sooner and gybed earlier instead of eating. Barometer 1,016·5, a drop of 5·5mb in the past twenty-three hours. This was a steady drop, indicating a weather change on the way.

The log entry for 0330 on the 4th reads: 'With the wind piping up and in the upper 30s at times, *Gipsy Moth* was beginning to run wild. Chiefly due to the old pal, the tops'l. So I hoicked myself out of my very comfortable sleeping-bag and dropped the tops'l. I also dropped the mizen stays'l to give the wind a better run into the big jib forward of the mizen stays'l. This also allowed the mizen to be squared off more with more effectiveness. . . . However, the barometer is dropping steadily and the wind rising, so there may be too much of it presently. The barometer is 1,012, down 4·5mb in seven and a half hours.' This was an average drop of 0·6mb per hour. I expected the wind to freshen but it was nothing to worry about.

An hour later: 'The true wind is 216°, SW by S, 25 knots. *Gipsy Moth* is running before it so the relative wind is only 18 knots. Sailing speed 7¾ knots. I had to change the big vane to the smaller one. The big fella was bending over below the horizontal and I think this was reversing the effect because *Gipsy Moth* put in one or two noisy gybes. The noise came from the mizen. I had it vanged down so fortunately it could not come right across, otherwise there might have been breakage. Now I want to gybe but am pondering on dropping the mizen first. The barometer has dropped a millibar in half-an-hour. Although the wind is not very much yet, the sea is getting up and the riding pretty rough. I think it would be much easier for the self-steering gear without the mizen. A nuisance because it is a cow to muzzle, that mizen.'

0550: 'Dropped and furled the mizen—quite easily in spite of my criticism of it. *Gipsy Moth* is under good control now, though rolling uncomfortably. Two or three seas boiled over on to the stern, but I hope they go with a front passing through. I hope the Met set-up is much like last night and that the weather will ease presently in the same way. But I don't really believe it will because the barometer is now dropping pretty fast; 1·5 millibars in fifty-six minutes speaks to me of a gale or worse. Anyway it is daylight and the sun shone for a minute or two which was cheering, but it looks pretty grey and murky now. I had one small casualty in the night's operations: I lost my favourite little torch; it slipped out of my mouth while I was changing the windvanes. It was most valuable for such jobs, enabling me to see the blacked-out side of the vane while using both hands to fasten it. Now I think some soup before something else cries out to be dealt with. This is the third night out of four since leaving Horta that I have been done out of most of my sleep. — There's a big sea just come aboard; I suppose I must fit a washboard or two in the companion. I don't want a sea down below.

0831: 'I was having a zizz after a bowl of pea soup and was woken by a squall. The windspeed instrument showed over 40 knots, which with *Gipsy Moth*'s 10 + knots—I had the log on the double scale which only reads to 10 knots—meant *Gipsy Moth* was bouncing along with a wind of at least 50 knots. The rigging had a relentless tone, not a screech or a scream but a tone sounding powerful and irresistible. The important point for me was that *Gipsy Moth* was going too fast in a rough sea, slueing, twisting and rolling. I had to act or breakages would occur. I felt awful, roused out after what seemed only minutes of sleep. I felt weary to the marrow. However, that big jib had to come down. It turned out an easy job. The jib made a shattering, ear-hurting din as I lowered it, but din wasn't going to hurt, as long as the jib didn't flog itself into pieces. The foot and bunt of the sail went into the sea and I hoped *Gipsy Moth* wouldn't overlay it with the keel as she bored and heeled when a wave pushed the stem; but when I returned to the stem after securing and hardening the halyard fall at the mast, the sail was docilely lying on deck against the sail net along the stem lifelines. A wave must have obligingly dumped it there for me. I didn't even get splashed until I returned to the cockpit after bagging the sail and stowing it in the forepeak, when a wave washed my legs. I think, and hope, it was only a squall causing the hurroush, but the barometer had just dropped 3·5 millibars in the past two and a half hours, 1·4mb per hour. I have only three more actions left me now, that I can think of at the moment:

1. Reef the remaining sail, the main stays'l. I had a row of reefing eyes added to it for that purpose.
2. Set the storm-jib which is about half the size of the reefed stays'l but needs two blocks for sheeting inboard; or
3. A smaller vane. My No. 2 vane is doing excellently at present and I hope it will be all right.

As far as the foresail is concerned, I have to have something forward whatever is blowing, otherwise *Gipsy Moth* won't steer downwind, but broaches and lies broadside on to the waves which is a bad position. The true wind is now 241°, 48 knots. Well, breakfast seems a good idea. Thank heaven I'm not feeling seasick. I think I will skip my exercises this morning though. I feel weary and I did have a lot of exercise in the past nine hours even if the wrong sort.'

1155: 'Baro. 1002·3; down 1·6mb in one hour and 26 minutes. True wind 254°, 45 knots. *Gipsy Moth* is sailing at 8 knots under the one sail, the main stays'l. A lot of spray is flying along horizontally with sundry swishes of water into the cockpit. I fear this is getting worse and I am debating whether to rig the storm-jib.'

1445: 'I dropped the main stays'l after rigging the storm-jib, which required quite a lot of jobs doing for it; such as, finding a shackle for its tack and shifting the mizen stays'l vang to make way for a snatchblock to lead the storm-jib sheet along the deck to the cockpit. It was blowing hard and raining hard and there were batches of big seas which made it all rather a long job. In the end it did not seem to have slowed down the speed at all. I noticed 9 knots on the dial just now but I suppose it might have been worse if I had left the bigger stays'l because the wind is now gusting up to 57 knots. My next worry is the windvane; will it hold out or ought I to change it for a yet smaller one. I have an R/T session due tonight and I notice that the mizen topping-lift is around the top insulator on the backstay aerial again. As the mizen is down and furled on the boom, the topping-lift is holding the boom, and I shall be unable to free the backstay unless I drop the boom right onto the deck. A snorter sea has just filled the cockpit and the water is pouring into the cabin under the washboard, but there is nothing I can do about it for the moment. The drains in the cockpit are small and the cockpit big. I think the drain is blocked or partially so. I suppose I had better don my armour again and go and bale it out. What a chore and a bore. Later; O.K., it has drained off. The duckboards are jammed above the floor with general confusion of sheets etc., but that can soon be cleared up. I'm for a wee snooze.'

1742: 'The wind vane bust in two and hell was let loose as *Gipsy Moth* headed across wind. I put on my stormwear at once and hunted for another vane. I got the old vane disentangled and off but needed to turn downwind to fit another one. I could not get *Gipsy Moth* to point downwind using fixed tiller lines. In the end I fixed it. All I worry about at present is that I was thrown across the cockpit and landed on my kidney against a wooden edge. It hurts like hell although I rubbed it well with arnica. Having only one kidney I am concerned. If that one is bust I shall be poorly placed in an hour or two's time.'

I figured that if the kidney had been bust, the body might not be affected for several hours though I would have had it when the blow occurred. For four hours I waited fearfully and then joy surged back that I had escaped. Other troubles dwindled by comparison. It continued horribly painful whenever I made the slightest movement.

'The cabin is getting into a rubbish heap as waves throw the boat one side or the other and anything loose flies through the air. Water is coming over the floor and I must bale some out. I let the mizen down on to the stern deck to try and free the topping-lift, but it was quite impossible because of the wind. One good thing, the barometer which dropped 2 millibars between 11.55 a.m. and 2.0 p.m., has practically stopped dropping since then; but even if it starts rising now I reckon it will be a long job, this storm, and the worst is usually just after the barometer starts to rise. What I do not understand is having all this dirt with such a high barometer, which I consider 1,000mb to be. The true wind was 278°, 57 knots. *Gipsy Moth* was doing 9 knots downwind. The rough DR since noon yesterday was 200 miles, less, say, 10 per cent = 180 miles in a direction 45°, which placed *Gipsy Moth* at 43°N23½°W. The sea was an impressive sight. The flying spray from the whipped off wave crests made a carpet 6–10ft deep covering the ocean as far as one could see, like a layer of ragged sea-mist.'

2026: 'The baro. has gone up 0·5mb in the past two and three quarter hours. It is hellish on deck. I did several jobs. Rigged a snatch-block to port for the storm-jib sheet. This enabled me to bring the clew of the storm-jib nearer amidships which would decrease the speed a little. (I was hit then, my hand, while writing, by a tin flying over from the other side of the boat.) Also I slacked away the boom of the main stays'l because its topping-lift was chafing against one of the storm-jib sheets. I rigged a light in the port shrouds, but I doubt if it will be any good on a night like this. I doubt if visibility is more than half-a-mile. Below, I baled out four bucketfuls of oily water under the cabin sole. I don't think there is any more I can do and I shall turn in. It is a good thing to get some rest if possible so as to have some ginger in case of emergency. I have not seen the wind indicator go over 60 knots but there are some very hefty gusts.'

The next narrative log entry in the main log was not until 9 May, five days later, at an hour before midnight. The 2026 entry in my log of 4 May was also the last entry in the navigation section until 0640 the next morning, the 5th, when I noted the rough position for putting out an SOS; but that was only half a line of figures. It was not till 1500 on 5 May that I again wrote log narrative, and then it was in a notebook which I could use while lying in my bunk.

Exactly what happened and when is hazy in my mind. For one thing my sense of time went completely haywire. It seemed an age between some of the events which later proved to be only hours. Before midnight I was lying on my back on my bunk, tensely braced against the starboard side next to the engine casing. Presently I slept. I was woken when *Gipsy Moth* was struck by a wild wave which nearly threw me out of the bunk. I lay still for a few seconds and then decided that the leeboard would not keep me from being thrown out. I must get out and fasten a rope somehow from above to underneath the bunk. I had just got out to do this when the first big knockdown occurred. I felt the boat start to hurtle, grabbed the handhold and held on like a fanatic. Stuff from the galley shelves flew across the cabin to the chart table. I thought, 'Christ! What luck; thirty seconds earlier I would have been still in the bunk and thrown across the cabin over the engine casing.'

I left things where they landed; it wasn't any good putting them back. I fixed a rope from the handhold above to the lug near the head of the bunk. Also I unfastened the galley belt and anchored it to the handhold farther aft. I got back into the bunk and lay trying to sleep but I was too tense. I don't know how long it was before I decided the speed was dangerously fast; the speedometer read 12 knots at times with only the little storm-jib set. *Gipsy Moth* was taking a terrific pounding. I thought I must be using the wrong tactics in running downwind. Every yacht behaves differently in a storm. Maybe I ought to head her into the wind to take the way off her. I got out to go and lash the helm down a-lee. As I stood beside my bunk putting on hard weather clothes, *Gipsy Moth* was thrown again. As I began to leave the floor, I grabbed the rope or strap and hung on with all my strength. 'God!' I thought, 'this is no good.' I felt desperate. 'What can I *do*?' This knockdown was more violent than the first; I expected it to be. I went into the cockpit, disengaged the windvane and lashed the helm hard down to a winch at the lee side of the cockpit. *Gipsy Moth* refused to head up to wind and would only lie beam on to wind and seas, and she was *still* doing 4 or 5 knots. I told myself it was better not to go forward and drop the storm-jib, that I might need it to control the boat. The truth was I shirked going forward to work the foredeck. Violent seas were breaking across. I was not sure what was best to do and, just out of my bunk, took the easiest course. I decided to leave her as she was until daylight.

I went below and lay on my bunk in oilskin trousers and sea-boots. Suddenly I had a premonition. The seas were far worse. Anything would happen and it was only a matter of how long before it did. That rope and strap would never hold me in with a worse knockdown. I was lying there like a trapped animal. God! How weary I was. What could I do? I got out to put on my life-harness and hook it to the steel beam above the bunk. It might keep me from being thrown more than two or three feet. I was scarcely on my feet before the third and biggest knockdown occurred. I was aware of terrific forces and had a lonely feeling as if I was being hurled into space, lost to the world, a feeling I have known in earthquakes.

I was pinned against the cabin roof looking down, as if from a dream-like height, at the frames in the bilge, stripped of all the floorboards. My back was against the roof and my thigh against the mizen mast where it passes through. I was lying on the cabin roof and the boat was above me. I had a spasm of fear that it was going to fall on top of me. Then I was only curious to know what was going to happen. I had flashing images of the mast torn off and tearing open the deck to let the boat go down like lead. I was tumbling from the ceiling. I was seeing badly. I remember putting up my hand and noting that my spectacles had been knocked half off; I remember pushing them back and being surprised that they had survived. I think all this occurred while I was tumbling. Then I was lying partly on the piece of floor beside my bunk. I began to lose consciousness and made an effort to flop into the bunk before I passed out. Things went distant and unreal but I recovered.

My impression was that *Gipsy Moth* had been hurled with terrific force off the crest of a wave into the trough ahead. The first thing I did was to look at the mizen mast beside me; it was still there. It looked all right, but I could see that the engine casing had moved and I feared that either the engine had moved on its bed or that the mizen mast had bent. Everything movable on the port side of the boat had been catapulted across to starboard and I could see a shambles. Below the chart table, debris was feet deep; broken plates, bottles, food, fruit—as if a cartload of rubbish had been tipped there. The light, however, was still on; a marvel on a black night of storm. How long would it last if the batteries had been upside down? There was a light in the main cabin. I did not remember having one there. It was the light at the head of Giles's bunk, switched on by the impact.

It had happened at two minutes to midnight. The clock had stopped when hit by a bottle. Hundreds of fragments of the bottle were stuck into the woodwork as if embedded there for ornament. The clock was at the top of the cabin doghouse between two windows. If the bottle had struck and smashed the window water would have been cascading in.

I must look to see what the damage was. I could hear above the din of the storm heavier regular thumps and bangs. Something had broken adrift on deck. I scrambled over the debris in the main cabin, going forward to look at the main mast where it passed through deck. The deck appeared intact and the mast all right up to it. I worked my way aft, hopefully switching on the mast spreader lights and wading through the heaped-up debris beside the companion. The hatch would not open and I had a nasty clutch of panic that I was shut in below. My side and thigh were so painful that I was feeble. I got myself into a better position on the companion steps where I could use both hands to tug at the hatch end. It opened a crack. I worked it open; but still feared that I could not get out. The hood with its steel frame was crushed down on top of the hatch and at first it seemed as if there was not enough clearance to slide the washboards up out of their grooves and away. It was only fear; I worked the top board up and free and it was easier to get the second one out of its grooves, making a gap big enough to squeeze through. In the cockpit I trod on a rubbish dump of duckboards, entwined with ropes. At the time it did not strike me as amazing that they were still there. Both masts were still standing. Both spreader lights were on. What astonished me more than anything was to see both paraffin lamps hanging still alight in the mizen shrouds. The lifelines were sagging, but all else appeared more or less secure. I felt a surge of great relief. I had had enough worry with broken booms to dread a broken-off metal mast bashing the hull in a storm. I looked for the storm-jib; all that remained were a lot of streamers up the forestay, flogging with loud cracks and bangs. Pieces of the mizen stays'l had been broken out from the ties holding it furled to the boom and were banging about. The sail was already torn and I shut my mind to it. Then I was amazed to see the self-steering windvane waggling normally. It was agonizing to move about because of my thigh and the pain in the small of my back.

I must have blundered heading across wind. I freed the helm, engaged the self-steering and trimmed to run dead downwind. I left the storm-jib alone. Its loss seemed to make no difference to the speed and once again *Gipsy Moth* was charging downwind at 10 knots. Once I saw the speedometer reading 12·5 knots. *Gipsy Moth* was now under bare poles but I daresay the fragments of the storm-jib and the flapping pieces of the stays'l would increase the speed. I could think of nothing to do about it. I think the wind was not very great; I never saw the indicator over 60 knots; even with *Gipsy Moth*'s own speed added, the wind did not, I think, exceed 70 knots except in gusts. The seas were the danger; they were terrific. During the day I had seen them like Cape Horn stuff, but steeper and shorter, with more frequent breakers. They had looked vicious. If only I could take way off the boat; *Gipsy Moth*'s own speed through the water caused the danger. What possible ways were there of doing this? It was a waste of time to put out a sea anchor, the warp would not last ten minutes before it parted due to the snatching load. The same thing applied to streaming warps by themselves. I had been through all that. I could not think of anything.

I went below and lay down in my life harness, which I fastened round the steel knee bracing the deck beam to the mizen mast chainplate beside my bunk. I hadn't been lying there long before I became aware that the water in the bilges was increasing fast. The floorboards had been floated free and were knocking against each other. I got up and looked for a leak. There was already about a foot of water in the main cabin. It was dark stuff, like black coffee, impossible to see through. I could not find any inrush of water. The leak must be under water. The violent impact when the yacht landed must have started the bolts holding the $7\frac{1}{2}$ ton iron keel to the wooden keelson or else pulled the keelson away from the frame. There wasn't a hope of finding a leak in that foot-deep black water.

I felt depressed and frightened. How many hours before *Gipsy Moth* sank? I was deeply sad. There was so much in Life. It was dreadful for death to tear me away from all the people I loved. But it looked as if this was it. There could not be a rougher sea or a rougher night for trying to launch the rubber dinghy from the foredeck. It would be blown away at once. Even if not, how could I get into it, or get water and provisions aboard? Why, I shouldn't even be able to keep them on the deck of the yacht. For God's sake, where is the brandy? A half glass would be like a comforting friend. I craved that warm glow, that dulling of fear, that damn all, who cares. But I turned it down; only clear thinking and good judgment would give me a chance here—and I had forgotten that the galley bottle was in fragments.

'God helps those who help themselves.' I fossicked out two plastic bags and a spinnaker bag and began filling them with any suitable food handy. I worked my way through the main cabin, treading on the edge of the settee bunk which was now being washed by the water, swishing from side to side. Thanks to Sheila's storage plan, some most suitable foods were to hand—dried fruits and nuts, peanut butter, biscuits, some rolls of bread and a lot of oranges from Horta, which would give me some liquid if unable to get water. I put aside the 5-litre jar of honey which Peter had got me. If I could get just that on board it would be food enough for months of existence. Water would be the big problem. All the 20-litre jerricans and 5-litre flasks of water were in the forepeak and I doubted whether I could open the hatch in the foredeck to get any of them out from under the pile of bagged sail. There was nothing to be done about that before leaving the ship. After the big knockdown I thought it would be safer to lie on the floor between my bunk and the engine casing, instead of in the bunk. I pulled the heavy wooden ditty-box into the cabin beside the chart table, where it was useful as a stepping-stone to pass over the water to the main cabin settee. It was three to four feet long, and over a foot high. Then I thought 'to hell with it! I'd rather risk the bunk in a dry sleeping-bag.' I looked round for somewhere to put the food bags but there was nowhere dry now, except my bunk. I regretted having moved the ditty-box; I could have piled them on top of it. I piled them on the floor beside my bunk. They got wet inside which I think may have been due to condensation.

'Am I being stupid not putting out an SOS?' I hate asking for help. And it was a ridiculous thing to do; how could any ship rescue me in this stuff? In any case I had been running before the storm for several hundred miles without a fix and couldn't give an accurate enough position for any ship to find me. On the other hand if I did get into the dinghy, the 400 miles to the nearest land, Portugal, would be a long drift without a sail and I might have no water. I was being stupid; there might be a ship nearby and it might mean the difference between life and death. I went over to the set. To my surprise it was working. I could hear quite well through the receiver but when I used the transmitter to put out the SOS, the meter indicated no signal passing through the aerial. The mizen topping-lift was twisted round the top insulator on the backstay aerial again.

I could think of nothing else I could do. I reckoned this was one of the tightest jams I had been in; I was dead beat with sheer fatigue, fear, tension and depression. Only a sleep could give me a chance of a clear brain to think up something to save me. I looked at the water level. I reckoned I had several hours before it reached the level of my bunk. I decided to sleep. To hell with it all! I flopped into my bunk, fell into a deep sleep and did not stir for two or three hours. When I awoke it was daybreak. I felt refreshed and clear-brained. 'What can I do to help myself?' I started to review and think. The water level in the cabin seemed about a foot below the level outside, perhaps somewhat less. Was there a chance of its rising no farther as soon as the two levels were the same? I wished I knew the answer. Even if the water continued to rise above the waterline, that is to say if the yacht continued to sink, would there be enough buoyancy forward and aft of the two watertight bulkheads to keep the hull afloat even if the cabin was full up and the decks awash? They had a considerable capacity between them. If so, I should still have a chance of bringing the boat to port, camping meanwhile in the cockpit with my bags of food and sleeping-bag. In any case when the water levels inside and out of the cabin were level, surely the inflow would be slower. Would I not have a chance of keeping the level there with bucket-baling? One thing I was determined on; nothing would make me abandon *Gipsy Moth* until she sank under me.

I had one Thermosful of hot water and I mixed up a honey and hot water to get over my queasiness. I think it was also excellent food though I did not feel hungry. After that I had a spoonful of honey at intervals.

The water was now up to the level of the settee and the noise of its surging to and fro, with the floating floorboards banging from side to side of the cabin, was like the seas breaking on Brighton beach after a storm. It nearly damped out the noise of the storm and deck gear. 'Of course I must send out an SOS. There might be a ship quite handy, and she might possibly rescue me.' I worked out what I thought *Gipsy Moth* had done and in which direction she had sailed since the rough DR position of the previous evening. I jotted down 43½°N 19½°W, and logged the time as 0640 GMT. I set about transmitting an SOS. The receiver was working well but no transmitter light came on. I gave it a biff with the palm of my hand and to my surprise it lighted up. I duly put out an SOS. I hoped it went on the air, though the instrument indicated almost no signal passing through the aerial. There was no response. I felt deserted. I was on my own.

After the knockdown when I had first heard the water in the bilges I had tried the electric pumps. The switches were at the foot of my bunk. They hummed for a while and then I tried the switches separately; only one hum. Then I thought 'How stupid to waste current on bilge pumps!' When I was in the cockpit to re-set the helm, I had tried the manual bilge pump. It required a lot of pumping to lift the water from the bilge just to the pump. I had to sit on the edge of the cockpit seat, bent double, head down level with my knees to avoid the sweep of the tiller. The water only spurted out intermittently until I had drawn off a bucketful, and then the pump jammed. I thought of opening up the pump to clear it but what was the good of a pump which had jammed after a bucketful? The idea of trying to empty a half full yacht with it was ridiculous and I left it, with a surge of anger at the futility of the thing.

I was gradually firming up my mind to keep the yacht afloat somehow or other until I got it to land. At first after the knockdown I had hated the idea of losing my life, now I began to hate the idea of losing *Gipsy Moth*. I got a bucket and staggered along from the chart table to the cockpit with ten buckets of water, which I emptied on to the side deck. In those seas it would have been difficult enough to carry a bucket of water through the boat if fit and fresh; with my damaged thigh and side it was agony. I went back to my bunk, flopped down, and fell asleep for a few minutes. When my kidney area had such a bang I thought the kidney must have been bust or so badly damaged that it wouldn't last more than a few hours; but I was still alive. Then I had thought that *Gipsy Moth* would be foundering in a few hours and that that would be the end of the road for me; but *Gipsy Moth* was still afloat and I was still alive. So I got up and dumped another batch of bucketfuls into the cockpit, to let it run away through the drainholes. With each bucket I carried I modified the drill in some small way. Bending my body a little forward and to the side eased the pain in my back; there was an important handhold above the chart table seat and the engine casing gave support to my right thigh when I moved my left leg forward, and so on. I kept a tally, making a cross for each bucket, and always aimed at a definite number, holding out for reward a flop down and a short rest on completing the batch. Then I would relax completely and often slept for a few seconds.

I think it was after the thirtieth bucket that I noticed a hole in the deck inboard of the toerail. It was on the lee side and was either under water when *Gipsy Moth* was heeled or else the seas swishing off the deck would run along the toerail from both fore and aft down to it, swirling into the boat with a kind of whirlpool action just like water emptying out of a bath. It was near the forward end of the cockpit where I had emptied the first buckets of water over the side of the cockpit on to the side deck. Hell! What a joke. The water from those first bucketfuls must have mostly returned at once through the hole. It was so ridiculous that I couldn't help laughing. But although there was enough swirling in from the water on the deck to sink *Gipsy Moth*, I still felt sure there was a big underwater leak.

I remembered almost the last thing that Sid Mashford had said to me when I left Plymouth: 'Don't forget that if you have a leak, a piece of towelling is an excellent stopgap if you can pack something over it.' I tore a corner off a green towel. I could not think of any suitable piece of plywood which was handy, so I cut a piece from the side of a Tupperware box. I hunted out the glass jar of tacks, stuffed a dozen into my mouth, and with a tomahawk which I kept to hand, crawled along the side deck. A stanchion had torn out, leaving the hole in the deck. I stuffed a torn-off piece of my underpants into the hole, spread my square of towelling over the top and held it there by firmly tacking down the piece of Tupperware. It wasn't easy because the hole went right up to the toerail. Every few seconds the sea would wash over the side deck while I knelt there.

In the afternoon I lay in my bunk, and resumed my narrative log in the notebook. Wednesday 5 May, 1500: 'Wind 25 knots, gusting to 45 and more occasionally. Speed 5·5 knots under bare poles. I had got together all the things that I needed for leaving ship in the dinghy except four, which I did not want now because of the storage difficulty. It was hard to find anywhere to put anything except on my bunk. The four were water, lifejacket, sailing gear and spare pump for the dinghy.*'

---

* For anybody unfortunate enough to be in a similar situation I offer overleaf, without comment, a list of my 'abandoning ship' stores, which I made when I later unpacked the three bags:

1905: 'Wind 35 knots. Speed 6 knots. Still no sail up and won't be for the foreseeable future till the gale is over and the sea down. I have a strong impression that the water level inboard is a little lower. So far I have removed 124 buckets two-thirds full. I would have done more this spell had it not been for pressing jobs on deck.'

My biggest, longest sheet, which had been attached to the storm-jib, had been chafed through and washed overboard. It had then got itself wound round the steering oar several times. To free it I had to lie full length on the counter and use a boathook plus a long arm. Then I noticed that one of the self-steering tiller lines was nearly worn through and would part at any time, though I felt sure it would happen at night when it would be most difficult to deal with. Replacing it was quite a job as it passes through four blocks or pulleys and the main tiller must be kept operating while fitting the new line. 'I cannot get at the galley for something hot to eat because of the water. It makes an incredible row with all the floorboards afloat, knocking against each other

---

No. 1 bag (polythene)

5 pkts biscuits	prunes/walnuts in	1 pkt Vita Wheat
kitchen paper roll	Tupperware box	Sunglasses
2 boxes matches	7 oranges	Dishcloth
1 pr socks		

No. 2 bag (polythene)

2 currant loaves	Aertex pyjama top [I	1 pkt prunes
5 bread rolls	dredged the	1 pkt almonds
1 lemon	bottom half out	1 pkt raisins
lightweight woollen	of the bilges much	1 pkt dried apricots
jersey	later]	1 red distress flare
1 pr long woollen	2 pkts figs	Very pistol
underpants	3 dried bananas	

Handbag (spinnaker bag)

8 oranges	1 box wheat germ	1 hand mirror (for
2 spoons	3 bars wholenut	sun-flashing)
1 fork	chocolate	6 tins baked beans
Toiletry bag (inclu-	2 caps	spectacles
ding Codeine,	2 tin openers [1 U/S]	1 pr pliers
comb, antiseptic	1 sleeping-bag (in	1 pen
ointment, etc. and	polythene bag)	1 pencil
1 pr gold cufflinks!)	5-litre jar honey	

and bottles and half the yacht's stores and gear. However, yesterday I was sure it was only a question of how long before she sank.' This shows how my sense of time had gone haywire; the knockdown had occurred that same day.

At two o'clock on the morning of the 6th the relative wind was 23 up to 40 knots, and *Gipsy Moth* was running at a speed of 3 to 5 knots with the wind on the quarter. Two or three big waves swept over the deck and poured quite a lot of water below the companion, but two and a half hours later the wind had eased to 28 knots, and while massaging my thigh and my back with arnica ointment with my left hand while I ate digestive biscuits and peanut butter with my right, I was planning to set the main stays'l first thing after daylight.

An early job was to get to the chronometer, which I had forgotten about completely. I supposed it had stopped for want of winding, as it only runs for 56 hours.

0835: 'The chronometer is O.K. It records that it is only forty-four hours since I wound it. All this in less than forty-four hours! It seemes incredible. A bonanza! I found a roll of dry paper.'

1009: 'Well, I have done several jobs. Item 1—Raised the main stays'l. Item 2—Secured the pieces of mizen stays'l with some more ties. It looks as if it is simply that the seam sewing has given way. It wasn't hoisted at the time but the wind got into the furl. Item 3—I noted that the starboard navigation light and its housing have carried away. Item 4—Charged the batteries to full meanwhile. Item 5—Freed the mizen topping-lift from the back-stay insulator. I should be able to use the R/T now. Item 6—baled out 21½ bucketfuls of water, making a total of 145½ buckets. Water obviously lower. I had to use the small bucket at times to fill the big one. Of course I am working at the near end of the lake, which is shallower than the midships part. All this would be easy if it were not for the pain when moving. I am having a rest and will then try for a sun shot and then have another go at the water. If I could get rid of that and start drying things it would be a cheering step forward. I was quite dry working on the fore-deck but got a souser in the cockpit just as I was finishing. I don't mind that except for its keeping my padded jacket wet. Now for some cold fodder. Another 40-bucket go at the water and I reckon I could use the galley and get something hot.

'I got a sun shot at 1139 and a second one at 1243 which gave me a fix at 43°45'N 16°25'W. Course for Plymouth 52°, distance 651 miles. Rather a rough position due to big seas. More precision later, I hope.

'Another 40½ buckets; total 186. Full ones too. Now dipping in the main cabin. I am getting a drill for it now. One learns to avoid the movements which hurt. I reckon that another 80 buckets will quieten the noise and get rid of swishing water. I have fond memories of Brighton beach but don't want to have it in the same small room for too long. I want to raise the mizen but I am determined to mop up this water first because my supply of energy is limited at the moment. . . .

'I baled until I had the deepest bilge empty. It has started filling again but that does not necessarily mean there is a leak. There may be a leak below the waterline, but the pockets of water lying outboard of the stringers and timbers will be finding their way to the deepest part of the hull for some time. I kept a tally and emptied 155 buckets. I measured the bucket, a two-gallon one, and reckon on average I filled it to 1¾ gallons. Total for the operation, 186 + 155 = 341. It may not sound much but carrying a full bucket 10 or 20ft in a yacht is a long way in a rough seaway. . . .

'What changes of fortune in a man's life. Two or three days ago I was as smug as can be with everything clean and tidy in the yacht ready for Sheila to come aboard at Plymouth. I was just reckoning the time to arrive. A few hours later I was collecting hurriedly the necessaries to keep me alive for a few weeks in a dinghy, thinking it only a matter of how long before *Gipsy Moth* sank. A few hours later I am still in the whole yacht, apparently undamaged below, making again for Plymouth.

'Some odd things turned up when I was baling out the ship. At the 106th bucket this afternoon, while baling in the main cabin, I noticed something under the water. I put my hand in the water, which is as thick as soup—or coffee perhaps would be a better description because I know there is at least 1lb of coffee in the water—and found my longest woodsaw lying at the bottom of the bilge. It had travelled all the way from a locker under Sheila's bunk in the forecabin, found its way round the mast, along the alleyway past the heads and half way through the main cabin. How did it get so far aft? It is 2½ft long. How did it get moved anyway with its row of teeth? At bucket 107 I drew out a full vacuum flask; this was Sheila's and it had been fitted with quite a tight fit into a slot above the little table beside her bunk; how did that get loose? Alas, it was smashed inside and only full of bilge water. At bucket 109 I drew out a full bottle of Courvoisier brandy. There were no labels left on the bottle but the stamped bottle glass identified it. It is my favourite brandy, given me by Raymond Seymour of Whitbread's. It was undamaged, another bonanza.

'These finds started me thinking and at bucket 113 I thought "Why not try to light the Aladdin heater?" It had been under water for some time but you never know unless you try. I opened the door and there was a large clump of nasty pulped trash inside, pulped paper and debris washed into the bilge. To my surprise a 24-watt opaque bulb was sitting on top of this heap. There is certainly an opening to the side of the stove so that one can put in one's hand to adjust the wicks, but it seemed very odd to find that bulb there above all that. Also it boded ill for the fate of the drawer containing all my bulbs, fuses and electrics generally, because that is where it had come from. Well, I put a match to the wick and it lighted at once. Astonished, I tried the second burner and that lit too. Now they are still going full blast, another big surprise. More good luck, because they are badly needed with everything in the boat more or less soused. I stopped work when I touched rock bottom, so to speak. Every bilge must be loaded with gear. Item—Where are 9 bottles of paraffin and probably the same number of grog of various kinds? There is no sign of any of them. Now for a try at a hot meal, the first for years it seems. I must log the heading, etc. but now I have dug out the proper log from the plastic bag where I had it ready for abandoning ship, and will resume entering up in that.'

On Friday 7 May, I was recording at 0600 that 'all's well. It seems to me that it is only comparison (though that's not quite the right word which I want) which counts in life. Here I am feeling happy, contented, undoubtedly pleased with the prospect of a whole lot of interesting problems to solve and actions to take.' I wondered how many people have been damaged by being hurled against the roof of a boat cabin? Thinking about it I figured that my leg hit the mizen mast where it goes through the cabin roof. Everything else shot right across the cabin so I would have done the same had something not stopped me, and that could only have been the mast. I know I was pinned to the roof because I was looking down into the bilges straight before my eyes. But they appeared to be above me. At the time I recall saying, 'Oh God, she's upside down; will she right herself?' But that must have been some effect of centrifugal force as she was picked up physically and thrown by the sea or the wind or both. She could not have been upside down because the masts were quite undamaged and not even displaced as far as I could see. Recalling the leeway *Gipsy Moth* made in rough cross seas in the Caribbean and the reasons I deduced for it, I am certain that this was the answer.

'Massage first, then as many exercises as I can do in the bunk. There is nowhere to stand for the others yet. One can't very well do leg swinging à la ballet school or 300 jogs while balanced on the curved frame timber of the bouncing hull. After that if I'm as mobile as I seemed to be when I got up just now, I'll be a devil and double the sail area by raising the mizen. Then a temporary aerial is needed so that I can get the Colorado time signal. The chronometer is probably still accurate because it has stood some pretty hefty shocks already successfully, but of course I can't tell. The previous aerial made use of one of the lifelines but evidently was put out of action when the stanchion pulled out of the deck. Voorwaarts! Oh! and then I must have a hunt to see if I can find an egg intact. How delicious fried eggs would be for breakfast! I know one egg that won't answer the roll call because it stuck my chart folds together and when I tried to open the chart the paper surface pulled off, spoiling the chart.

'Anyone reading this might say, "Why on earth is he meandering along over the paper when there is so much wanting to be done?" My answer would be that I am not in a hurry; at present I am not going to do a single thing unless I have to. I want to recover from my body blows first and that requires time. I don't want even to feel hurried. The only way to make a success out of a situation like this is to act as if it were one's normal way of living. I am going to turn it into a normal way of life, sailing this craft with my body damaged. I learned this from that great explorer Stefansson. His maxim was that successful polar travel depended on first making Arctic travel one's way of life. And there is dear old Lao-Tsze's remark, "The journey of a thousand miles begins with a single step."

'It is all a little overpowering when I start working on the debris. I feel like an earthquaked peasant picking over the ruins of his cottage. This job needs a month to clean up. I simply cannot get into Sheila's cabin. It is one great dump of interlocked boxes, gear, all my clothes, two suitcases, one of which I can see open upside down while there is no sign of the other, stool, curtains, vacuum cleaner, newspapers, all hotch potched in a cabin-filling heap 3½ft high. If I pull anything out where can I put it? First I must hunt for my navigation instruments. I took two sun sights and want to work out an accurate position. Perhaps this tin of anchovies, these saucers, bowls, cups and vacuum flask tops won't mind if I move them off my chart table. There is a place to put them in the galley. What oddities turn up. When I opened my cutlery drawer in the galley which is usually filled with many knives, about 20 forks, spoons, teaspoons and the rest, so that there is not a blank square inch in it, there was not a damn thing except one solitary fork. The drawer was closed. I needed one of the spoons and hunted round for a while and finally ran them to earth in the adjoining cupboard in the dustpan and under some big scrubbing brushes; but many are missing. Where do these things get to?'

Friday 7 May, 1407: 'Run 113 miles. Sun fix 44°53'N 14°19'W. Distance to Plymouth 532 miles. Rig: mizen and main stays'l.'

2255: 'Just now I slipped with a saucepan half full of water and went a purler. Critics might assert it was due to this champagne cocktail I'm drinking. If so I shall be having a worse fall after this second one. I fear, however, that this is going to be a rough night.'

Saturday 8 May, 0629: 'Out of my bunk after donning oilskin pants and sea boots. I have a technique now for putting on boots while in the bunk; I make use of the engine casing to push my foot against it. I had to get out to gybe because the heading had fallen off to 120° instead of 65°. A horrible movement due to heading across the seas raised by the previous wind. I felt slightly seasick by the time I got back to my burrow but a spoonful of honey fixed that. I've just had to go out again because the mizen boom was whanging across with gear-breaking force due to the lumpy sea and *Gipsy Moth* being so close to sailing downwind. I thought the vang tail had worked loose but it had not. The trouble is that the eye to which I usually downhaul the boom when running carried away with the stanchion which pulled out of the deck. Why worry, the sun is shining and *Gipsy Moth* is 140 miles nearer home than this time yesterday. 424 to Plymouth.

'Today, after some breakfast, I emptied the bilges which are too full again; I still think that may be due to blocked up water working through the limber holes and past the frames and stringers. Up forward I think all the bilges are still full because of the limber holes being blocked. Last night I penetrated to the heads. It really is somewhat depressing; my razor, hairbrushes and all such accessories gone. They may be in the bilge, but there is still too much black water there to see through. Even if I recover them, I don't fancy using them. I may not find the razor in which case I shall have to turn up in Plymouth looking like Rip Van Winkle escaped from jail. I spent quite a time mopping up and clearing limber holes to let the water find its way to the lowest part of the hull, where I could scoop it up. As a result, with 14½ bucketsful taken out, the hull is pretty clear of water. It would require a cloth to mop up most of the rest. This of course is wonderful, but when I look round I want to shed a tear to see the boat I had clean and tidy for Sheila and Giles to sail in with me. Now it is as if living on a rubbish dump. Total bucket talley 362½.'

That Saturday evening, I had a blessed nine-minute R/T call to Sheila. She told me not to come into Plymouth on the Monday or Tuesday because fifty foreign and British NATO warships were going in on Tuesday, and recommended that I 'slow down and wait outside till Wednesday.' That was certainly the easy way but I hate being in a crowded sea area at night, alone, when I need sleep, and I now had only one navigation light. *Gipsy Moth* seemed to have picked up Sheila's message because she decided to put on a spurt to arrive ahead of the warships. At 0700 on Sunday 9 May she had 285 miles to go and had averaged 158mpd for the past sixteen hours, so she intended to arrive early on Tuesday. She was making 9·5 knots fluctuating to 10·5 with no fuss or difficulty in a wind S by W, 27·5 knots. The rig seemed to suit her very well—main stays'l and mizen with the tops'l. 'The tops'l is setting beautifully and it seems the mizen stays'l and big jib only spoil its effectiveness with the wind on the quarter.' Later I dropped the mizen and then lowered the tops'l about 10ft down the mast, after which I changed down the windvane. That seemed to work well and may prove a good rig for running when one does not want to pole out. The pressure on the sails is farther forward and I think it is much easier on the self-steering.

Clearing up continued all the way to Plymouth. A lot of the work would have to await the attention of the boatyard. For example, the floorboards all had rounded edges where they had been battering each other in the cabin surf, and a lot of fitting and painting would be needed. But I found my razor at last, in the bilge under the heads floor. My hairbrushes also turned up, thickly matted with filth and never usable again. The third and fourth drawers up in the fixed chest of drawers in the cabin were full of photographs, newspaper clippings and ship's papers, such as my passport, *Gipsy Moth*'s registration certificate, the radio licence, the visitors' book full of addresses, and many unack-nowledged telegrams and letters. All went under the water and were mostly pulp. Perhaps those many people who helped me before and during the voyage, and those who sent me letters and telegrams, all of whose names I faithfully recorded, will accept this account of *Gipsy Moth*'s knockdown as my reason and apology for not writing to thank them for their kindness.

At 2200 on that Sunday, 9 May, *Gipsy Moth* was running into the Channel nearly blind, with visibility down to a mile through light fog and no fix for 217 miles. It was not until 1625 the follow-ing day that I got a sight of a hazy sun through the fog. This put *Gipsy Moth* on a position line which gave the distance off Plymouth but no indication whether she was heading north or south of the Lizard.

Gradually the D/F bearings of the Lizard changed from NNE to N by E, and although I was having trouble with the D/F loop and reckoned it to be giving readings 20° in error, this indicated that *Gipsy Moth* was moving to the south of the Lizard.

Tuesday 11 May, 0300: 'I awoke to stillness—I mean no steamers around and the Lizard siren sounding a mournful, fear-inspiring long and short, seemingly near. I found the heading had gone to 30°, so got agitated in case *Gipsy Moth* had turned and made for the rocks as soon as I fell asleep. However, I reckoned the mournful moaning blasts came from the NW so that if I could keep going eastwards I should be all right. And I need not have worried about the silence; because now the air is again throbbing with steamer engine noise and several are around

Gipsy Moth. I actually saw some steamer lights for a few seconds so the fog must have thinned. To hell with fog—and calms—and especially the two together. *Gipsy Moth* has only done 8 miles in the past three hours. I reckon she is at present right in the middle of the westbound steamer lane and just a few miles south-east of the Lizard. Spending a night here becalmed in fog is not my ideal location for peace of mind.' But with the dawn the fog gradually lifted and it was a fine, sunny, calm day with a light breeze. All day *Gipsy Moth* ghosted along at 1·5–2·5 knots. At noon she had only 24 miles to go.

The breeze strengthened and as I passed Rame Head it was too strong for the big windvane and I had to change it for a smaller one. I passed the great breakwater across Plymouth Sound at nightfall and my beloveds, Sheila and Giles, came out to meet me in the Flag Officer's launch, lent to Terence Shaw by Admiral McKaig. Soon after midnight we were all eating scrambled eggs in the Royal Western Yacht Club while I was telling my tale.

Gipsy Moth was home again after sailing 18,581 miles in twenty weeks and four days elapsed time. I had spent five days in Bissau, twelve days in El Bluff, and seven days in Horta, so that the total sailing time was 120 days, which gave an average distance logged per day of 154·8 miles, and per week of 1,083·9 miles.

X

CAN IT BE DONE?

Yes, and soon. The first singlehanded craft to sail 4,000 miles point-to-point in 20 days could well be a multihull which, if it can be kept from capsizing in rough weather and if the single-hander avoids the mistakes I have recorded in this book, could do it easily.

Absolute speed in sailing is going to be the important new field of effort to interest yachtsmen, especially singlehanders. If I have made any records I like to claim them, but I do believe that standards of speed must be established and properly recorded. Up to now there have been a number of loose 'barside' claims about speeds made under sail. The reader of this book will have noted what great differences occur between a day's run as logged, as measured fix-to-fix, and as made good towards the target according to calculation; and again, the difference between the total of, say, five days' point-to-point runs compared with the straight line calculated distance between the first and last of the five days' positions.

For the record, I took 22·3 days over the 4,000 mile point-to-point run instead of the 20 days I aimed at; but this was 38 per cent faster than my fastest 4,000-mile straight line run in *Gipsy Moth IV* in 1966/7. In addition, *Gipsy Moth V* made good 2,000 of the 4,000 miles in under 10 days, if the two runs of 1,017·75 in one five-day period and the 995·5 miles in an earlier one during the same voyage are added together. The 1,017·75 at an average of 203·55mpd was a lot faster than the best five-day straight run which *Gipsy Moth IV* made good in 1967 (884·75 miles at an average of 176·99mpd). On the way down from Plymouth to Bissau, *Gipsy Moth* sailed in two days, noon to noon, 431·6 miles, a distance point-to-point of 405 miles. Then there was a single day's run of 200 miles point-to-point on the way south to the Equator and a three-day run of 601 miles or 200mpd on the way north from it.

When a speed is claimed as a record, competition and

development benefit; rivals have a definite target to attack, know the advantages that can be taken, the mistakes that can be avoided. What interests me is whether *Gipsy Moth V* could sail 4,000 miles in 20 days and what changes to boat or gear I would make before another attempt.

First, the route. Undoubtedly that 50 miles of Bissau estuary which had to be negotiated, followed by the day of ghosty winds until clear of the mainland, is a great handicap. Through greed or love of romance, depending on the viewpoint, I stuck to Bissau for a starting point. If I had cut the distance from 4,000 to 3,780 and started from Dakar instead of Bissau, I reckon it would have put up the average speed considerably. But I loved the idea of 4,000 miles and 20 days; it has such a splendid ring about it. When it comes to a rival setting out to beat me over my own course, it will be nice for me in my deckchair to think of him starting with the challenge of that appalling yet truly romantic estuary drag.

After that bad start I cannot complain about the wind for the rest of the run; but it became clear that *Gipsy Moth* was not fast enough in winds under 25 knots. Could I speed her up for another attempt? If so, how? *Gipsy Moth* only clocked 9 knots on the speedometer for 295 miles out of the 4,000. Undoubtedly this was underregistering about half a knot during the second 2,000 miles, and I think that she probably did altogether 600 miles of the 4,000 at 9 knots sailing speed or 216mpd. With luck the fix-to-fix run for 216mpd logged would be 208. There is little margin; nineteen days at that speed would only allow 152 miles reserve for a calm on the 20th day. To clock up 4,000 miles straight *Gipsy Moth* had to be driven at between 8·6 and 9 knots sailing speed for 24 hours a day for 20 days. On thinking it over I reckon I was lucky that she did clock up a total of 2,012 miles in two five-day runs out of 20 days sailed.

So, obviously, to have a chance another time she must go faster. Could she have been speeded up? She was the right monohull for the job, but she was badly trimmed. To starboard, she had a 41-gallon water tank (say 435lb full) under Giles's berth and a 41-gallon Diesel fuel tank (say 380lb full) under the chart table, a total of some 815lb set as far outboard as possible to give greater cabin space.

The main counterbalance was to be provided by the 26-gallon water tank at the forward end of the cabin, the Baby Blake lavatory in the heads, and the galley. But as I pointed out when I took delivery, the centres of gravity of the water tank (say 285lb full) and the Baby Blake and hand-basin (say 50lb) are only about a foot to port of amidships, while the Primus stove full can only weigh about 10lb.

In addition to this, the Perkins 4107 Diesel engine (525lb) was aft of the mizen, and the six batteries (say 420lb) were aft of the engine. The result of this was that *Gipsy Moth* had a heel of several degrees to starboard, and was badly down by the stern.

I tried to remedy this as best I could by careful stowage of my stores amidships and by, for example, stowing in the forepeak 120 litres of water in jerricans (say 275lb), two anchors, 20 fathoms of chain, plus the sails and anything else Sid Mashford and I could think of, but there is a limit to what one can do in this respect and I reckon that the bad trim cost *Gipsy Moth* anything up to ¼ knot.

On speed runs I think one of the most important items is the self-steering gear. Time after time I had to take in sail because *Gipsy Moth* slued up to windward or, with the runner up, turned downwind. The sail which had to come in was nearly always the tops'l, because it made *Gipsy Moth* gripe up into wind. I hated dropping that sail; it pulled like a shire horse (and as I write I have on order one double the size for more speed, so the problem will be greater). At first I thought this slueing was due solely to bad balance caused by the weight aft, but on consideration I think that the self-steering needs more power. Great power is needed to check a 29-ton boat from slueing to starboard when the stern is slapped hard to port by a wave and the tops'l sheet also pulls the stern to port while *Gipsy Moth* lays over to port in a 25-knot wind. The Gunning gear was excellent—I was always admiring its performance—and for *Gipsy Moth* I think it only needs the skeg and oar a foot longer and a modification to give it more scope in its lateral swing through the water and double the power.

Few sail changes are needed. I shall be arranging for the 450 medium-sized running sail which I needed so badly when *Gipsy Moth* was sailing at full speed until the pole folded under the strain of the 640. The storm-jib which was torn into strips in the storm has been redesigned but that does not affect racing speed.

There is not much to say about the broken gear. Although I would have come much closer to my 4,000-mile target if the poles had stood up, I doubt if I would have made up that 465-mile shortage on target in the 20 days. Nevertheless, gear must be strong enough for the job for which it is intended and Robert Clark has specified new poles which should be 75 per cent stronger.

There is one problem which has me completely foxed at present, but somehow it must be solved. How can a yacht with a hull as fast as *Gipsy Moth*'s be slowed up in a storm? God spare me from another trouncing like I had in the North Atlantic! Streamed warps would be gone in twenty minutes with a fast yacht, due to the snatching, and a drogue would be snatched off in ten minutes. I carry one for use at a mooring to keep the yacht tide-rode instead of wind-rode and I noted when lying at Mashfords' mooring at Plymouth on return that it was hard to recover the drogue against only the tide. Spoilers, as on the underside of aircraft wings to spoil the airflow over the wings and cut down the speed for landings, are the ideal thing; but to fit these to the curved hull of a yacht would be a hopeless proposition. I had an idea for slipping an inflatable rubber ring over the stem to work its way down to the keel before filling it with air to make a sort of horse collar. I think it would be a wonderful brake, but what one can think up in an office chair and what one can do in a storm are two very different things.

No one could succeed in this project without luck, and throughout this voyage I had the most amazing good luck. Consider those broken spinnaker poles, for instance: fifteen feet of jagged-edged metal boom attached to a full-bellied 600sq.ft sail beating about like a mad balloon could be a lethal weapon and also could do great damage to deck and gear. Yet in no case did the broken halves actually part until I broke them apart myself. There were a number of falls I had, many of which could have been serious. There was that terrific bashing I had when I was thrown across the cockpit, which could so easily have finished off my remaining kidney. What amazing good luck!

Then there was the matter of my leg when I was thrown up against the roof of the cabin. Judging by the pain afterwards and the fact that I was knocked partly unconscious, I think it was lucky the leg was not broken, which would have been awkward with the boat half-full of water and the leak to be mended. Time after time it struck me how good my luck was. There was the landfall at Nicaragua when it seemed again and again as if something were trying to drive *Gipsy Moth* ashore, and in each case I awoke in time. Was all this luck, or a capricious handout by Providence, or was it due to *Gipsy Moth* being blessed in a service aboard in the Beaulieu River by Tubby Clayton and Rector Baddeley of St James's Piccadilly, our parish church? I do not know. If I try carrying this examination of luck into *Gipsy Moth*'s own behaviour I feel my brain will twist into knots.

But I would like to retract something I wrote in my book *Gipsy Moth Circles the World*. Sailing up the Atlantic in May 1967, on passage toward Plymouth from Sydney, I said that after the Southern Ocean it was like entering an enchanting lake. At that time it was. Most yachtsmen experience the North Atlantic at its best and mildest in summer. But as I discovered in *Gipsy Moth V*, in mid-winter the deep depressions chase each other across from Newfoundland south of Iceland just as they do in the Southern Ocean. This is not the place to compare them in detail, but I think this quotation from Alan Villiers's excellent book *The War with Cape Horn** illustrates the power of the sea—and exactly what I mean:

> The *Marion Josiah*, a 2,400 ton sailing ship, lost three men when coming up to Queenstown in winter 1906. A great sea pooped her, smashing the wheel, washing away the mate and two helmsmen. The mate and one helmsman went overboard. When the sea cleared the decks, it was found that the other helmsman had been washed along the deck and smashed almost to pulp against the for'ard house.

I was lucky to survive the storm which hit me in the North Atlantic.

But as Captain Slocum, whose kindly spirit must surely sail with every singlehander, said to himself: 'Let what will happen, the voyage is now on record.'

* London, Hodder & Stoughton; New York, Scribner: 1971.

February 1971

As would be expected, Sir Francis Chichester's new project is interesting and majestically ambitious. Put in the simplest terms, it is to sail singlehanded, non-stop for 20 days at an average speed of 200 miles a day.

Why 200 miles per day? And why 20 days? I cannot tell you. Perhaps because both are nice round numbers, while their product of 4,000 miles is rounder still. What may be said definitely is that it is a soaring aim worthy of one who has a habit of success. But frankly I cannot believe that there will be success this time. Two hundred miles a day entails an *average* speed of 8·35 knots, and that average has to be sustained for two-thirds of a month, entailing appreciably higher speeds being maintained for part of the time; and this in a boat handled by one man. No fully manned offshore racing yacht has ever made such an average for—I think —even a week. But there is one important difference: Chichester has chosen what should (and indeed *must*, if he is to succeed) be a course in steady fair winds; and they must be continuously strong as well.

The down-wind course is in the tradition of ocean-going commercial sail, which depended on the belts of the Trades and could not have operated otherwise, when deep-laden hulls were driven by square rigs unable to lie closer to the wind than 65–70 degrees. The fastest among such ocean carriers sometimes made 400 miles a day, but this was rarely achieved and not held for more than a day or so at a time. In terms of relative speed, Chichester is aiming at an appreciably higher figure. The clipper ship running through the Trades at 400 miles a day had a relative speed

$$\frac{\text{speed (knots)}}{\sqrt{\text{length (feet)}}}$$

of about 1·1. Chichester, to reach his target, must make a relative speed of 1·3.

Speed being a function of length, clearly Chichester has required the longest ship he can handle alone. Yet is she big enough for the intended speed? She will need every fraction of her length to maintain that average of 8·35 knots. We hear a great deal about the maximum theoretical speed of sailing yachts being equal in knots to 1·34 multiplied by the square root of the waterline length in feet. This speed for *Gipsy Moth V* is only 8·7 knots, so it is fortunate that the widely endorsed supposition is untrue. It is the sailing length, or length of the hull immersed when sailing in full career, that is important, and this in a yacht with overhangs is appreciably more than the waterline length (static). The faster types of yacht will under ideal conditions exceed their supposed theoretical maximum speed as derived from the waterline length. I estimate *Gipsy Moth*'s maximum speed on a broad reach in calm water as about 10 knots, or 240 miles per day; but such a speed could be held only for minutes rather than hours or days.

The yacht's sailing length when running down wind at high speed is about 49ft. This happens to be the same as that of the American offshore racer *Ondine*, which in 1963 made a day's run of 248 miles, averaging 10·2 knots. The reports of this were fairly reliable, and it was regarded as a memorable performance; and bear in mind that the period involved was 24 hours only and there was a large crew.

Once *Gipsy Moth V* exceeds about 7·25 knots, she begins to be over-driven, throwing up a considerable wave system and running along a steepening part of the resistance curve. At her necessary average speed of 8·35 knots her resistance will have increased by some 50 per cent compared with that at 7·25 knots. At 9 knots, a speed that will have to be held for appreciable periods to maintain the average, the boat is sailing on a wave longer than her static waterline, the crest of the stern wave being right aft along the counter. These facts reveal the degree of hard driving that must be entailed in holding the required speeds. And the boat will be in broken water, which raises the resistance and is particularly harmful in the high speed regime. Moreover, the source of power has to be constant. In human terms this means that one man for 24 hours a day should be trimming sails already operating at near their maximum output of power, to assure the last atom of performance. The rig is a staysail ketch.

Some notable speed performances are recorded of two earlier

APPENDIX

Clark designed yachts. In 1949 *Naiande*, of 26·3ft LWL, maintained a speed giving $V/\sqrt{LWL}$ of 1·67 for 3 hours, and in 1946 the 31ft LWL *Corinna* was recorded as holding a speed ratio of 1·63 for 1 hour. These were moderately heavy displacement full keel yachts. There is a record of a 32ft waterline sloop that made the 132 miles' passage from Ajaccio in Corsica to St Tropez in 19 hours. This gives a $V/\sqrt{L}$ ratio of 1·25, and for a passage of this length the performance may be regarded as excellent. But *Gipsy Moth V* must maintain a speed-length ratio fractionally more than this for thirty times the distance! In 1951 Pat Ellam and Colin Mudie in the tiny and light displacement *Sopranino* maintained a speed-length ratio of 1·03 on passage from the Canary Islands to Barbados.

The crucial technical factor that must make Chichester's objective so difficult to achieve is due to the size of the boat in relation to the required average speed. The following resistance figures may not apply precisely to *Gipsy Moth*, but their general proportions are correct. When the yacht is sailing at a comfortable clip of 6·5 knots, her resistance is about 45lb per ton of displacement. When the speed is raised to 7 knots the resistance becomes about 60lb per ton. At 8 knots it is 100lb; at the required average speed of 8·35 it is 125lb. But to maintain this average it would seem that she must spend part of the time sailing at about 9·5 knots; for inevitably there must be many occasions when the speed will drop below 8·35 knots—when, sailing singlehanded, the trim will be less than perfect, when the wind will let up (specially near the coasts) or swing right aft. At 9·5 knots the resistance jumps to no less than 250lb. This speed, as it happens, gives a speed-length ratio of 1·45, which is comfortably in excess of the oft-assumed 'theoretical maximum'. As shown above, it is nothing of the sort; but it is unquestionably a speed that cannot be often reached or held for long, let alone exceeded. Yet Sir Francis, alone and with a 57ft two-masted yacht on his hands, must for some periods flog her up to and beyond this speed, near the hydrodynamic limit of performance, and hold her there. It is a tremendous ambition.

It is the fact that the yacht must be held for such long periods in the extreme upper part of her speed range that gives the operation the air of impossibility, and makes one wonder whether anyone but Sir Francis could have the confidence to attempt it.

He will have to double the average speed made by Geoffrey Williams when he won the Transatlantic race. To assist him he will have more sail area and free winds. I have suggested that 10 knots is the maximum speed of *Gipsy Moth*, and one that only under the rarest conditions could be reached. Sir Francis must hold an average for 20 days and nights of 83 per cent of this speed to achieve his object.

During his circumnavigation in *Gipsy Moth IV*, Chichester's best average was an 8 days' run at 176 miles per day. This magnificent performance is, I believe, a record in any singlehanded craft for such a period, single or multihull. But in *Gipsy Moth V*, despite her greater length, it is going to be necessary to maintain a higher relative speed ($V/\sqrt{LWL}$ of 1·3 instead of 1·1) for a period of two-and-a-half times as long. If this record is achieved, it will—technically, so far as the boat is concerned, physically so far as the man is concerned—be a staggering performance. And apart from the boat and the man, it should be emphasized again that the Trade Winds will have to behave immaculately. Calms or light winds will cripple the venture. The voyage may be no less than 4,000 miles but it resembles a runner trying to establish a record for the 100 yards. He cannot afford to ease off for even a few seconds.

*   *   *

August 1971

Following my notes in February, on the project of crossing the Atlantic at an average speed of 200 miles per day under sail single-handed, Sir Francis Chichester has now provided me with detailed information on the results achieved. This evidence of a 22 days period, when the object was to achieve the highest possible speed together with its accurate measurement, provides, I believe, the most valuable data ever to have been offered on ocean speeds under sail. From henceforward, whenever the subject is under discussion, no one will be wise to neglect using it as a yardstick of the possible though, in fact, rarely attainable.

It is easy enough on the basis of the physical principles involved to disprove many of the speed claims made for sailing ships and yachts. But how hard it is to find reliable records. So far as the fastest speeds of the clippers are concerned, we shall now never have them. We have had very little on yachts too, at least of dependable results covering appropriately long periods. Hence the table of noon-to-noon runs achieved by Chichester during 22 days crossing the Atlantic (pages 92–3) is a record of permanent value, the lack of which hitherto has given wings to many ethereal claims.

The object was to sail 4,000 miles non-stop and singlehanded at an average speed of 200 miles per day. I described it in February as a 'soaring aim' unlikely to be successful. 'If this record is achieved, it will—technically, so far as the boat is concerned, physically so far as the man is concerned—be a staggering performance.' Well, it was not achieved; but the performance was impressive enough. It was closer to the target than most of us would have guessed.

To summarize the results briefly: the voyage extended from 1130 on 12 January to 1925 on 3 February. The time for the 4,000 miles run was 22⅓ days, giving an average of 179·1 miles per day. In the course of the whirlwind rush two spinnaker poles were broken, and for 3 days 8 hours of the last 5 days' record run, during which an average of 200 miles per day *was* maintained, the two poles were set lashed together. To achieve the object of 200 miles a day the average speed over the whole passage would have had to be 8·33 knots. The actual speed was fractionally less than 7·5 knots.

This average for 22 days in a vessel 42ft LWL and 57ft LOA throws a new light on possible speeds under sail. It may be 0·83 knots less than the target. But it is also quite as much more than most judges would formerly have considered likely.

Turn now to some of the best day's runs (see table). The longest was 231·5 miles on 30–31 January. The average speed was then 9·6 knots. I wrote in February: 'We hear a great deal about the maximum theoretical speed of sailing yachts being equal in knots to 1·34 multiplied by the square root of the waterline length in feet. This speed for *Gipsy Moth V* is only 8·7 knots, so it is fortunate that the widely endorsed supposition is untrue.' It is more reasonable in this connection to consider the sailing length of the hull, which is more than the waterline by the length of the overhangs that may be effectively immersed when sailing in full career. In *Gipsy Moth V* I reckon this to be about 49ft. On this basis her relative speed above would be in excess of 1·36.

When making 9·6 knots, the length of the wave created by the yacht in her progress would have been 51ft, or only 6ft less than the overall length of the yacht. Sir Francis Chichester has written, 'Your forecast of the behaviour of the yacht during this last voyage, which totalled 18,581 miles logged, was amazingly accurate, even to the stern wave being continuously level with the counter when she was sailing her fastest.' But this, of course, is the inevitable hydrodynamic condition when driving at such speeds. The more amazing thing is that such speeds were held for so long in a yacht singlehanded in severe ocean conditions.

It will be seen from the noon-to-noon fixes that more than 200 miles was made on 8 days, or for some 36 per cent of the period at sea.

Chichester tells me of two other periods during which *Gipsy Moth V* maintained more than 200 miles per day. The first was on the passage from Plymouth to Portuguese Guinea, when in two days, noon to noon, a run was made of 431·6 miles for a point-to-point distance of 405 miles. On the passage home, he says, 'I diverged for a jaunt to the equator and tried for a faster 5-day time. During 3 days *Gipsy Moth* made good, noon fix 31 March to noon fix 3 April, 601 miles.' Shortly afterwards a 5-days run of 932 miles was achieved.

He has also written: 'I only succeeded in sailing at an average of 9 knots or more during the 22 periods during the first two-thirds of the 4,000 miles run. These 9 knots periods totalled 295⅓ miles. During the last third of the 4,000 miles, 9 knots speed was only averaged once according to the log, but the underwater units of the speedometer were much worn and greatly under-reading. This I discovered afterwards. I think 9 knots was exceeded during 21 periods of the last part of the passage. Of course, some of these periods were short, at an hour or two.'

Nine knots average gives a distance of 216 miles per day. It will be evident that since, on the fix to fix distances recorded in the table, averages of 215·5 and 231·5 miles were attained on two days in the latter part of the voyages, speeds of 9 knots must have been held for appreciable periods, as Chichester deduces. Here, incidentally, we may see one of the many sources of error in speed records, apart from the gay imagination. Logs sometimes under-read. They also over-read, and since wishes so often beget records, this fact is overlooked. The distance between two fixes must be the basis of claimed record speeds. Where the clipper ships were concerned, doubts of speed claims were sometimes most powerfully reinforced by doubts about the fixes recorded. It appears to have been the habit of some Masters to find it conveniently impossible at times to make (or at least to record) an observation. This occurred in the case of the *Champion* on the day following one when the mileage claimed was an astounding 465 miles. In a hectically competitive trade, some of the captains may have been guilty of fixing their fixes.

Of the boat's behaviour and the general effect of her naturally high speed, due to length and light displacement, Chichester tells me: '*Gipsy Moth V* was the design of boat I wanted for the job, but I found two effects of her speed which I think will be something new to reckon with in fast ocean racers:

'In a storm her speed was a great disadvantage. I could not slow her down. Running under bare poles, I once noted the speedometer reading 12½ knots. When I tried to slow her down by heading into the wind after setting a new small storm jib, she would not point into the wind with the helm hard a'lee. I reckon she would have sailed into the wind at 8 knots if I had trimmed the rudder for it, and this would have been suicide. Soon afterwards the storm jib was blown into strips and ribbons and the two 1½in braided nylon sheets parted. I think this occurred during the worst of the three knockdowns: perhaps afterwards but not before. There was too much din to tell.'

The fact that, even with the helm hard down, the yacht could not be coaxed into the wind is disturbing, but a similar effect was apparently experienced by USN destroyers during a Pacific hurricane. After running before mounting seas until yawing and rolling became dangerous, it was found that the destroyers could not be headed up. No doubt the windage and water resistance of their high foc's'les contributed to this. As a result one or more was lost by capsizing. But it will be evident that the yacht of light and fine lined type, capable of gathering high speed very quickly, can be a source of danger in a high wind and sea, which the slower and heavier type would not be. The volatile character of the former might, under such conditions, be exchanged with advantage for the relatively stodgy performance of the latter.

Incidentally, the speed of 12½ knots under bare poles recorded above may cause suspicion. Unless the log held this speed for at least a minute or so one would be inclined to regard it as a momentary effect of the violently disturbed wave motion on the underwater unit, or perhaps an inertial effect on the needle of the indicator. But this does not call into question that the yacht was travelling dangerously fast.

Talking with him, I gained the impression that Sir Francis Chichester still believes his object could be attained. I confess that even in the pleasant atmosphere of a St James's Street drawing room when a warm June evening makes everything hopeful, and miles of monstrous seaway are taken lightly, I remained sceptical. But then, last February I should have been sceptical of what actually has been achieved.